# The Birth of
# BALLETS-RUSSES

**PRINCE PETER LIEVEN**

BALLET PETRUSHKA

*Design by Alexandre Benois*

# PRINCE PETER LIEVEN

---

# THE BIRTH OF
# BALLETS-RUSSES

**TRANSLATED BY L. ZARINE**

DOVER PUBLICATIONS, INC.
NEW YORK

This Dover edition, first published in 1973, is an unabridged republication, with minor corrections, of the work originally published by George Allen & Unwin Ltd., London, in 1936. The frontispiece and the plate facing page 129 originally appeared in color. A new foreword has been written specially for the present edition by Catherine Lieven Ritter.

International Standard Book Number: 0-486-22962-9
Library of Congress Catalog Card Number: 73-80556

Manufactured in the United States of America
Dover Publications, Inc.
180 Varick Street
New York, N. Y. 10014

TO
# FRIEDA CRAMER
**THE TRUEST AND BEST
OF FRIENDS**

# FOREWORD TO THE DOVER EDITION

MY father, Peter Lieven, was born in Moscow in 1887 and was educated both in Russia and abroad. He graduated in the Faculty of Jurisprudence of Moscow.

He was an avid amateur musician and, though he had lost the sight of one eye in a hunting accident during his youth, his other eye opened wide to the colour and spectacle of the stage. It was only natural that he should have been led to a consuming interest in the then nascent Ballets-Russes, bringing together, as they did, a constellation of talent from so many arts. He became a familiar and keen observer in musical centres throughout Europe.

With the time of troubles occasioned by the First World War and the Russian Revolution, he emigrated first to Sweden and then to France, where he worked as a correspondent of a Swedish newspaper. The present volume is a summary of his recollections of the early years of the Ballets-Russes and the people who helped to create it.

During his later years he was host to many celebrities, including Rachmaninoff, Backhaus, Horowitz and Heifetz, in his house on the Lake of Lucerne. He died in Lucerne in 1943.

CATHERINE LIEVEN RITTER

*March, 1973*

# PREFACE

THE chief figure in this book is actually Alexandre Benois. Many books have appeared recently on the Diaghileff Ballet, interest in the subject has revived, and the study of the art has been renewed. Excellent though some of these books are, they all fail, in my opinion, to give Alexandre Benois his proper importance. It is as if there was a conspiracy among authors to dismiss him with a passing reference, forgetting that he and he alone played the main part in the creation of the *Ballets-Russes*. Perhaps this neglect is due to the fact that he ceased regular collaboration with Diaghileff quite early in the history of the *Ballets-Russes*. Indeed, his influence no longer dominated after 1911. Already at that time he was beginning to drift apart and to have other interests. But the truth is that by the year 1911 the *Ballets-Russes* were already an accomplished fact with their future clearly foreshadowed. They might be repeated, might even be developed, but the creative act had already taken place. They had been tried and proved. And, perhaps for that very reason, Benois abandoned them.

It was not my set intention to write a book about Benois. My purpose was to reveal as truthfully as possible the steps which led to the creation of a new branch of theatrical art.

In unfolding that story I could not help making Benois the most prominent figure.

For a complete understanding of the nature of the Diaghileff Ballet it is more important, in my opinion, to understand the period 1885–1911 than all that followed

9

afterwards. And in this first period the whole story centres round the personality and the artistic urge of Benois.

During the preparation of this book I frequently met and talked with Benois. In my pages I often directly acknowledge my indebtedness to him. More often, however, in an endeavour to avoid overloading the text with such sentences as "Benois says" or "Let us hear what Benois has to say," I speak in my own person, though it is his words and opinions that I am reporting. I cannot separate his contribution from my own; I need only say that, if the reader finds any colour and vitality in my pages, he may be sure that it is due to Benois.

Regarding the importance of Benois in the development of the ballet and his influence on the group of friends, I had, besides my own recollections, other sources of information at my disposal. In this connection I wish to express the warmest gratitude to Prince Argoutinsky-Dolgoroukoff for his valuable information and very useful help.

I am also greatly indebted to the stage manager, Serge Grigorieff, whose unfailing kindness, faultless memory, and wide culture were extremely helpful. He alone among those great ones of the past is still active to-day—long may he continue so. For his valuable assistance with this book I am deeply grateful.

I must also acknowledge my debt to Les Archives Internationales de la Danse in Paris. To the principal of this museum of choreography, M. Rolf de Maré, and to the curator, M. Pierre Tugal, I owe very great thanks for granting me the privilege of verifying some of the material of my book.

The reader will be aware of three omissions in the

following pages. In dealing with Diaghileff and his collaborators, I have no chapter on Igor F. Stravinsky. The
reason for this is that Stravinsky has already published a
book about himself, where the reader can find all that he
wants to know. Secondly, I make no mention of Serge
Lifar, the brilliant dancer and talented *maître de ballet* of
the Paris Grand Opera. The truth is that Lifar's connection
with the ballet dates from much later than the period with
which I am mainly concerned, and consequently he does
not come within the scope of this book. Thirdly, at the
very end of the book, where I mention the *Ballet de Basil*,
I do not deal separately with Leonide Massine, my reason
being that I did not wish to make a mere passing reference
to him in connection with the new ballet generation.
Massine, in my opinion, demands a book to himself. No
such book has yet been written, though undoubtedly
there is a very great need for it.

Finally, I must thank Mr. L. Zarine for the great care
and attention he has given to the translation of my book.
His friendship with many of the artistes and knowledge of
ballet greatly helped the work.

P. L.

# CONTENTS

# CONTENTS

15

16

# CONTENTS

17

# THE BIRTH OF BALLETS-RUSSES

# LIST OF PLATES

19

# THE BIRTH OF BALLETS-RUSSES

# I

## INTRODUCTION

IT is more than a quarter of a century since, in the Théâtre du Châtelet in Paris, *Les Ballets-Russes* made their first public appearance. That is a whole generation ago, and yet, far from being forgotten, they continue to be played with success on the stages of various theatres in various countries.

The enthusiasm of the public for them is unabated, the old favourites still hold the stage, and new ballets are being offered us inspired by the restless creative imagination of the pioneers whose youthful enthusiasm twenty-five years ago produced this bold new art-form.

What Western Europe knows as *Ballets-Russes* appears to us who were born and bred in Russia a separate branch of art. As children sitting in the boxes and stalls of the Maryinsky Theatre in St. Petersburg we connected quite different sensations with the word "ballet." These *Ballets-Russes* were a novelty not only for Western Europe but for us Russians.

We had never seen anything similar on a Russian stage before—the gorgeous décor, the choice of music other than ballet music, the daring, sometimes frenzied choreography—all these were new to us. We had not even been accustomed before to a performance consisting of several short ballets.

The evening of May 17, 1909, saw the birth of a new art. It would be quite wrong to imagine that Diaghileff merely transplanted abroad the Imperial Russian Ballet. The *Ballets-Russes* were the result of a complex process, of a special creative urge manifesting itself under special and sometimes unfavourable conditions. Various factors had to combine, various obstacles be overcome before this new art was possible. The century-old tradition in Russia of classical ballet, the availability of a corps of technically perfect performers, a group of enthusiastic young men with creative talent, a clever and daring choreographer like Michael Fokine, an organizer of genius like Diaghileff, with his power of surmounting all difficulties—all these were necessary, and it was also necessary for this organizer and his friends to sever their connection with Russia and create their art outside its borders. It was fortunate, too, that at this time dancers of great talent and even of genius were at the height of their powers. A Nijinsky occurs perhaps once in a century, and ballerinas such as Anna Pavlova and Tamara Karsavina are rare indeed.

But even the presence of all these separate factors is insufficient in itself to explain the origin of the *Ballets-Russes*. Equally important was the quickening atmosphere which made itself felt in Russian art circles at the end of the nineteenth and the beginning of the twentieth centuries.

The nineteenth century in Russia was a productive period for art. The creative drive can be detected everywhere.

In literature we pass from the great national poet Pushkin to Turgeniev, and from Turgeniev to Tolstoi and Dostoevsky.

The founder of Russian music, Michael Glinka, was followed by the famous "Big Five"[1] with Rimsky-Korsakov and Moussorgsky. The theatrical renaissance comes later: the early years of the twentieth century saw Stanislavsky's Moscow Art Theatre and Sava Mamontov's private enterprise in opera which gave us Chaliapine. The final manifestation of this art renaissance was the birth of *Ballets-Russes*.

To understand the process of their creation, to understand why they took the form they did, one must turn to the end of the last century to find the embryo from which they sprang.

[1] The Russian term "Mogoutchaya Koutchka" means literally "the mighty little heap." This was the name given to a group of friends and composers who created, from the sixties onwards, Russia's national music. There were five of them: Balakirev, Moussorgsky, César Cui, Rimsky-Korsakov, and Borodin.

# 2

## AB OVO

AT the end of the nineteenth century the young Russian schoolboy was quite different from those of his own age in Western Europe. The physical side of his life was undeveloped—sport and games were looked down upon. On the other hand, the intellectual life was held in deep respect. All the fire and energy of youth went into discussions on art, philosophy, science, into arguments about "questions" of the day. It would be a mistake to imagine these young men as long-haired, pale-faced, bespectacled members of the "intelligentsia,"[1] indulging in endless empty arguments and theories.

On the contrary they were as virile, gay, and high-spirited as their European contemporaries; only their enthusiasm took a different direction. Instead of seeking satisfaction in a game of football, they enthused about a Böcklin painting or the theory of labour value. School friends formed discussion circles, where they argued, shouted, quarrelled, and waxed in turn enthusiastic and indignant. All this, of course, was very naïve, but it was, too, a sign of youthful energy and high spirits.

[1] The word *intelligent* (intelligentsia) was coined at the end of last century by the minor Russian author Boborikin, and soon became in the Russian language a term defining members of the professional classes with "left" political tendencies. After the Kerensky Revolution the word *intelligent* acquired a definitely derogatory connotation in Bolshevist as well as emigré circles.

24

Just such a circle was formed by a group of intimate friends who were school-fellows from 1880 to 1890 in May's private school in St. Petersburg. May's was a college for boys of good family with well-to-do parents, who preferred this more expensive private school to the Government schools.

The group of young men we are concerned with were not only school fellows but close personal friends.

Shura (Alexandre) Benois, Valechka (Walter) Nouvel, Dima (Dimitri) Filosofov, Kostia (Constantine) Somov, Kalin, and Skalon met together every day. They even formed a sort of club, and jocularly called themselves the "Pickwickians." High spirits, wit, and irony were the distinguishing features of this group. They adopted an attitude of not taking things seriously. Before long they were joined by another young man, Levushka (Leo) Rosenberg, who later took his grandfather's name of Bakst. Benois was elected "president" of the club, and Bakst "speaker." It was the latter's duty to keep order at the meetings by striking on a bronze bell, the property of Benois' mother. The unfortunate Bakst, the most good-humoured of persons, bawled at from every side, was quite incapable of performing his task.

The minutes of the club meetings were very carefully kept by Kalin, and somewhere to this day in Soviet Russia they are lying preserved among Benois' papers.

At the meetings papers were delivered on various subjects. Benois spoke on Dürer, Holbein, and Cranach, the sceptic Skalon delivered a speech on the after-life, Filosofov one on the reign of Alexander I, Bakst dealt with the history of Russian painting, and Nouvel with the history of Russian opera. It is true that these papers were seldom read to an end, that the "speaker's" bronze bell rang out continuously without the slightest effect, and that poor Bakst begged for order in vain; nevertheless the interests and enthusiasms of the youths centred round this intellectual sphere. Laughter, gaiety, and good-humour were imperative, and things of serious importance were mingled with friendly joking and banter.

Benois was the central figure of this group, and his influence was the dominating one. He was brought up in an artistic milieu. His father was a prominent architect; his mother, a Cavos, was the daughter of the architect of the Imperial Theatres, and grand-daughter of the famous conductor and composer, Catarino-Cavos. In the Benois family heredity proved so strong that three of the five brothers became prominent painters.

However, their leaning towards art was not of a professional or bohemian character. The Benois tradition was that of wealthy, cultured architects; they had never known poverty, acted as patrons of art, and were completely devoid of any narrow professional outlook on the arts.

In addition, their Latin (French-Italian) extraction gave their lives discipline and order. The father's house, elegant, rich in *objets d'art*, as much a social as an artistic centre, offered a hospitality full of that freedom and gaiety which only an inborn and thus stable discipline can give.

From early childhood Alexandre Benois's artistic tendencies were strong and well defined. He collected art publications from abroad—the *Gazette des Beaux Arts*, *Die Kunst für Alle*, *Bilderschatz*, the *English Art Journal*. His love of the theatre revealed itself in marionette shows in which he and his friends manipulated the puppets. He was a young man of initiative and resource, temperamental and enthusiastic, infecting others with his enthusiasm, captivating them by his imagination and looked up to as their leader.

Bakst and Benois first met in the spring of 1890. They talked together, and Benois, deciding that Bakst was one of "themselves," introduced him to the Pickwickian circle. Young Bakst was a curious yet charming person. Red-haired, very short-sighted, almost ridiculously self-complacent, he was remarkably good-humoured. His friends made him the object of much good-natured banter on their part. He was teased about his weakness for smart clothes and his care of his appearance. Bakst met these inoffensive gibes with good-humoured laughter and with ready retort.

"Shut up, you old Jew," someone would shout.

"Shut up yourself, you penniless son of a lord," roared back Levushka.

At this time he was the only Jew in the circle. The son of rich parents who had lost their money, he was the only professional among the friends. He was studying at the Academy of Art, and was already earning a little to help his family. He was a most unselfish person, and his life's ambition was to put his family "on their feet."

In the Vasili-Ostrov quarter of St. Petersburg, on the far side of the river, there was at that time a whole colony of rich foreign merchants who led their lives in their own way. In this colony lived the family of Valechka Nouvel, who remained until the very last Diaghileff's close friend and collaborator.

Nouvel had a place of his own in the group of friends.

He was hypercritical to a degree, voicing his own opinion—generally far from complimentary—on almost everything and everybody. Periodically he became unbearable. Once or twice a year there were unpleasant scenes with him. Like Bakst, he too was the object of the friends' banter, but in his case it was seriously intended. At the same time the company was not complete without him. He was the piquant spice which every good dish needs to give it full flavour. Music was his main interest. He could read a score with ease, and altogether was a great connoisseur. In these early days he even composed songs, but presumably this exhausted all he had to say, as he showed no inclination later towards creative work.

"Led astray" to balletomania by Benois, like the rest of the friends, Nouvel, with Benois, once managed, during carnival, to see Tchaikovsky's ballet *The Sleeping Princess* six times within a week, actually attending two performances in one day.

Even to this day Benois remembers by heart every note of this ballet, and Nouvel can play anything from it on the piano.

Rather later, in the early part of 1890, the "Pickwickians" were joined by still another member—Alfred Nourok. Several years older than the others, Nourok's strange but charming personality produced an undoubted effect on the friends. He was full of affectations and could be truthfully accused of posing, but the pose was a witty, cynical, attractive one. He tried to conceal his Jewish extraction and liked to be taken for an Englishman (he was educated in England). His philosophy was cynical, and he aspired to the reputation of drug-fiend and rake. His mannerisms were odd, and were defined by the friends, in Hoffmann's word, *skurrilität*. It was through Nourok that the friends' interest in Hoffmann took root, an interest which later, during the ballet period, was so clearly evident in many productions. He was a witty and biting conversationalist, and in spite of his pose he led a very quiet and orderly life.

Another important member of the Pickwickians was Dima Filosofov. A typical Russian nobleman, he was the son of rich parents, who, though outside Court circles, were socially prominent. Filosofov was a highly cultured youth, and the friends often held their meetings at his home, a pleasant, gay house completely free from snobbery and Court intrigues. During the time of the Pickwickians, and later in the period of *Mir Iskustva*, Filosofov was one of the most important and active members of the group. Later he became absorbed in religious mysticism, and dropped his connection with the circle. He played no part whatsoever in the creation of the *Ballets-Russes*, but he is important, if only because he had a provincial cousin at school in distant Perm in the Urals, on the borders of Asia. In August 1890 this cousin, having finished school, came to St. Petersburg and through Filosofov made the acquaintance of the "Pickwickians." This cousin was Serge Diaghileff.

Thick-set, plump, fresh-complexioned, with sensuous red lips and perfect white teeth, Serioja (Serge) Diaghileff was a typical sturdy provincial. He had a ready laugh, without irony, with an animal-like gaiety. Benois says that he laughed so heartily that one could see the back of his mouth. It was only by degrees that Diaghileff was accepted in the circle as one of "themselves." Until 1895 he remained

"Dima's cousin," Filosofov providing the link between him and the friends.

He was greatly under the influence of his cousin Filosofov. From 1895 onwards, when he began to take an interest in painting, Benois became his mentor in matters of art, but Filosofov's influence in intellectual matters in general was apparent until the beginning of Diaghileff's enterprises abroad in 1906.

Diaghileff's father, a manufacturer in the Urals, was a nobleman who, once rich, had now lost all his wealth. Diaghileff grew up in Perm, which at that time was still the cultural centre of the Ural province. His stepmother was a good musician, and her home was the musical centre of the town. His father, Pavel Pavlovitch Diaghileff, was an ex-officer of the exclusive Imperial Chevalier Guards.

At first the "Pickwickians" were annoyed by Diaghileff's provincialism. He was gibed at for his foppery, for posing, for what they called his "hussar" manner. In the theatre and in company Serge would suddenly leave his friends to talk to people whom he thought "important." At heart he was a good fellow suffering from shyness, yet with the desire to shine. It appears that at this time he himself had no great opinion of the "Pickwickians." As a provincial he was rather shocked by the unrestrained and sometimes indecent jesting of the group.

His artistic bent, too, evident even on his first arrival in St. Petersburg, ran on different lines from the others.

He came to the capital to study singing and musical composition. Despite their enthusiasm for Tchaikovsky, Diaghileff and the friends did not quite agree even on this point: Diaghileff was interested in the composer's "broad melody," the friends in the dramatic and expressive side of the music.

On the other hand, the friends found Diaghileff's "By the Fountain," a scene from Pushkin's *Boris Godounov* composed in the spirit of Moussorgsky, insipid and dull. His singing also produced no great enthusiasm in the friends; his voice was strong but unpleasant to listen to in a room, and the friends found it full of false pathos and lacking in taste.

As it happened, however, Diaghileff's musical studies did not last long. Rimsky-Korsakov bluntly advised him to give up composition, and his singing never came to anything. Nevertheless, for the rest of his life he retained a professional attitude towards music. Later, music was the only branch of the ballet with which he was able to deal without outside aid. His musical collaborators respected and took notice of his advice, which was given, of course, in the form of categorical orders.

It is worth while to refer to Alexandre Benois's own words regarding this period:

"During his first years in St. Petersburg Serge paid little attention to art. His interest lay in the theatre, in social connections, in his musical lessons, least of all in his university studies. He avoided art exhibitions, never entered a museum, and was a rather casual frequenter of our circle, where the usual topics of conversation were painting, sculpture, and the plastic arts. . . . Later, coming into a modest inheritance from his mother (£6,000), he took a little flat of his own, furnished it, and began in a diffident sort of way to collect pictures.

"It was at this time that he made several journeys to

Europe in the company of his cousin Dima. How thoroughly and energetically he undertook this business of travelling may be guessed from the fact that in one month abroad he visited twenty-four museums and fourteen studios. His impressions left by these journeys were confused, but the important thing was that they brought him into contact with the West, towards which he began to look more and more steadily.

"Largely owing to his travels abroad, he began to lose his provincial outlook and to become gradually the Diaghileff who undertook his mission, the Diaghileff known to all of us who had dealings with him at the period of his great achievements. It was at this time, too, that he became accepted in our circle on terms of intimacy and equality.

"Diaghileff was not a creative genius, he was perhaps rather lacking in creative imagination, but he had one characteristic, one ability, which none of us had and which made of him what he later became: he knew how to *will* a thing, and he knew how to carry his will into practice. Many a time Bakst, Filosofov, Serov or I tried our hardest to infect with an idea of ours the inert and indifferent Diaghileff. How his lethargy annoyed us! It is strange to think that this tireless worker was actually upbraided by his friends for his laziness. And then suddenly the position would be reversed. Once *convinced*, Serge, his eyes alight with the love of action, began to dash about busying himself with all the details necessary for the realization of the plan. Once having taken a matter in hand, he adopted it as his own, and from that moment the initiators of the plan, the originators of the idea, carried it out obedient

32

(sometimes not very obedient!) to the wishes and commands of Diaghileff.

"One of Diaghileff's special characteristics was his mania for making the personal acquaintance of painters, authors, and others. At first we misunderstood and even disapproved of this. It seemed to us exaggerated, perhaps snobbish, curiosity, almost immodesty. Later on I saw it quite differently. Diaghileff had an insatiable desire to make personal contacts, to get the 'grasp' of a person. Like many other men of action, he read little and unwillingly, more for information than for interest. Writing he simply detested—despite our long friendship, I have only about thirty letters of his. But all this was due not to laziness, but to his 'gluttony' for people, to his 'appetite' for intimacy. He had real fascination, real charm. If he wanted something, it was scarcely possible to gainsay him. And his powers of persuasion arose from his intuitive understanding of people, from his 'grasp' not only of their external character but of their innermost depths. In the most offhand and casual fashion he would find out sacred personal secrets. His 'cultivation of notabilities' was the outcome of quite a special curiosity which was closely bound up with this amazing gift of 'grasping' people. He who was too lazy to read a novel, and who yawned at the opera, was capable of long and careful study of the author of a novel or the composer of an opera. This was a passion with him—and a passion he knew perfectly well how to conceal. Though he could be cynical and cruel in his judgment of a person, some fundamental truth almost always lay behind his censure, a truth too which everyone was not capable of detecting. I often thought that if Serge

33

had been a doctor, he would have been a genius of diagnosis."

Soon after 1890, that is, after Diaghileff's final acceptance in the circle, a new period of its existence began. The naïve papers, discussions, and arguments about society stopped. The "Pickwickians" had grown up. Benois was twenty-five, and married. What was previously a childish diversion became a matter of serious import. A desire to appear before the public, to create, to express themselves, became apparent.

At this time the friends were interested almost solely in painting. Accordingly, Diaghileff's first attempts at organizing were connected with this branch of art. After the first two or three exhibitions, in which he proved his organizing abilities, he became in fact the leader of the group, the practical architect of their ideas. These first attempts, which, like everything he did, had a great but controversial success, led soon to the formation in 1898 of what is known in the history of Russian culture as *Mir Iskustva* (the World of Art). Though this movement has no direct connection with the ballet, I shall have to go in some detail into *Mir Iskustva*.

PLATE I

ALEXANDRE BENOIS IN 1890

MADAME A. BENOIS
*From a drawing by L. Bakst*

PLATE II

FACSIMILE OF COVER OF "MIR ISKUSTVA"
*Designed by C. Somov*

# 3

## EARLY DAYS

THE description of the youthful "Pickwickians" was indispensable to indicate the artistic embryo from which the *Ballets-Russes* sprang. The main constituents were already present there. Benois, with his painting and balletomania; Bakst, the future genius of costume; Nouvel, staunch and constant friend and helper—the whole Pickwickian atmosphere was saturated with potential ballet. But their group still lacked one element, perhaps the chief element—the practical genius of Diaghileff. With the coming of *Mir Iskustva* the group had already crystallized. Diaghileff undertook and put into practice the ideas and aims of his "artistic legislature." From the inception of *Mir Iskustva* up to the War of 1914, the period of the journal, the work for the Russian Imperial Theatre, and the ballet seasons abroad, the structure of the group is exactly what it was when *Mir Iskustva* was formed. With rare exceptions, it is always a joint enterprise of Diaghileff with the erstwhile "Pickwickians," who became the editorial board of *Mir Iskustva*, and ultimately the "fireside talkers." In nearly all the ballet productions of the brilliant pre-War period one can detect the artistic influence of the editors of *Mir Iskustva*, and often there are traces of the earlier youthful enthusiasms of the "Pickwickians."

What was *Mir Iskustva*? There was certainly a journal of that name, there were exhibitions, there was a society;

but it would be nearer the truth to call *Mir Iskustva* a movement, a group of young enthusiasts, with Diaghileff at the head, banded together to strive for their artistic ideals.

There was nothing of the clique about this movement. The friends detested "ists" and "isms," considering such things artistic ostentation and vulgarity. They simply strove on behalf of every manifestation of the original and creative in art, wherever it was to be found, whether among advanced "moderns" or in established classics. On the other hand, anything they considered devoid of talent, insincere, lacking in artistic truth, they severely condemned.

Their independence and outspokenness in this direction had simply no limits. They spared neither celebrities and people of influence, nor, on occasion, friends. Their brief, incisive, sometimes mercilessly frank criticisms produced a sensation in art circles. This practice gave, intentionally or otherwise, a tone of controversy to the journal and made for it not a few enemies. Persons and groups who had been offended attacked *Mir Iskustva*. The friends were labelled with the word then in great vogue, "decadents," and cursed back in turn. Even at home Benois became accustomed to the ironical greeting, "Here comes our decadent!"

The opposition and rebuffs which the friends met with in their work, far from subduing their fire, only added fuel to it. They threw themselves with greater ardour into the fight for the vital and creative in art and against the static and mediocre. Very soon, probably in the first year of the journal, they were successful in their efforts. *Mir Iskustva* and the group won for themselves the position of the most advanced and vital force in Russian art. They were abused and detested by many, but it was impossible to ignore them.

There are many reasons for the comparative ease of this victory. Firstly, *Mir Iskustva* embraced the greater part of the young creative talent of Russia. The Diaghilevian corps gained highly gifted adherents in Moscow (such as Serov and Levitan). Secondly, its success was due perhaps to the absence of anything narrowly sectarian in its outlook. Last, but not least, it was due to Diaghileff.

Even in this first attempt he was able to show his flair for success. The *Mir Iskustva* exhibitions, the external appearance of the journal, and its actual contents—all these were not only first-class but hitherto unknown in Russia.

No difficulty was too great for Diaghileff; expense was immaterial to him, and he did not worry about financial profit. When an exhibition had to be arranged in the Academy of Arts, the walls of which were hung with huge canvases, Diaghileff without a moment's hesitation draped the walls with pleated cloth, covering the academy pictures. On this cloth he hung his own exhibits. The cost was unimportant; he always knew where to find a patron, and the sensational success justified his daring.

The external appearance alone of the journal *Mir Iskustva* was unusually magnificent for St. Petersburg of those days. Unable to find a suitably elegant type, they unearthed old eighteenth-century founts and used them. Paper of the desired quality was difficult to get. They used *vergé*, which was new to Russia. Great technical difficulties had to be overcome in attaining the necessary quality of illustration. For a whole year the blocks for the journal were ordered in Germany. On one occasion Diaghileff and Bakst spent

37

a whole night at the printers' while woodcuts were being printed from several wooden blocks.

Perhaps the main reason for the success of *Mir Iskustva* was the harmonious working of those who took part in it. The editorial office of the journal was a home where friends gathered. There everything was discussed jointly, performed jointly without either rivalry or envy. Everything was done in the spirit of friendship. While Bakst drew a vignette, Diaghileff cut out photographs for the printing block, Filosofov acted as printer's devil, Benois corrected proofs, and somewhere in a corner Serov or Nourok wrote a trenchant article. In a word, the same friendly atmosphere of common enthusiasm as in the past had prevailed among the "Pickwickians" prevailed now in the editorial office of *Mir Iskustva*.

The influence of the group on the artistic life of Russia proved immense. In the history of Russian culture, especially as regards artistic taste, this movement was a dividing line which marked the beginning of a vital and productive renaissance. Interest in Russian art reawakened, and the wider public began to take a more cultured attitude towards its artistic heritage. People began to demand more originality and vitality in contemporary art. Taste improved, and this improvement extended to all branches of art, even to house decoration.

No historian of Russian culture can afford to neglect *Mir Iskustva* or the six years during which it lasted, for without it we should be unable to understand the new vigour which is shown in Russian art at the beginning of the twentieth century.

* * *

Before long the group had tangible evidence of their success.

The newly appointed Director of Imperial Theatres, Prince Serge Wolkonsky, still a young man, enlisted in his service two important members of the new movement. Filosofov was appointed a member of the Repertory Committee of the Dramatic Theatre, and Diaghileff was made a junior assistant of the director.

Proud and excited, and filled with a sense of their importance, they rushed with the news of their appointments to Benois, who was living in the country just outside St. Petersburg. What was to be done? Many plans were suggested. Meetings and discussions followed. In the editorial office of *Mir Iskustva*, and sometimes at the homes of Benois or Filosofov, elaborate plans were made. The group became a kind of unofficial consulting committee of the Imperial Theatres directorate.

The directorate published a year-book intended to sum up and evaluate the work of the previous season. As might be expected, it was a dullish, official publication. Diaghileff was put in charge of it. You may imagine what he and his friends did with the next number. There was an article on the scenic art of Gonzago, the great eighteenth-century decorator, a lengthy eulogy of the late director I. A. Vsevolozhsky, and an article on the architecture of the Alexandrine Theatre.

The number was attractively and profusely illustrated. When the 1900 edition finally appeared it was so brilliant that it won the approval even of the Tsar.

But this activity was insufficient either for Diaghileff or his friends. It is true that they were also engaged simultaneously in minor tasks. Benois was given the production at the Hermitage Theatre of *Cupid's Revenge*, the opera by the mediocre Court composer, Alexander Taneev. Somov designed the vignettes for the programmes, and Bakst was given the costumes for the French play, *Le Cœur de la Marquise*. But all these were trifles. They wanted to expand their work, to find an outlet for self-expression.

The idea occurred to the friends that they would like to produce Delibes's ballet, *Sylvia*. Diaghileff approached the director, and won his consent. *Sylvia* was a fine old ballet, but it had passed from public memory. The group of friends set about planning the details of this production, and the work proceeded furiously. Benois was given the general production of the whole ballet and the detailed production of the first act.

Constantine Korovin, from Moscow, was given the second act, and Benois's nephew, Eugene Lanceray, the third act. The costumes were designed by Bakst. Even their Moscow friend, Serov, unwilling to be left out of the work, designed the costume for an old faun. Work was in full swing, and soon everything was nearly ready. The chief part was given to Preobrazhenska, and the two brothers Legat were also given parts. . . . Suddenly the storm broke.

A delegation from the higher grades of the Imperial Theatres directorate interviewed Wolkonsky. They protested against the commission of such important work to a junior assistant, saying that it was a contravention of the rules and must not be allowed.

Wolkonsky summoned Diaghileff, and informed the latter that he was regretfully unable to entrust him with the official production of the ballet. An unpleasant scene followed, in which Diaghileff reminded Wolkonsky of his previous promise and threatened to give up the editing of the year-book. Wolkonsky, changing from a friendly tone to one of command, ordered Diaghileff to continue with the year-book. Diaghileff refused. Thus began in February 1901 the differences between Diaghileff and his group and the Imperial Theatres directorate. The other members of the group wrote to the director refusing to collaborate further with him, and the quarrel became prolonged. There was an attempt at reconciliation in the editorial office of *Mir Iskustva*, which was visited for this purpose by Wolkonsky and his Moscow assistant, Teliakovsky. Nothing came of this, however. Both sides remained obdurate.

On the following day Diaghileff received from the directorate an official letter demanding his resignation. Greatly upset, he rushed to the Grand Duke Serge Michaïlovitch, who immediately went to his cousin the Tsar to intercede on Diaghileff's behalf. After much suspense Diaghileff received the Tsar's answer: "If I were in Diaghileff's place, I would not resign."

Overjoyed, Diaghileff reported this to his friends. In high glee, and relying on the Tsar's words, they were confident that they had won their case.

This was on a Friday. Saturday was the day for the report of the Minister of the Imperial Household to the Tsar. What Rydzevsky, who was acting in place of the absent Minister, said to the Tsar remains unknown, but when, lying in bed on Monday morning, Diaghileff opened the official gazette the first thing he saw was his own dismissal under paragraph three.

41

Dismissal under this head was a serious matter. It happened only in cases of embezzlement and dishonourable conduct, and the Crown Service was closed for all time to the person dismissed.

Throughout his whole career this was probably the heaviest blow which Diaghileff ever suffered. All his plans and hopes fell to the ground—and through no fault of his own. He was cut off from the Imperial Theatres and from Russia. It was as if the ground had fallen from beneath his feet. It is true, of course, that several years later Diaghileff was readmitted to the Crown Service in the Chancery of Petitions, but this was only a matter of form, a kind of compensation to him, and he himself did not take it seriously.

The possibility of creative theatrical work in Russia on the scale he wanted was denied him for ever. We, however, must remember that but for the *Sylvia* "scandal" Diaghileff would probably have remained in Russia, and the *Ballets-Russes* perhaps would never have come into existence.[1]

The reconciliation of Diaghileff with Court circles took place slowly and was never complete. He was, for example, never appointed gentleman-in-waiting, a post that was his due by birth and merit. His enterprises never met with full and unqualified support from Russia. The definite nature

---

[1] It is curious to remember that five months after this occurrence, the director himself, Wolkonsky, was forced to resign, following an incident with a ballerina who was a close friend of the Grand Duke Serge Michaïlovitch, who interceded on Diaghileff's behalf. The ballerina appeared in a ballet in a costume which was not according to the director's regulations. By an order of the director she was fined. What was the astonishment of Wolkonsky when he saw in the theatre that the fine had been remitted by personal order of the Tsar. Wolkonsky was obliged to resign.

42

of the break was clearly revealed in 1905 in connection with the Exhibition of Russian Portraits organized by Diaghileff in the Torrida Palace. The exhibition was promoted by the Grand Duke Nikolai Michaïlovitch, and the Emperor gave it the honour of his patronage.

Diaghileff showed colossal energy in the organization of this exhibition. Muffled in a heavy fur coat in biting cold weather, he travelled in sledges over nearly the whole of Russia, visiting many out-of-the-way estates to collect pictures, sometimes unearthing Old Masters in lofts and barns. The results of his labours proved to be brilliant. An enormous quantity of pictures hung in the Torrida Palace. It was the first important representative exhibition of Russian paintings through the ages.

The decoration of the Palace was entrusted to Bakst, who fitted up the large gallery as a charming garden for the sculpture.

The Grand Duke Nikolai Michaïlovitch gave a dinner at his palace for the organizers and their friends. It was evident at this dinner that the Grand Duke, in view of the Tsar's displeasure with Diaghileff, intended to throw him overboard at the last moment. A friend of the Grand Duke, the rich old eccentric Dashkov, who was present at the dinner, could not restrain himself. He began to shout and stutter at the Grand Duke, roaring that, devil take it! that was no way to behave. The old man became so excited that he had a heart attack, and Benois had to take him home and calm him. They sat till four in the morning and finished three bottles of liqueur.

The Grand Duke repented, went to see the Tsar, and put things straight. Nevertheless, although on the opening day Diaghileff accompanied the Tsar, giving him information about the pictures, their relationship did not improve. The strain and mutual distrust was apparent. It was then that Diaghileff decided to try his fortune abroad and take the exhibition to Paris.

# 4

## TOWARDS THE BALLET

TO explain Diaghileff's activities in Europe purely by his failure to keep on good terms with official Russia would be a mistake. A Western outlook had always been characteristic of the group of friends. They belonged to St. Petersburg, the gateway to Europe. Even in 1893 Benois had been in correspondence with Muther of Munich, and had written, unknown to the other "Pickwickians," the Russian chapter for the German's *History of Painting*.

Again, several of them had foreign blood in their veins. But at first, despite or perhaps because of their Westernism, they had intended to spread Western enlightenment in Russia—not export Russian culture abroad. Perhaps they had contemplated a mutual exchange of ideas between Russia and the West, but they had certainly never foreseen the undertaking of a Western crusade. Now that their opportunities in Russia were gone they were *forced* to turn to the West.

In 1906 the exhibition in a slightly altered form was taken to Paris. Twelve halls of the Salon d'Automne were filled with Russian pictures. As before, the decoration was done by Bakst, and even his garden was reconstructed on a smaller scale in the Grand Palais, on the banks of the Seine. A wonderful catalogue was published, and Benois read a paper on Russian art. The enterprise was certainly successful, but not in the same overwhelming way as when the *Ballets-Russes* took Europe by storm.

45

The more advanced Press praised the exhibition, and the select few admired it. Many pictures were sold. Still, the great mass of the people were indifferent. In fact, it was a *succès d'estime*.

In 1907 Diaghileff undertook another enterprise, this time in music. The season of Russian concerts at the Paris opera will always remain in my memory. Diaghileff had collected—as only he could—all the greatest talent in Russia. The young Feodor Chaliapine sang as only he could sing in his prime. I remember how, after the solo from *Boris Godounov*, the German musician in my box, who despised Russian music on principle, with a face as pale as a sheet, had to go into the foyer to recover his composure.

Rachmaninoff, still in his youth, played the piano.

In this connection I remember a little display of chauvinistic displeasure at *ces sales étrangers*. Rachmaninoff, recalled after his number by the repeated applause, at length sat down to play an encore. Suddenly the silence which had fallen was broken by a piercing cat-call from the gallery. The pianist turned and looked in the direction of the interrupter with a look of astonishment. Then his face lit up with a modest, good-natured smile. He seemed to say, "All right, have your little bit of fun. I have to play, anyhow."

The applause shook the house.

Rimsky-Korsakov, Alexander Scriabin, and Josef Hofmann took part in this triumph of Russian music. The idol of the Russian public, Arthur Nikisch, conducted. It was magnificent. I myself have never heard a more brilliant performance of Russian music. That was one of Diaghileff's special feats—to show Europe Russian art in greater perfection than it was known in Russia itself.

\* \* \*

In the same year in St. Petersburg there occurred what must be counted the first step in the direction of the *Ballets-Russes*—and Diaghileff had no part in it.

As far back as 1902 Benois had toyed with the idea of producing a ballet on the subject of *Le Pavillon d'Armide*, for which Tcherepnin composed a preliminary score. A long ballet in five acts was contemplated.

The Vicomte René de Beaugency, entering the pavilion of the wizard Marquis, falls asleep and sees in a dream a Gobelin tapestry come to life. Armida and her train descend from the tapestry and begin to dance. The Vicomte watches, and finally joins in. Next morning, waking in the pavilion, he finds a shawl on the ground where Armida had left hers in the dream.

This mingling of fantasy and reality, and the weird figure of the wizard Marquis, are characteristic of Benois's genius. There is evidence here of his enthusiasm for Hoffmann, that terrifying and fantastic German romantic.

In 1903 Benois and Tcherepnin took *Le Pavillon d'Armide* to Teliakovsky, who followed Wolkonsky as Director of Imperial Theatres. Teliakovsky asked if they had the music. When they replied that they had a provisional score the director wished to know whether there was a waltz! Benois and Tcherepnin, who considered the matter of waltzes irrelevant, were offended, though there actually was a waltz, and Tcherepnin played it. Nevertheless, nothing came of this visit, and the subject was dropped for the time being.

47

In the spring of 1907, having come to Paris for the production at the Opéra Comique of Rimsky-Korsakov's *Snow Maiden*, Tcherepnin called on Benois and told him that now was the chance to produce *Le Pavillon d'Armide*. Benois returned immediately to St. Petersburg. Kroupensky, one of the assistant directors of Imperial Theatres, arranged everything satisfactorily. During the whole of the summer Benois worked on the scenery and costumes, and Tcherepnin finished the musical score.

It was during this period that Benois first made the acquaintance of a man who played a vital part in the creation of the *Ballets-Russes*—Michael Fokine. A young man at this time, he was regarded by those who hoped for a revival of ballet as the most promising choreographer of the day. He was considered a first-rate dancer and a bold and original choreographer. Benois was in need of just such a man. Fokine was given charge of the choreography of *Le Pavillon d'Armide*, and meetings, discussions, and work followed.

At one of these meetings Fokine remarked to Benois:

"I have in mind a pupil who is just finishing at the school. He is very talented. Do you think we might invent some sort of part for him?"

"Who is he?" asked Benois.

"You don't know him. His name is Vazlav Nijinsky."

"Do you think it worth while to make a part for him?" asked Benois.

"I certainly do. He's a very brilliant dancer."

The rôle of Armida's slave was inserted. Tcherepnin hastily composed the music, and Fokine introduced a variation and *pas de trois*. It was in this *pas de trois* with

48

Fokine and Pavlova that Nijinsky made his first independent appearance on the stage.

But the collaboration of the former "Pickwickians" with the Imperial Theatres seemed doomed to misfortune, and here again there were "incidents." Benois invited Diaghileff to a rehearsal. When the latter entered the theatre he was approached immediately by the police inspector attached to the theatre, and requested to leave. He had to comply.

A second incident followed. Kroupensky commanded a performance without having a dress rehearsal, and at the same time his proposed programme placed *Le Pavillon d'Armide* (which had already been abridged) to follow Tchaikovsky's long ballet, *Lac des Cygnes*. This meant certain failure. Benois could not restrain himself, and he gave an outspoken interview to Bakst's journalist brother, Isaiah Rosenberg. In this article Benois "tore to pieces" the whole Imperial Theatre directorate, referring to Assistant Director Kroupensky as "a nobody in official uniform." Benois shut himself up at home and had decided that everything was over, when he was suddenly informed that Director Teliakovsky had swung to the opposite extreme; he had called for *two* dress rehearsals. Work was recommenced. Still another hitch occurred. Matilda Kchessinskaya, probably annoyed about the second dress rehearsal, refused to dance Armida. The position was desperate. Benois, running into Anna Pavlova in the wings, told her of this new calamity.

"How many days are there before the performance?" she asked.

"Six," said Benois.

"Very well; I shall practise the part and dance it," replied Pavlova.

So it turned out. Pavlova saved *Le Pavillon d'Armide*, and gained Benois's lifelong friendship.

Diaghileff, of course, attended the performance, and went into raptures over it. The friends met and discussed possibilities. It was decided that *Le Pavillon d'Armide* was the very thing to take to Paris.

* * *

In 1908 Diaghileff had already undertaken a big enterprise in Paris, when he presented at the Grand Opera his first theatrical venture in Western Europe—Moussorgsky's *Boris Godounov*, with Chaliapine in the main part. The complete production had been taken from Russia—scenery, principals, chorus, and almost the entire orchestra. It was an Eastern caravanserai moving westward. What a fine sensation it must have been when these wanderers, complete with bag and baggage, took possession of the Opera. It was just like home: everything and everybody was Russian. Sanin was manager, and the scenic artists were Juon, Benois, and Golovin. Diaghileff had slightly altered the opera for Paris—not without objections from his friends. He was afraid to stage the famous "tavern scene" with the drunken monks. But on the other hand he preserved the crowd scene of revolt which was censored in Russia for political reasons.

Diaghileff even stressed this scene, and explained it to the journalists as *la révolution Russe*.

The dress rehearsal, which in Paris is even more important than the *première*, passed off with great success.

50

The friends were delighted. They went straight from the theatre to the Café de la Paix to celebrate their triumph with a gay supper. Till early in the morning the whole party roamed the empty streets of Paris, and Diaghileff's top hat was set at a very jaunty angle. They were still young and high-spirited. Diaghileff was staying at the Hôtel Mirabeau in the Rue de la Paix, and Benois lived in an hotel behind. Through their open windows they talked, shouted, and sometimes sang across the yard to each other. Complaints from a neighbour, who fetched the police, brought these serenades to an end.

*Boris Godounov* was performed eight times at the Opera. It was well received. It was even a striking success, but again, as on the previous occasion, it appealed rather to the advanced Press and the *élite* than to the general public. If it had been an unsubsidized private enterprise, it would certainly have been a financial failure.

\* \* \*

Meanwhile active preparations were being made in St. Petersburg for the Paris season of the following year. The success of *Le Pavillon d'Armide* influenced the choice of programme, which, it was decided, should include ballet as well as opera. Among the operas chosen were *Prince Igor* by Borodin and *Pskovitianka* by Rimsky-Korsakov. The title of the latter did not satisfy Diaghileff. Nobody would understand it, he complained, proposing instead to re-name it *Ivan the Terrible*, which everyone could understand. As usual he had his way, despite protest from the composer's widow (Rimsky-Korsakov had recently died). The only concession made to her wishes was to put

*Pskovitianka* in brackets underneath *Ivan the Terrible* on the programmes.

In addition to these two operas it was decided to stage *Judith* by Serov and the prologue from Glinka's opera, *Rousslan and Ludmila.*

The ballet repertoire was not immediately decided. Fokine's relationship with the Imperial Theatres became strained at this period. The directorate gave him no productions and interfered in his work. Fokine began to undertake private and charity performances. In collaboration with Benois he produced *Harlequinade* to Clementi's *Sonatinas.* But even in this he had many difficulties to encounter. Performers engaged in active theatrical work were not allowed to take part in these charity performances, and Fokine had to rely on old and retired dancers such as Maria Petipa, Enrico Cecchetti, and Bekeffi, all of them over fifty.

Another of Fokine's private productions was important in connection with the *Ballets-Russes.* This was a short ballet performed to Arensky's music, *Nuits d'Égypte.* Benois was delighted with this performance, and began persuading Diaghileff to include it in his repertoire. He found this a difficult task; Diaghileff disliked Arensky's music, and only gave way after much argument—and then with reservations.

The music was quite changed. Leaving the Arensky music only as a background, Diaghileff introduced into the body of the ballet music from various different sources: a little of Rimsky-Korsakov's *Mlada*, Glinka's "Turkish Dance," the "Persian Dance" from Moussorgsky's *Hovanschina*, and finally the "Bacchanal" by Glazounov. The result was

52

better than might be expected from such a mixture, and it achieved fame later as the ballet *Cléopâtre*.

When the matter was discussed at meetings, held often at Fokine's home, it was seen that Bakst and the choreographer whispered to each other a great deal behind the backs of the others. Eventually it appeared that the subject of their whisperings was one of Fokine's private pupils—a handsome, talented, and rich young girl, Ida Rubinstein. Bakst, with his peculiar Jewish loyalty, was loud in her praises. "She is a goddess," he would shout, and Fokine, too, spoke highly of her. The friends discussed the possibilities of giving her the part of Cléopâtre. The difficulty was that she was not yet sufficiently trained. However, when Fokine promised to be responsible for her training it was decided to entrust her with the part, although none of them except Fokine and Bakst had actually seen her, and indeed they did not see her before her arrival in Paris.

Diaghileff completed his programme for the ballet and opera season in France with two more ballets, *Les Sylphides* and *Le Festin*.

If you meet anyone who remembers the Paris season of 1909, the talk will inevitably centre round the ballet performances, and not the operas, which are scarcely remembered. Even *Prince Igor* is memorable only for its "Polovetz" dances. Fokine's inspired choreography in these wild dances and the poetical décor by Rœrich overshadowed the music. And this was typical of the season as a whole; the ballets completely outdid the operas in popularity. Diaghileff and his friends found their true vocation, and their future was decided by this season. They had ranged from painting to concert music, and from that to opera, and they understood finally that their real task lay in the ballet and nothing else. Ballet, the most international of languages, offered the biggest field for success and the greatest opportunities for creative originality. In the West the ballet had declined and was neglected: it had come to be regarded as a mere adjunct to opera; there was no school of ballet in Paris, no accepted style or technique. The male rôles were played by women *en travesti*. In the shape in which Diaghileff presented it, as an independent, self-contained art, ballet was a striking novelty to Western Europe, a strange resurrection of something long since defunct and forgotten.

On the other hand, the old classical ballet still reigned in Russia, which had a magnificent school and a tradition and style which were sacredly preserved. There were still in Russia companies of first-rate performers, a vast reserve of talent from which suitable material could be selected without difficulty. But the rigid form of Imperial Ballet lacked one thing: bold, creative thought. It was just this which Diaghileff and his friends supplied. Their youthful prodigality of ideas was inexhaustible, and their leader, Serge Diaghileff, knew how to bring their creative ideas to life before the public.

From 1910 the whole activity of Diaghileff and his friends was concentrated on ballet.

# 5

## IMPERIAL BALLET

IS it correct to call Diaghileff's Paris productions of 1909 the Russian Ballet? It would be wrong to reply to that question with a simple direct affirmative.

The answer is, of course, in the affirmative, but certain qualifications and reservations must be made.

The fact is that when in 1909 the Théâtre du Châtelet was resounding with applause, it was for something which had not yet been seen in Russia and which we Russians could see only by visiting Paris, London, and later New York.

Nevertheless, but for Russia these ballets would not have been possible. Russia contained all the essentials of *Ballets-Russes*, and the whole act of creation was performed by Russians in Russia. Without the Imperial Ballet, without its school and traditions, the Diaghileff productions, different as they were, could not have been created. No art is born suddenly; like man, it must have parents and ancestors.

During the nineteenth century the Russian Imperial Ballet had experienced several vicissitudes of fortune. During the thirties it was still in full bloom, and the great national poet Pushkin was writing immortal verse in praise of the classical dancing of the ballerina Istomina.

After the death of the famous French choreographer Didelot ballet began gradually to decay, though it never became completely extinct. It always retained a small but

55

loyal public. Although the balletomanes were rather mocked at and ridiculed, they still persisted in their loyalty to the art.

The Imperial Ballet was never given as an adjunct or *divertissement* to other arts. Wednesdays and Sundays were set aside for performances of nothing but ballet, and the half-empty auditorium contained a special public—a mixture of children accompanied by their mothers or governesses, and old gentlemen with binoculars.

The preservation of ballet in Russia was due in great part to the Imperial régime with its Court atmosphere and abundant wealth. Artists often continued on the stage long past their prime. The famous *maître de ballet*, Marius Petipa, was in charge of the ballet at the Maryinsky Theatre for approximately sixty years. This helped to preserve tradition, but tended also towards lethargy. Gradually the older generation of balletomanes died out and interest in the art declined. By the eighties ballet survived only feebly. It is true that it never fell to the depths of the Paris ballet, for the male parts were always danced by men, and by such wonderful dancers too as Gert the Magnificent, Kchessinsky, Gorsky, Stukolkin, and others. In Paris the ballet had sunk to nothing more than a display of pretty women in tempting costumes. In St. Petersburg on the other hand, all the performers down to the youngest ballerina had their names on the bills and programmes.

Not only in Paris but throughout the whole of Western Europe the independent life of ballet had ceased in the latter half of the nineteenth century. The famous seventeenth-century ballets of Milan and Naples were defunct. The impoverished rulers of a dismembered Italy could no

PLATE III

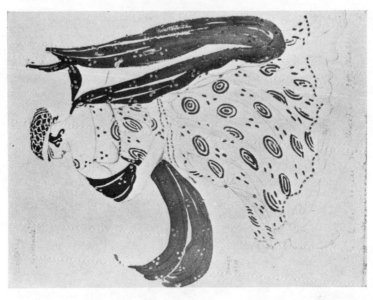

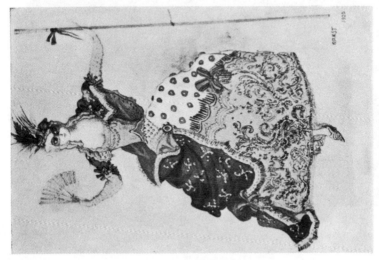

COSTUMES
*Designed by L. Bakst*

PLATE IV

MARIUS PETIPA

*Archives Internationales de la Danse*

longer afford to support independent ballet companies. There were only occasional performances in the Scala, mostly at carnival time. The ballet schools in Milan and Naples still survived, however, and these schools provided the whole of Europe with competent *maîtres de ballet* and first-rate touring ballerinas.

One of these ballerinas played a large part in the revival of Russian Ballet. This was Virginia Zucchi, who was invited to St. Petersburg for a season in 1885.

I myself had not the good fortune to see her, as she was before my time, but judging by the accounts of those who did see her Zucchi was something quite out of the ordinary. If, even to-day, you asked Matilda Kchessinskaya what is her most vivid recollection, she will reply without the slightest hesitation: "Zucchi!" She appeared in the ballet *Pharaoh's Daughter*, and her success was not only pronounced but even "sensational." In the severe old Grand Theatre people went mad about Zucchi. Prince Vassilchikov presented her with the famous "Kachinski" diamonds. When the conductor (who at that time sat immediately in front of the stage with his back to the orchestra, and part of whose duties it was to hand presents to the artists) handed Zucchi the case, and she opened it, the whole stage was illuminated by the huge brilliants. This gift, odd though it may seem, did Zucchi harm. In St. Petersburg such excesses were disliked.

Zucchi seems to have been a dancer of great temperament and exceptional dramatic art. Her technique was that of a *terre à terre* dancer without any great *élévation*, but she had the rare gift of a magnetic personality which made itself felt at once across the footlights.

On Alexandre Benois, who was then quite a youth, Zucchi produced a lasting impression.

"She was an inimitable mime and a striking dramatic actress," says Benois. "When I saw Zucchi I fully realized for the first time the dramatic possibilities of the ballet. Later, collaborating with Diaghileff, creating dramatic ballets instead of the former fairy-tale ballets, I involuntarily recalled the youthful sensations which this marvellous artist produced in me.

"In the ballet *Pharaoh's Daughter* there is a scene in which Zucchi crosses the stage in flight from the pursuit of a lion. The miming and acting of Zucchi were so convincing that watching her gave one a sensation of fear. And this, even although the lion which pursued her was grotesque in the extreme. The rough cardboard dummy of a lion, with sagging legs, as if going through the steps of a foxtrot, slung on crude wires, was dangled over the stage. Yet Zucchi had only to appear, even with this caricature of a lion, to send a shiver down the spine of the spectator."

*　　*　　*

The invitation of Zucchi to the Maryinsky Theatre was given on the initiative of the Director of Imperial Theatres, Vsevolozhsky.

In the ballet history of the eighties it is difficult to give enough credit to this man's immense personal influence on the revival of ballet. Vsevolozhsky was not a professional artist—no director was in Tsarist times. The connection of the Court with the theatre, the necessity for the director of continuous personal contact with members of the reigning family, and finally his direct subordination to the

58

Minister of the Imperial Household, induced the Tsar to choose for the post of director persons belonging to the highest circles of St. Petersburg aristocracy. The Director of Imperial Theatres, indeed, had to know not only how to deal firmly and skilfully with the artistes under his control, but also (and this was perhaps the more difficult task) how to keep on good terms with the grand dukes and influential Court circles. He had to be fair to both parties and to retain at the same time his own independence of judgment. Vsevolozhsky had the noble birth and the independent spirit essential to the post.

Besides his natural tact, coolness, and knowledge of handling people, he also possessed fair artistic talents. He was well versed in music, including contemporary work, and was a not inconsiderable designer. He often designed costumes for the productions in preparation, and if his designs were not distinguished by originality, they were quite competent and appropriate to the convention of the ballet at that period.

Vsevolozhsky's initiative had specially happy results in the sphere of ballet. It was he who commissioned a ballet from Tchaikovsky, then at the height of his power. The project was not immediately carried out. The first idea was to base the ballet on the fairy tale *Undina*, but the scenario composed by the musician's brother was unsuitable. Then Vsevolozhsky himself undertook the writing of the story, and produced a charming variation on Perrault's *Sleeping Beauty* theme which caught the imagination of the composer, who almost immediately, in December 1888, began to compose the music.

The first performance of *The Sleeping Princess* took

59

place in the Maryinsky Theatre on January 3, 1890—a very important date in the history of ballet.

At the dress rehearsal the Tsar and members of the Imperial family were present. The front-row stalls were occupied by grand dukes and their suites, and in the boxes were members of the highest aristocracy.

From every point of view the production was a success; Vsevolozhsky's story was charmingly developed, and Marius Petipa, whom Zucchi's visit had given a new lease of life, excelled himself. His choreography was varied, witty, and elegant. Regarding the music, which was dedicated by the composer to Vsevolozhsky, there can be no two opinions; it is certainly one of the greatest achievements of Russian music. Tchaikovsky himself, in a letter to Yurgensson in January of the same year, says: "*The Sleeping Princess* is probably one of my best compositions."

As regards the public the ballet was also a success, and though it was scarcely a sensation it played to full houses for a very long time.

These two events—Zucchi's visit in 1885, and the presentation of *The Sleeping Princess* in 1890—are dividing lines in the history of Russian ballet. Their success revived interest in the ballet, which once again became fashionable, and from then until the present time that interest has never waned.

On the evenings of a ballet performance the theatre was full. Guards officers in uniform mingled with grey-haired Government officials and beautifully gowned women; here and there was the hard glitter of diamonds; friends in the stalls approached the parterre boxes to greet and talk with acquaintances. . . . There were many faces one recognized,

PLATE V

VIRGINIA ZUCCHI

I. A. VSEVOLOZHSKY, SELF-CARICATURE
*Archives Internationales de la Danse*

faces one had seen on the evening before at a ball and on another day at a party. Amongst the public in the boxes were many children, the boys in sailor suits and the girls with bows in their hair. How infinitely joyful and exciting it was to go to the Maryinsky Theatre, to drive up in the closed carriage with wheels grinding on the snow, to be met at the box by an attendant[1] in braid and shoulder-knots and long white stockings. Generally he knew you; he had greeted in the same way your own mother when she was a little girl. You took off your outdoor clothes in a small padded withdrawing room.

The auditorium was very magnificent in a rococo style, done in cream and Nattier blue, which harmonized with the gilt bas-reliefs. There was a great deal of velvet and soft hangings, and a huge chandelier of cut crystal lit up the whole auditorium. The orchestra tuned up, the public poured into the theatre; how one's heart beat when a little

---

[1] These attendants were also keenly aware of the ancient traditional atmosphere of the theatre. On one occasion the Director of Imperial Theatres, Vsevolozhsky, invited to his box the wife of an old friend of his, Zografo, who had newly arrived in St. Petersburg. It was the duty of the Kapelldiener of the director's box to announce the arrival of the guest to the director. Between him and Madame Zografo there occurred the following dialogue.

"Whom may I announce to the director?"
"Madame Zografo and children."
"Princess Zografo?"
"No, Madame Zografo."
"Countess Zografo?"
"No, I say."
"Baroness Zografo?"
"No, I tell you just Madame Zografo."

With a look of reproach, the Kapelldiener withdrew and through the partition he could be heard saying into the speaking tube: "Inform the director that the wife of *General* Zografo has arrived in his box."

man appeared at the prompter's box, sat down, raised his baton, the lights went out, the first soft strains of the orchestra began, and the curtain rose silently. The mysterious, wonderful dream had begun.

Probably all we Russians have an inborn love of the theatre. Even now, if I close my eyes, I can feel again the faint hot-house smell of the Maryinsky Theatre.

As a child, I remember once one of the grown-ups in our box pointed out to me one of four dancers, *coryphées*. "Look at the one on the right. She is a dancer with a big future. She is called Pavlova the Second." This was the future Anna Pavlova. I can still see clearly the extraordinarily graceful poise of her head and the delicate lightness of her movements.

Promotion in the Imperial Ballet was very strict. It was very rare that a dancer was preferred out of rotation. Promotion from *corps de ballet* to *coryphée* and from *coryphée* to prima ballerina was long and difficult. The rapid advancement of Pavlova and Karsavina were rare exceptions.

\* \* \*

In the early years of the twentieth century the popularity of the ballet was increasing. Performances were always well attended. Balletomanes increased and multiplied. These were mostly dignified Government officials, and they occupied the greater part of the stalls. In the front row old Vintulov, with his long white side-whiskers, was always to be seen. Not far from him sat the civilian "general" Bezobrazov, clean-shaven and heavily built; and the ballet critics Skalkovsky, Plesheev, and Zheltouhin were also

always present. Never without their binoculars, the balletomanes, these severe critics and upholders of tradition,
"observed, judged, and counted." None of the technical
defects of a ballerina escaped. They religiously counted the
famous thirty-two *fouettés* of the virtuoso Kchessinskaya,
discussed and evaluated the talent of a beginner, her grace,
her elevation, her temperament. These people were known
to the artistes behind the footlights, who knew and expected
their criticism.

The boxes were nearly always occupied by families who
subscribed for the seats. There was always someone in the
grand ducal box on the left of the orchestra, and the
director's box on the right was always filled with young
people. In the 1907–8 season some of the boxes were taken
by clubs and regiments. The exclusive Yacht Club and the
English Club had boxes, and so had the Hussars and the
Horse Guards. It was almost impossible for an ordinary
private individual to book a box for the season.

\* \* \*

The theatrical life of pre-War Russia was distinguished
by strict morality. It was very rarely that an actress or
ballerina was a kept mistress. No Rolls-Royces or even
Fords waited for the ballerinas at the stage door. No one
was admitted behind the scenes except those connected
with the work. Only members of the Imperial family had
access to the *coulisses*. But then the theatres were the
personal property of the Tsar; the Imperial family felt they
had a right there, and they could not be refused admission.

I remember an episode at the Moscow Art Theatre
which was very characteristic of the theatrical morals of

63

the time. The young actress Baranovskaya, who was to have the chief part in a play *The Life of Man* about to be produced, was unexpectedly called to Director Stanislavsky's office "for explanations." She left his room looking as white as a sheet, and in reply to questions from her colleagues said, "I am leaving. Stanislavsky has thrown me out." After much interrogation the cause of the trouble was discovered. It appeared that Baranovskaya had been seen in the street with a powdered nose, and Stanislavsky had been informed. In his room he said to her:

"It appears you do not understand the spirit of our theatre. It is only cocottes who powder their noses. You do not suit our tone. You had better leave."

Stanislavsky was only with difficulty persuaded to revoke his decision.

This incident of "Baranovskaya's nose" is, of course, an exceptional case, but it is significant of the theatrical atmosphere of the time.

\* \* \*

The Imperial Ballet Schools were conducted in monastic fashion. They were boarding-schools where girls and boys were educated at the expense of the Crown. The girls and boys were kept apart, only meeting at their joint ballet work. The lady supervisors and instructresses were strict disciplinarians. There was no communication with the outside world. They were rather like finishing schools for young ladies of high birth, except that dancing was taught instead of deportment. The severe uniform in which the pupils were dressed gave them all a similar impersonal appearance. Owing to the fact that the pupils were boarded

64

and trained at the expense of the Crown, there was a certain Court atmosphere about the schools, and the discipline was very rigid. The children studied for eight years—two years as day pupils on trial and six years as boarding pupils. The child's family had to practically part with it for that period, since the schools had absolute power over the child's life. Visitors were not allowed, except occasionally during rehearsals, when outsiders connected with the work would attend. A charming picture greeted them in the practice hall of the schools. Young girls about fifteen to eighteen in *tutus* with bare arms and shoulders, without make-up, were grouped here and there at the sides of the hall, whispering and sometimes laughing together. The girls curtsied in greeting, and the boys clicked their heels and bowed. After eight years of intensive teaching and training the pupils immediately made their début on the Imperial stage, a company of marvellously trained, technically perfect adepts of their art.

Even as children they were accustomed to the stage. Many classical ballets contained scenes in which the Ballet School appeared—for example, the famous mazurka in *Paquita*. The children performed brilliantly, and this charming dance invariably drew rounds of applause. The pupils were brought to the performance in closed carriages and taken back to school immediately after their appearance on the stage.

The atmosphere of peace and tradition which reigned in the Imperial Theatres was due partly to their absolute financial security. The usual deficit, which generally reached the figure of two million gold roubles (£200,000) was covered from the Privy Purse.[1] Profit was a secondary consideration and was no essential part of the policy of the theatres. Every theatrical worker had an assured future; they knew that, having served their term of years, they would receive a pension and have a comfortable old age. The whole atmosphere of the old Imperial St. Petersburg explains the strange fact that the Imperial Ballet could carry on a tradition of their art which went back almost without change to Noverre and Vestris. Even at the beginning of the twentieth century the eighteenth-century ballet was preserved in them alive, even if somnolent.

The calm and assured tradition of the Imperial Theatres was perhaps similar to that which prevailed in Court society. A century of internal rest and peaceful progress had produced a sense of security. On the very eve of the disaster of 1914 St. Petersburg society was convinced that it was firmly established, and its position, stable for more than a century, seemed unshakable. Only people outside that circle could understand the falseness of such a conviction and foresee the possibility of a future catastrophe.

In spite of the noticeable revival of interest in ballet, in spite of a succession of wonderful new ballets based on the work of the finest Russian composers of the day, the conventional style of ballet remained unaltered. Marius Petipa allowed not the slightest deviation from tradition. Tchaikovsky's three ballets, *Lac des Cygnes*, *The Sleeping Princess*, *Casse Noisette*, as well as ballets by Glazounov,

---

[1] In Russia there were three sorts of Crown Properties: (1) State Property; (2) *Oudeli*, which consisted of the joint property of the House of Romanoffs; (3) the Privy Purse—the property of the reigning monarch. This included miscellaneous things, for example, the whole Altai district of Siberia.

including the famous *Raymonda*, were all produced in the same style of fantasy. *Meaning*, without which no ballet is truly creative, was quite neglected; the choreography was always worked out within the same traditional framework.

The *prima ballerina*, like the tenor in Italian opera, always came forward for her solo dance, while the *corps de ballet* remained waiting up-stage. There was no conception of the ballet as unified whole; it was divided into numbers, *pas seul*, *pas de deux*, *corps de ballet*, etc., just as the old Italian opera was divided into arias, duets, and choruses, and during the performance of these numbers the others on the stage made no pretence of acting.

The scenery was excellent in its way, no expense being spared, but it was pompous in style, with little sense of colour or design. For example, the representation of an inn would cover the whole stage as if it were a hall in a palace. More attention was paid to producing the illusion of reality than to the artistic purpose of the décor, and great pains were taken with perspective, the aim being to make the stage look as deep as possible. Almost every ballet had as a background either a lake or a fountain. This custom was so firmly established that the dancers in the last row of the *corps de ballet*, whose main function was to perform classical arm movements, were called *les ballerines près de l'eau*. The décor was not allowed to be intimate or poetical or to express emotion. It was sumptuous, but its function was merely to provide a decorative background for the performers.

The costumes, in charge of Monsieur Ponomarev, were also conventional, almost to the point of uniformity. All the female costumes were based on the short, projecting *tutu*, which is now nearly forgotten. To this was added the necessary local colour—a Greek design for classical ballet, hieroglyphs for Egyptian ballet, and so on. The male costumes were designed principally with a view to comfort and were generally variegated in colour.

Ballet music was for a long time monopolized by two composers, both ballet conductors of the Imperial Theatres, Minkus and Pugni. The latter was admittedly a talented composer of ballet music, though he was not by any means a musician of the first rank.

Ballets could be divided into four types:

1. The Heroic Ballet, like the *Bayadère*, in which the heroine died in the first act and reappeared later in spirit form. At the end of the ballet everything collapsed like a bubble bursting; this was carried out very effectively, columns, scenery, and everything quite disappearing.

2. The Romantic Ballet, like *Esmeralda*, based on Victor Hugo's *Notre Dame de Paris*.

3. The Eighteenth-century Ballet, such as *La Fille mal gardée*.

4. National Ballet, based on some Russian fairy tale, in national costumes and with characteristic national dances. Such was *Konek Gorbounok*.

All these productions were distinctly substantial affairs —they gave you a lot for your money. *La Fille mal gardée* was in four acts, and *Pharaoh's Daughter*, lasting four hours, had two prologues and an epilogue. All this was certainly brightened up a little with the introduction of ballets by Tchaikovsky and Glazounov, but the general style and tradition of production remained the same.

68

My comparison of classical ballet with Italian opera was not accidental; the parallel does exist. The production of Italian opera concentrated on the voice and the art of the singer, and the orchestra provided scarcely more than an accompaniment, its dramatic function being kept in the background; in the same way the classical dance was the central part of the classical ballet and the music was merely an aid to the dancer.

The Italian opera's disregard of the dramatic aspect of the art was almost incredible. The famous tenor, Masini, who possessed a voice of unsurpassable beauty, did not even make a pretence of acting; he simply approached the prompter's box and sang. In one opera there is a scene in which the soprano, grieving over the prostrate form of the dying tenor, sings a long aria. Masini, tired of lying still during this scene, rose and walked to the wings, leaving the poor prima donna to sob over an empty stage. When the moment approached for Masini to sing again, he returned to the stage and lay down as if nothing had happened.

The treatment of the music in classical ballet was not much better. Rimsky-Korsakov, in his *Reminiscences*, complains that his *Mlada* was rehearsed without an orchestra, without even a piano, the only accompaniment being provided by two violins. Neither ballet master nor dancers, nor the musicians themselves, could understand the first thing about the orchestration. When the orchestra was supposed to play a *tutti* with trombones *fortissimo*, Petipa rehearsed light aerial movements, and when the score demanded the soft tone of strings mass ensembles were staged.

When the Imperial Theatres directorate commissioned Glazounov's *Raymonda*, Marius Petipa gave the composer

69

a libretto in which the music was already divided out minutely, sometimes into passages of four, eight, and sixteen bars. In *The Sleeping Princess* there is a scene known as the Panorama, where Prince Charming with his suite advances towards the castle of the Sleeping Princess. During this scene the back-cloth moves. At one rehearsal it became apparent that the music would finish before the scene had been completely unfolded. Tchaikovsky was urgently requested to add enough music to last out the few yards of material. This additional piece of music has remained known as the "Yard Music." It did not seem to occur to anyone to cut down the scenery.[1] The music had to be written to the dances, just as the librettists in their day had to set words to previously composed arias.

The rehearsals of *Raymonda* were also conducted to the accompaniment of violins, and when Glazounov protested

[1] I produce as an example a portion of a memorandum given by Marius Petipa to Tchaikovsky for the first act of the ballet *Casse Noisette*:

"1. Music for dance—64 beats.
2. The tree is lit up, sparkling music for 8 b.
3. Children's entrance. Boisterous and gay music—24 b.
4. A moment of astonishment and admiration. Tremolo of several b.
5. March of 64 b.
6. Entry of the Fops. 16 b. Rococo (tempo—menuet).
7. Gallop.
8. Drosselmeyer's entrance. Rather frightening and at the same time comical music. A broad movement of 16 or 24 b. The music changes character gradually—24 b. It becomes less melancholy, brightens and finally passes to gaiety.
   Fairly serious music—8 b., rest, repeat the same 8 b. and rest again.
   4 b. with startling chords.
9. 8 b. in Mazurka time. 8 more b., Mazurka. A further 16 b. of Mazurka.
10. Waltz, staccato and with well-marked rhythm."

M. TCHAIKOVSKY: *The Life of P. I. Tchaikovsky.*

that this distorted the meaning of the music, Petipa answered that he could not help it because he could not pick out music played on the piano.

Little attention was paid even to the story of the ballet. I myself, for example, could never follow the story of *Raymonda*. It has a wicked Saracen, a noble knight betrothed, a Hungarian king, a duel, a goblet with magic drink, and of course Raymonda herself, who, it appears, does not want to marry the Saracen; it has a finale and a *divertissement*—in a word, it has everything but meaning.

The first evidence of reformation began in the opera in the fifties, when Wagner and Bizet and later, in Russia, Dargomizhski, Moussorgsky, and Rimsky-Korsakov put dramatic content into their operas. The ballet was affected much later, and the beginning of the new outlook must be ascribed to Isadora Duncan, who was the first to bring out in her dancing the meaning of the music; she was the first to *dance* the music and not dance *to* the music. She altered the whole direction of the dance from pure movement to movement expressing sound. It was a pity that as a dancer Duncan was a dilettante and did not possess an adequate technique. Then, too, she was alone, and if her art can be called plastic it certainly was not ballet.

It was left to Diaghileff and his friends to complete the revolution by making music the basis of the ballet. This was Diaghileff's chief innovation and constitutes the main difference between *Ballets-Russes* and the Imperial Ballet. The acceptance of the principle of the primary importance of the music had implications which led the Diaghilevians far.

When the music became the guiding factor in ballet and the dancers had to express its meaning, the greater part of

71

the older ballet music proved to be quite unsuitable in quality for the increased scope of the new art. For this reason the new ballets were produced to music either written specifically for them or—and this was the general practice—music which, though not written for the ballet, was of sufficiently high quality to provide suitable material for creative work. *Carnaval*, for example, was created from one of Schumann's compositions for the piano; *Les Sylphides* from a collection of Chopin's piano music; *Sheherazade* from one of Rimsky-Korsakov's symphonic poems, and so on.

Once the purpose of the dance was to interpret musical meaning then there could be no further idea of special interpolated dances or numbers (*pas seul, pas de deux, pas d'action*, etc.). What was required was a co-ordinated unity of dramatic action. And this, in turn, changed the whole character of the performance, which became clearer and more logical in its story. Even the character of the dancing was changed and became often more expressive than "plastic." The movement became more fluent and "dramatic," the poses bolder, and the technique less rigid.

The same causes led to the introduction of performances of several short ballets in one evening. Schumann's *Carnaval* cannot be prolonged for a whole evening; Rimsky-Korsakov's *Sheherazade* occupies only about forty minutes; and Debussy's *L'Après-midi d'un Faune* is even shorter. In brief, not only the character of ballet, but even the structure of the whole performance was altered.

It is impossible to deny that this revolution introduced to the ballet much that was excellent, vital, and artistic, and many changes were based on the elementary demands of common sense. But, as with every revolution, every break with tradition, much that was good was also lost. While Diaghileff was producing his ballets one often met lovers of the old Imperial Ballet who were deadly enemies of Diaghileff and his enterprises. They considered that Diaghileff and his friends were distorting and spoiling the essence of ballet, that they were introducing Western Europe not to the Russian ballet but to a kind of decadent parody of it.

I shall not enter into a detailed discussion of this point of view. I do not agree with it, and I consider that the achievements of the pre-War *Ballets-Russes* attain heights which are rare in the history of art.

However, it is possible that I can understand this point of view, even though I consider it wrong.

In the old Imperial classical ballet there was a great deal that was unforgettable. Its conventionality, perhaps even its absurdity, contained a whole tradition, comprised the whole charm of the past. Those lengthy evenings, those spectacular ballets with the stage filled with male and female dancers, those pompous décors, those conventional, graceful movements and technically brilliant classical dances by ballerinas light as air—I have a great affection for all those, they are as dear to me as my childhood years and as the old St. Petersburg of bygone days.

It is difficult to separate one's youthful recollections of ballet from the whole atmosphere of the social life of Imperial St. Petersburg. Only there and in those surroundings, in the general Court atmosphere with its elaborate functions and social life, could Imperial Ballet have existed, with its costly upkeep, its conservatism, its extreme loyalty to tradition, its rigidity, its splendour.

# 6

## 1909

AS soon as *Le Pavillon d'Armide* production had determined the friends to take ballet to Paris, Diaghileff and his friends threw themselves into the work. In spite of the lukewarm reception of *Le Pavillon d'Armide* by the general public, and in spite of attacks from all quarters on the friends and on Fokine, they had faith in their work. They were not aiming at a revolution, they did not want to be, at any cost, "the last word." They were simply carried away by their enthusiasm to create what they saw to be necessary. Far from being revolutionaries, they were in fact young people with rather conservative tendencies. Diaghileff alone showed any inclination to "shock the bourgeoisie" by being advanced, daring, and even impudent. There was much wrangling within the group on this account. Even in the *Mir Iskustva* period the friends protested against Diaghileff's attempts in this direction.

The production of *Le Pavillon d'Armide* proved a revolution in spite of itself. Diehard balletomanes would not accept it; they misunderstood and abused it. Even the eulogy written by the famous critic Beliaev in an endeavour to save the situation was of no avail. The production was not accepted as an official directorate one, but as something foreign. Anna Pavlova, who saved *Armide*, found herself unexpectedly embroiled with the Imperial Theatres

74

over it. Assistant Director Kroupensky commenced intrigues, and the brothers Legat turned against Fokine, with the result that the latter threw himself even more whole-heartedly into the work of the Diaghileff circle. For many years he was happy in his work for the friends. It was only later, in Paris, that, damped by the moving into prominence of Nijinsky, he began to change and, as if purposely to make difficulties, demanded an enormous salary (in the neighbourhood of £10,000 a year)—and got it.

The friends had no special axe to grind. They simply created what they wanted to create. Even the national question did not bother them too much. Certainly they could not ignore it.

"We must take to Paris something Russian," they said to each other. "We can't do otherwise. We're going for a *saison Russe*."

The ballet *Le Festin* was chosen as a concession to nationalism. This collection of Russian dances in national costumes had to justify the general cosmopolitan character of the repertoire. Nevertheless, it did not prevent the *Ballets-Russes* from being accused in the French Press of "internationalism." The fact that universality is one of the main traits of Russian psychology, that to be "international" is natural to Russians, was not accepted in the West. "To become a real Russian, a true Russian, may only mean to become a brother of all men, to become universal, if you like" (Dostoevsky, *Speech on Pushkin*). The West expected from Diaghileff not only Russian national colour but something like Eastern Asiatic exoticism which the Press and public demanded of anything

75

Russian. For the following season they had to make a greater effort in this direction.

\* \* \*

Since 1908, when *Boris Godounov* was staged at the Paris Opera, Diaghileff's enterprises had been honoured by the high patronage of Grand Duke Vladimir Alexandrovitch (maternal grandfather of Marina, Duchess of Kent). The relations of Diaghileff and the Grand Duke rested on a friendly basis of mutual confidence. The Grand Duke approved of the idea of including ballet in the 1909 season and promised his support. The financing of the enterprise was a difficult matter, and various channels had to be utilized.

In Riga, in the Baltic provinces, Diaghileff found a very rich galoshe manufacturer who was prepared to give him financial support. This patron of art promised the large sum of £10,000. Unfortunately, the manufacturer was offended at not receiving the patent of nobility which he had expected. Diaghileff undertook to set matters right. He obtained from the Grand Duke a promise to sign the petition himself, and the affair would probably have been settled satisfactorily. The handling of this business was Diaghileff's personal matter. The friends had only heard it mentioned briefly in conversation.

"Well, Serge, how are the galoshes?" they would ask.

"All right. Things are moving," Diaghileff would answer.

But all Diaghileff's affairs in Russia seemed doomed to misfortune. The Grand Duke fell ill and died soon afterwards. Not long after his death his widow, Maria Pavlovna, received Diaghileff very kindly, and said she would try to do everything her late husband wanted. But she absolutely refused to sign the letter of petition. This was disastrous, as the whole foundation of the business was based on the promised £10,000. Diaghileff lost his temper and did not mince his words with the Grand Duchess, who took offence, refused to extend her patronage to the enterprise, and wished to have nothing more to do with Diaghileff.

For the second time in his life Diaghileff had the ground taken from beneath his feet; but, as ever at critical moments, he did not give way to despair. Telegrams were immediately dispatched to Paris, and, with the aid of the impresario Gabriel Astruc and friends there, the situation was saved.

Such crises often occurred in Diaghileff's enterprises. Negotiations would go on till the very last moment, and when they collapsed it seemed as if disaster must follow. But Diaghileff always knew how to extricate himself from the most desperate situations, and the very risks he incurred appealed to the adventurous streak in his nature.

The break with the Grand Duchess Maria Pavlovna had unexpected results in another direction. Diaghileff's company had previously been granted the use of the Hermitage Court Theatre. When Benois arrived there for the first rehearsal he was met by an unusual sight. Agitated and depressed, the artistes, huddled in corners and sitting on the costume baskets, were whispering together anxiously . . . rehearsal was "off." Diaghileff himself was not to be seen. The stage manager, Serge Grigorieff, took Benois aside.

"What's the matter?" asked Benois.

"We have been forbidden to use the stage."

"What? Impossible! There's some mistake."

"Oh, no. It is an official order."

"Where is Diaghileff?"

"He has gone to look for other premises."

At last, after much anxious waiting, the telephone bell rang. Diaghileff had found new premises in the German Club on the Ekaterinsky Canal, and everyone had to hurry there.

The whole company hastily bundled themselves and their baggage into cabs. The new premises proved excellent. The newly decorated German Club was clean and spacious. The hall had a large stage, and there were large ante-rooms where the artistes had tea and refreshments when not engaged in work. Everyone who shared in these six weeks of intensive work retains pleasant memories of the premises. Whether this was due to the place itself or to the spirit of youthful enthusiasm in which the work was carried out it is difficult to say. In any case, they all felt at home there. The work proceeded in a spirit of pure friendliness, and every heart was filled with hope for the future.

Benois confesses that during the whole time he worked there he felt as if in a dream. The actualities of life seemed colourless and dead. He was haunted by his work, moving about in his intervals of leisure as if half-conscious, like a man in love.

Only a few friends were admitted to the premises. The balletomane Bezobrazov, a convert to the cause, and the critic Valerian Svetlov both came, highly delighted to be surrounded by young girls in *tutus*. Prince Argoutinsky, an old and true friend, who often acted a peacemaker among the friends, was always there. Although his praise or condemnation was never expressed in more than mono-syllables, the friends relied upon his judgment.

The creation of the ballets was worked out in two places. The group generally met on the day before rehearsal to discuss the next day's work. The music was played, and there on the spot Fokine gave the outlines of the choreo-graphy. Often demonstrating in the centre of the room and sometimes designing it on paper, he explained how he conceived the distribution of the score and discussed the general choreographic lines. The plan was discussed, repeated, re-discussed, and so on. Poor Tcherepnin had sometimes to play the same thing more than twenty times. Benois usually developed the dramatic side, in which Fokine was not at his best.

At these meetings, and even at rehearsals, Bakst was very quiet and self-effacing. His task was a specialized one. In his own sphere his imagination was full of fire, and he produced wonderful work. In the ballet *Cléopâtre* Benois suggested that the queen should be brought in on a palanquin resembling a sarcophagus. When she was taken out of the sarcophagus Cléopâtre was wrapped like a mummy. Bakst, who had to design the costumes, shut himself up for several days in the Hermitage Museum making sketches, with beautiful results. Cléopâtre was wrapped in a long strip of linen sumptuously designed with Egyptian hieroglyphs and motifs. When this wrapping was unwound, it stretched nearly the whole width of the stage and the tableau was very effective. It was, however, very inconvenient for the actress who had to play the mummy. In Paris Benois approached Ida Rubinstein when she lay wrapped up and asked her:

"Well, Ida Lvovna, how are you feeling?"

"All right, thank you," she replied from the coffin, "but I can't move."

If a fire had broken out the hapless Cléopâtre would certainly have perished.

In this ballet, Cléopâtre agrees to accept Amune to her couch of love if he is willing to pay for it with his life. For this scene Benois suggested hiding the amorous pair from the public by a group of dancing slave girls with shawls. This idea, too, caught Bakst's imagination, and the result was brilliant. The production was severely attacked for this scene on the score of indecency. But Benois did not wish his work to contain the ". . ." which so often appear in books. This would have required the removal off-stage of the lovers, thus interfering with the unity of action in the climax of the scene. In any case the lovers were not seen behind the groups of dancers, and Benois did not consider that the implication of the love act on the stage was either coarse or cynical.

The other ballets of the repertoire were rehearsed simultaneously with *Cléopâtre. Les Sylphides,* the ballet which Fokine had previously produced at a charity performance under the title of *Chopiniana,* was almost finished and required little work on it. The scenery and the whole style of the production was given by Benois the atmosphere of ultra-worldliness which was so congenial to him. For this ballet Benois designed a new skirt for the ballerinas, which displaced in future the short projecting *tutu.* It was a return, one might say, to the forgotten *tutu Taglioni*— a return to the romantic thirties. A long skirt, like a reversed tulip head, descended well below the knee and gave the ballerina's figure a more subtle and feminine appearance.

At the rehearsals in the Ekaterinsky Hall, Fokine became very dictatorial. He conducted the whole rehearsal, and everybody had to obey. He would not accept slipshod "approximations" in practice, and this severe insistence on precision was not greatly to the liking of the established ballerinas. All the details of the plan which had been elaborated on the previous day were repeated on the stage. The smallest fragments of music were played again and again until the movement was memorized. But Fokine also invented a great deal of material at the actual rehearsal. Just as a painter with a general idea of a picture in his head can realize the details only on the actual canvas, so the choreographic detail of a ballet can only be filled in on the stage itself. Fokine's rehearsals were long-drawn-out, exacting affairs. The performers were ready to drop with fatigue, but so fine was the spirit of the company that no one really minded. They were all very keen on their work, and after rehearsals their faces, even though drawn by fatigue, were still gay.

Sometimes during practice one or other of those connected with the work would ask Fokine questions on certain points. The rehearsal would be held up while directions of a dramatic or artistic nature were given, and then the work was resumed.

Diaghileff was present only occasionally. His activities were different. All the practical and organizational side of

81

the work was in his hands. He did not interfere in the artistic sphere either with criticism or advice, leaving the creative side to his friends and devoting all his untiring energy to the realization of the business.

Nouvel was always present. He also took no part in the creative work of the ballet, but even at this early stage he revealed the abilities which were to make him Diaghileff's right-hand man. Whenever a difficult letter had to be written, especially in French or English, Diaghileff depended upon Nouvel—and never in vain. He was, as it were, Diaghileff's "Foreign Minister," and his help was both necessary and important.

The "Polovetz" scene from the opera *Prince Igor* was rehearsed with great enthusiasm. Rœrich's designs for the scenery were remarkable. His task of representing on the stage the boundless expanse of the South Russian steppes was not an easy one. He designed a huge panoramic backcloth without wings. The low, squat tents of the nomadic Polovtzi were silhouetted against a red and orange morning sky, giving promise of a very hot day. A feeling of spaciousness was obtained by this sky, which ran right across the breadth of the stage. Rœrich's costumes also proved successful. There are no extant relics of the Polovtzi; nothing is known even of the extraction of this fighting nomadic tribe. But Rœrich was not a specialist in primitive cultures for nothing. He produced costumes for the Polovtzi which were a combination of the Yakut and Kirghiz costumes, and the result was both colourful and convincing.

The rehearsals had proved to the Diaghileff group that in Fokine they possessed a real and vital force. Something quite new had emerged at these rehearsals. Instead of the

PLATE VI

DÉCOR FOR SECOND TABLEAU OF "PAVILLON D'ARMIDE"

*By A. Benois*

PLATE VII

DÉCOR FOR FIRST TABLEAU OF "GISELLE"

*By A. Benois*

usual ballet dances full of decorum and restraint, the dancing developed a wild impetuosity. Sofia Fedorova, a thin, weakly-looking creature, probably with a touch of gipsy blood, became transfigured into a frantic maenad, and the whole company got "devil" from her wild spirit. Adolph Bolm and Rozaï danced as if possessed. Even the friends themselves, the creators, were gripped by these unbridled displays of passion.

*Le Festin*, the concession to "nationalism," was rehearsed more soberly. This ballet was a mixture. It had been collected bit by bit and patched together without much care. The music, too, was miscellaneous. The ballet opened to the march from Rimsky-Korsakov's *Le Coq d'Or*. There followed the "Lezginka" (the Caucasian dance) from Glinka's *Rousslan and Ludmila*, the "Gopak," a Ukrainian dance by Moussorgsky, the "Trepak" (a popular Russian dance from Tchaikovsky's ballet *Casse Noisette*), and the finale was danced to the last composer's Second Symphony. The scenery was simply taken over from the opera *Rousslan and Ludmila*, and the costumes were designed by Bilibin, Korovin, and others. That costumes were given to Bilibin proved that the heart of the friends did not lie in this ballet. Bilibin specialized in the illustration of fairy tales. His style was rather sentimental, over-realistic, and not quite in line with that of the collaborators of the Diaghileff group.

Considerable changes were made from the Maryinsky Theatre production of *Le Pavillon d'Armide*. "An artist," says Benois, "always retains a certain feeling of dissatisfaction with his creation. He always wants to add things and to change things. That is why I felt such satisfaction

THE BIRTH OF BALLETS-RUSSES

in altering *Le Pavillon d'Armide* for Paris." The ballet was shortened and a few scenes were transposed. Some adaptations were due to the size of the cast, which was smaller than in St. Petersburg. For example, the "Awakening Hours" were reduced from twenty-four to twelve. As the *divertissement* following the revival of the Gobelin tapestry seemed rather long, the Turkish dance and the waltz were omitted and the "Dance of the Masks" was abbreviated. Nevertheless, sufficient remained—the "Dance of the Jesters," the *pas de trois* with Nijinsky, and a large, complicated *pas d'action.*[1] Rozaï made a special hit in the "Dance of the Jesters." Fokine invented for him a jump finishing on a bent leg and demanding great acrobatic technique. Among these jesters there also appeared a dancer who had just finished his course at the school, Boris Romanoff, who was to make quite a name for himself as a choreographer.

\* \* \*

After the death of their sincere friend and patron, the Grand Duke Vladimir Alexandrovitch, Diaghileff's company had no longer any strong support in Russia. Labelled as revolutionaries and decadents and abused by the Press, they felt no security at home. On the contrary, they felt that they were pariahs, that no one wanted them except a few friends. In the end they had to seek even financial support from their friends in Paris, Astruc, the Comtesse de Greffulhe, and others. They turned their backs on Russia and faced the West.

[1] *Pas d'action* is a term given to a complicated dance expressing a scene of a dramatic character.

So in the spring of 1909 they moved to Paris without having given a single performance in Russia. The new art, unseen in Russia, was transplanted, and began to flower in foreign lands, where it remained for many years—so much so that the influence of *Ballets-Russes* in Russia itself was seen only much later and as if by repercussion from the West. *Petrushka*—the peak of the Diaghileff achievements—was first performed on a Russian stage in 1921, ten years after its first production in Paris.

\* \* \*

The company set out for Paris at the end of April. From its external appearance no one could have guessed that this was the departure of the world's finest ballet company. Nearly all young people, dressed quietly, they were as lively as a crowd of holiday excursionists. Their luggage was of a miscellaneous and surprising description. Strapped hampers were mingled with impressive-looking trunks, everything was heaped higgledy-piggledy on the luggage racks, and nobody knew what was his and what was not. Gaiety was visible on every face, and even those who had seen them off showed signs of pleasure. They were undertaking an exciting and hazardous adventure in strange and foreign lands, and they were full of optimism about the future.

From the Gare du Nord in Paris they were immediately taken in various conveyances to hotels near each other on the Boulevard St. Michel. The new arrivals simply took complete possession of these hotels. Nothing was to be heard spoken but Russian. From fifth-floor balconies they would yell and shout to friends on lower floors. They sang and danced in the hall, and in fact made themselves completely at home.

The arrival in Paris was a great thrill for the company. Hardly any of them had ever been outside St. Petersburg before and everything was new. They strolled through the streets like gaping provincials and felt very happy. Old friends and the new ones they soon made in Paris began to look after them and tried to amuse them. It was pleasant and exciting to show the town to people with such youthful freshness. They had many excursions in the Bois de Boulogne. Benois remembers particularly one of these expeditions in which Prince Argoutinsky, four ballerinas, and he scrambled all six into a cab and jogged round the Bois for hours.

Their French friends were surprised by the modest behaviour and bearing of these artistes; they had nothing of the "music-hall" style about them. Probably through excitement the new arrivals were unable to speak French, though they had learned it at school and knew it quite well.

Shortly before the company's arrival in Paris there arrived from Moscow a man whose part in the Diaghileff ballet was of no small importance, but who always remained unknown to the public. This was the technician, Karl Fedorovitch Valz.

In 1908, when Diaghileff was producing *Boris Godounov* at the Grand Opera, he had a great deal of difficulty with the technical side of the production. Almost on the eve of the dress rehearsal (*première*) the Opera's chief technician warned Diaghileff that some of the scenery was not hung and that it was impossible for it to be ready in time. No one knows whether this was the result simply of inefficiency or of an intrigue which, arising from hostility to foreigners, was intended to discredit the performance.

Diaghileff thought the matter over.

"So you can't guarantee to be ready with the scenery for the performance?" he asked.

"No, I can't," was the answer.

"Very well, we shall play without it. The opera will be performed without scenery, and the responsibility will lie on you."

Only this threat of exposure saved the situation. The scenery was in place in time.

After this experience Diaghileff decided to take his own technician with him to Paris. K. F. Valz was the Moscow Grand Theatre technician. He had formerly been a scenic artist, but, having seen the brilliant work of young Moscow artists like Golovin and Korovin, he abandoned this occupation and began enthusiastically to help them in the technical execution of their aims. He was exceptionally devoted to Diaghileff and his enterprise, and the two men were very fond of each other. Diaghileff knew that he could thoroughly rely on Valz, any discussion with whom generally ended up by his saying: "Don't worry. It will all be ready in time." And it is a fact that without exception everything was always ready.

This Valz was a curious figure of a man. Small and wizened, perched on high-heeled shoes, he did not look more than fifty of his seventy-two years. Jet-black dyed hair and rouged cheeks gave an air of bravado to his jaunty, corseted figure. In spite of his age he was a passionate Don Juan and a positive danger to the virtue of young

87

dancers. He was the libertine at large, and, strange though it may seem, a great success in this direction.

Before leaving for Paris he had asked Diaghileff's permission to take four carpenters along with him. Within a fortnight of their arrival he had overhauled the whole machinery of the Théâtre du Châtelet. Though the equipment in this theatre was one of the best in Paris, it was inadequate for ballet. All the floor boards were changed, and a huge trap-door was devised, through which some of the company, Benois among them, often just saved themselves from falling during the work.

At the same time Diaghileff filled the theatre with an army of workmen to renovate it and to cover the floor, the passages, and the stalls with red cloth, which produced a gala appearance. What all this cost and where the money was to come from, heaven alone knew, but such considerations never hindered Diaghileff. It appears that this red cloth is still in the Châtelet, though in the past twenty-five years it has faded from red to a dull grey.

In the St. Petersburg production of *Le Pavillon d'Armide* there had been on the stage a fountain, which provided an atmosphere of freshness and enchantment.

Running into Valz at a rehearsal, Benois said to him:

"What a pity that we can't create the effect of spraying water."

"What do you mean? Can't? Your word is law. Give the order, and it shall be done."

"But how can you manage it?"

"Don't worry. It will all be ready in time."

And so it was. In the Paris production two beautiful fountains played on the stage, each superior to the St.

Petersburg one. The murmur of water could be heard through the whole theatre.

During the renovation of the theatre intensified rehearsals of the operas and ballets were going on. In dust and dirt and the noise of hammering they were adapting and finishing the production. With the exception of *Ivan the Terrible* (*Pskovitianka*), which occupied the whole evening, all the performances were mixed. Even the "Polovetz" dances were not presented as a separate, purely choreographic number, as was the custom later; the whole "Polovetz camp" act of the opera was given, complete with singers and chorus.

How much hurry attended all this work can be judged by the tragic fate of seven unfortunate sheep which Diaghileff bought for the pastoral scene that is one of the backgrounds in *Le Pavillon d'Armide*. They were intended to replace their cardboard imitations in St. Petersburg, and were to move in procession across the stage accompanied by a shepherd and a shepherdess. When the live sheep had been procured, they were stored underneath the stage and . . . forgotten. The poor animals died of hunger, and the pastoral scene had to be played without them. Even to-day Benois remembers this unfortunate episode with a pang of remorse and sorrow.

At the very last moment new artistes had to be engaged. For the first performances a substitute had to be found for Anna Pavlova. Probably Diaghileff, as often happened, delayed his negotiations with Pavlova until the very last moment. In any case, it turned out that she had another engagement and could not arrive for the start of the season.

Pavlova was one of the great "attractions" of the

company. The public had been promised her appearance, and Serov had made a beautiful drawing depicting her as a sylphide, using a delicate white line against a blue background. This sketch had been printed on the programmes and posters. Nothing could be done but submit to the inevitable, and Pavlova did not arrive in Paris until the fourth or fifth performance.

In this way, between work and a very modest half-bohemian mode of life, the time of preparation passed before the opening performance. The artistes would snatch a hasty lunch in the adjoining Bouillon Duval, one of the best known of the less expensive Paris restaurants. Nobody had a great deal of money and they had to be content with what they could afford.[1]

Meanwhile, Gabriel Astruc was displaying great activity, and he was not slow to announce it. Wearing a shiny "topper," he was an impressive figure of a man with a beautiful Assyrian beard.

"You will see," he would say, "how brilliantly I shall fill the auditorium for the dress rehearsal. Crowds of beautiful women will mingle with ladies of the highest society."

Who the "beautiful women" were was not quite clear, but on the evening of the dress rehearsal the auditorium of the Châtelet produced a brilliant effect.

Astruc was the business manager of the company. He had a great deal to do and did it well. He was a manager of a new type—not a dry business man, occupied exclusively

[1] Romola Nijinska's assertion in her book that the whole company was served by the Restaurant Larue is a pure invention, though Diaghileff entertained his friends and business connections in this expensive establishment.

with the business aspects of the affair, but an enthusiast who shared boisterously in the life of the company. He was rather a likeable personality, with a touch of the droll. He talked "big" and was inclined to take the credit for everything to himself. His attitude of the impresario of imagination with artistic pretensions was admirably suited to the whole atmosphere of the enterprise. This attitude, however, did not prevent his conducting financial matters very efficiently. And the financial side was no smooth matter. Money was sometimes required at the shortest notice. Astruc's office in the now demolished Pavillon de Hanover in the Boulevard des Italiens was luxuriously appointed. All the negotiations with the management of the Châtelet were done there, as well as all other discussions about new contracts.

During the final rehearsals Fokine was in a state of nervous tension, and sometimes had hysterical outbursts. "Throw out that pianist!" he shrieked at poor Pomerantzev, who, it must be allowed, was an amazingly good pianist. When such scenes occurred attempts were made to smooth things over, but these were not always successful. Pomerantzev had to be replaced by a small, lame, but very even-tempered gentleman, who now appears under the pseudonym of Betove on the French music-hall stage.

* * *

There was in Paris a whole clan of friends, admirers, and devotees of the ballet. Diaghileff's own circle of friends was composed of social figures and patrons of art. Monsieur and Madame Bernardaki, elderly Russian Greeks, were typical representatives. They were very rich, lived in a luxurious mansion, and were passionately enthusiastic about Diaghileff's work. Whole-heartedly devoted, old Bernardaki sat through nearly every rehearsal. He was a well-known figure in Paris. Madame Bernardaki had been a great beauty in her day, and it is even rumoured that King Edward the Seventh, while Prince of Wales, was numbered among her admirers and gave her a necklace with which she never parted. She organized receptions to which she invited all the leading members of the company, and she never missed an opportunity of singing the praises of ballet wherever she went.

Benois, who had spent many years in Paris, had a circle of friends of an artistic type. Foremost of these must be counted Robert de Montesquiou, whose friendship was of long standing, dating back to the time of the first Russian exhibition in 1906, when his remarkable and striking figure first appeared in Benois's flat. Well built and handsome, he possessed a risqué elegance, bordering on the eccentric, even a little "precious." He talked in a falsetto voice and posed. There emanated from him the epoch of Louis XV. In the garden of his house at Neuilly stood the bath of La Montespan, cut out of a single block of pink marble. A poet and an arbiter of fashion in Paris, he was known by his colourful figure. He trumpeted the praises of ballet on every possible occasion, even wrote several articles, and gave great service to the cause.

The Spanish painter, José Maria Sert, and Misia Edwards, whom he later married, were both warm adherents. She was a splendid musician, and everyone of importance in the art and musical world of Paris gathered round her. She had been friendly in the past with Toulouse Lautrec, and her house was constantly frequented by Renoir, Vuillard, Bonnard, Matisse, and others. Ravel she never called otherwise than "Mon petit Ravel," and Claude Debussy, then already a venerable figure, was always there. In her artistic salon in the Quai Voltaire she spoke enthusiastically about the ballet to her friends, and entertained and introduced to one another her French and Russian acquaintances. It was through her that Diaghileff later made the connection with Pablo Picasso.

Georges Devaillères, Maurice Denis, and Maxime Dethomas, who later became art director of the Grand Opera under Roucher, were also intimates of Diaghileff's circle and enthusiastic supporters. Jean Louis Vaudoyer, then quite a young man, was very handsome and elegant, with well-groomed moustaches. At this time he was only a quiet spectator of the friends' activities, hiding the deep emotion which he felt under his reserved manner.

All these artistic friends had an important influence on the success of the enterprise. They gave, as it were, an artistic *cachet* to the ballet in Paris. It was a baptismal blessing given by the elect of Paris.

At this time there was no general public for the ballet. Ballet had been forgotten, nobody was interested in it, it was no longer considered one of the arts. It is true that about this time there were vague indications of a general revival of interest in the art of dancing. Isadora Duncan was already creating a sensation through the whole of Europe, and dancing in general was felt to be "in the air." But there was not a special ballet public in Paris.

The circles connected with the Diaghileff enterprise were composed purely of painters and musicians. Except

93

for Montesquiou and Vaudoyer, there were no men of letters attached to the group, and literary figures were only attracted along with the general public. D'Annunzio did not appear on the scene until 1911, and Marcel Proust not till the 1913–14 season.

The artistic *élite* and the frequenters of the social salons of Paris, *les fervents des Russes*, noised the ballet abroad through Paris. It is owing to them that Diaghileff managed to create that atmosphere of intellectual snobbery of which he was such a master and which he knew, like the genius he was, how to exploit for business purposes. His *Ballets-Russes* seemed something apart, something with a flavour of its own, a sort of higher refinement of sensibility, only fully to be appreciated by the chosen few. To admit that one did not understand the *Ballets-Russes* became a confession of inferiority; it was to convict one's self of stupidity.

In the famous play by Robert de Flers and Caillavet, *Le Bois Sacré*, which was contemporary with the pre-War ballets, there is a line which sums up Diaghileff's showmanship in this direction: "Nous commençons à devenir des gens très bien, d'avoir des rélations très chic, très pourries, très *Ballets-Russes*," says Paul Margerie.

This genius for creating an atmosphere of intellectual snobbery around his enterprise was one of Diaghileff's great qualities as an impresario, and remained with him till the end. Even in all his post-War productions, even in those which had no artistic value, or for that matter success, one felt this character of "attraction," of uniqueness.

As far as the first ballets and all the pre-War creations of the friends are concerned, this characteristic was limited to

Diaghileff's method of presenting his dish to the public. There was not a suspicion of snobbishness, no attempt at it, in the creation of the ballets themselves. Such psychology was completely alien to Diaghileff's collaborators, who had no other purposes in their work than those dictated to them by their artistic conscience. The snobbery was the work of Diaghileff and his clever showmanship.

The loud approval of the salons and the artistic elect was not sufficient for Diaghileff. Despite exceptional over-work, worries, and cares of a practical nature, he found time for a conscientious Press campaign. He invited every well-known critic to rehearsals, entertained them to lunches, dinners, and suppers, explained the productions to them, talked to them persuasively, and made them his adherents and helpers.

On May 17, 1909, the evening of the dress rehearsal, the nervous tension of the Diaghilevians behind the scenes at the Théâtre du Châtelet reached a climax. Everybody was in an exalted state of mind. Nobody doubted that success awaited them. The joy of combat and the conviction of victory lent everyone wings—they went into the battle as if it were already won. "We'll show these foreigners," their flushed faces seemed to say.

On the other side of the curtain the scene was brilliant in the extreme. Astruc had done his work well. The "invitation" public was exceptionally elegant even for the Paris of that time. Astruc's beautiful women and society ladies mingled with artistic celebrities. Rodin, Ravel, Montesquiou, and many others could be seen in the stalls. There was a great deal of excitement, and one had the feeling that it was a "big night" in Paris. People talked and moved about from box to box. There was tense expectancy in the air.

When Nijinsky appeared in the *pas de trois* in *Le Pavillon d'Armide*, with which the performance opened, the audience gasped. Nijinsky seemed to belong to another world, he seemed to soar like some strange new bird. The classical purity of his dancing, produced strictly in the style of Louis XV, was something that had never been seen in Paris. His exit brought the house down in applause. "The Jester's Dance," in which Rozaï produced his special accentuated movements and jump, had nearly as great a success. The second item on the programme was the Polovetz Camp scene from *Prince Igor*. At the very beginning of the act the short dance of the Polovetz girls produced an impression. But when the now famous "Polovetz" dance was reached the public went mad. The wild waves of the Polovtzi rushed in their frantic dance one after the other right up to the footlights and there sank. They danced as if possessed. Sofia Fedorova's fire caught the imagination of the public, and the curtain fell to thunderous applause. It was not a success, it was a triumph. From that moment the fate of the Diaghileff ballets could not be doubted. The baptism was over; success was certain.

Soon after this, following the exceptional success of the "Polovetz" dances, a cinematograph company offered to film them. Everything was arranged, a field was found outside Paris to represent the Russian steppes, and a day was fixed. Unfortunately, at the last moment the scheme collapsed over money matters, and a valuable and very interesting document was thus lost.

At one of the following performances *Les Sylphides* was presented. This ballet had already been staged by Fokine in St. Petersburg with the title *Chopiniana*. Its presentation then was very slipshod. The scenery was collected from other ballets and the costumes were rather defective. But this did not deter the Diaghilevians from liking it and seeing what a beautiful thing could be made of it. Benois's production of it for Paris emphasized the elegiac mood which we feel in Chopin's music. The style, which was a return to the romantic days of Taglioni, was strictly adhered to. The whole production was penetrated with an atmosphere of sadness and ultra-worldliness. The moon shone on a dilapidated abbey, a cemetery, and a tomb, round which the ballerinas danced in white classical dresses with long drooping *tutus*. The Paris public accepted this ballet in the spirit in which it had been created, sensing the charm of its noble restraint. There were no noisy manifestations of delight, but the ballet did not call for those.

While the performances were going on work was proceeding with the ballet *Cléopâtre*, which had not been finished in St. Petersburg. The mysterious Ida Rubinstein arrived. She proved eminently suitable for her part. Her long, youthfully slender, peculiarly angular body seemed to have just descended from an Egyptian bas-relief, and her marvellous Eastern profile with narrow almond eyes was very appropriate to the rôle. Fokine had more than made good his promise to the friends in St. Petersburg; he had taught and trained Ida Rubinstein to perfection. She created such a dazzling impression that on the day of the performance she overshadowed all the other dancers, even Anna Pavlova, who appeared with her. She was young,

97

handsome, strange, and somehow mysterious. Robert de Montesquiou immediately fell at her feet and became her devoted admirer. This was not at all the usual romantic affair, but resembled rather the medieval platonic kneeling in adoration before the chosen "lady of the heart." It is said that even now in Ida Rubinstein's house there hangs over a sofa a portrait of Montesquiou. She has not forgotten her "true and faithful knight." *Cléopâtre* was a big success; the public were delighted with the dancers, and Fokine and Bakst shared the credit as authors. In spite of Benois's considerable contribution to this ballet, in spite of the fact that it was based almost wholly on his ideas, his name was not mentioned either in the programmes or the Press notices. This omission, which was hushed up immediately for friendship's sake, proved the beginning of the unpleasant quarrel which occurred the following year between the friends.

* * *

The success of Diaghileff's Russian season of 1909 was immense. Not only were the purely artistic merits beyond dispute, as witnessed by the enthusiasm of the Parisian elect, but it was obvious that Diaghileff's enterprise was in a fair way to catch the favour of the general public. Admittedly the season was too short (only twelve performances were given) to make it possible to win over completely the mass of the public, but the groundwork had been prepared. The performances were striking in their novelty, the spectacular boldness gripped the audience, and the spontaneous and unrestrained enthusiasm was thoroughly genuine.

98

The following extracts written by Benois at the time make interesting reading:

"In what did the novelty consist?" (he writes). "Not in the music—Paris was already acquainted with it from the 1907 concerts; not in the staging, for the opera—*Boris Godounov* had shown in 1908 what Russians could do in this direction; the novelty consisted purely in 'the ballet.'

"It is often said that the ballet is for children, hussars, and senile dignitaries. Perhaps that is true of the old ballet. Ballet is the most closely knit and yet the most free of theatrical forms. The very principle of ballet—to present a beautiful spectacle, to sway the mind of the spectator by means of beautiful forms, beautiful rhythm, beautiful combinations of movement—contains something truly divine and mystic. It was Russian culture which triumphed in Paris, the whole essence of Russian art, its conviction, its freshness, its spontaneity. . . . Our primitive wildness, our simplicity revealed itself in Paris as something more refined, developed, and subtle than the French themselves could do.

"The success of the ballets is based on the fact that Russians are still capable of believing in their creations, that they still retain enough spontaneity to become absorbed, just as children are completely absorbed in their play, in the God-like play which is art. This secret has been lost on the Western stage, where everything is technique, everything is consciousness, everything is artificiality, and from which have gradually disappeared the mysterious charm of self-oblivion, the great Dionysiac intoxication, the driving force of art."

Regarding separate ballets, Benois writes as follows:

"The purpose of *Le Pavillon d'Armide* was to show the Russian conception of eighteenth-century France, in the story itself as well as in the manner of its presentation, in the scenery, the costumes, the manners, the groupings, and the dances. This is what happened: to the French, who were accustomed to the chocolate-box pictures which the French stage presented as rococo, the Russian interpretation seemed over-ornate, the colours too bright, the gracefulness of the performers exaggerated. But then those Frenchmen who still retained the capacity of understanding that period from Versailles, the Gobelin tapestries, the Sèvres, the gold ornaments, and the bobbed wigs, those who understood the actual spirit which breathed through this delicate art, felt and understood the meaning of *Le Pavillon d'Armide*. Its aim was achieved; Russians had shown that they were not only supreme but that they could outvie the French on their own ground."

These words of Benois require perhaps some commentary. The fact is that *Le Pavillon d'Armide* was the creation of Benois, the grandson of a French émigré, who was brought up in the atmosphere of eighteenth-century Royalist France. The family tradition and his father's lively recollections of his own father helped Alexandre Benois to a clear understanding of that epoch. He loved it from childhood, and neither in Russia nor even in France could there be found a man with a deeper knowledge of eighteenth-century France. Doubtless a certain Russian flavouring was also present, but one cannot, in my opinion, call the production of *Le Pavillon d'Armide* a Russian conception of the Rococo epoch. It was just the lifelike quality, the truthfulness, the actual re-creation of the eighteenth century which astonished people with a knowledge of the period, who for this reason felt the artistic truth of the production. And this understanding of the period was peculiar to Benois alone and cannot be called a Russian understanding.

About *Les Sylphides* Benois writes as follows:

"The impression of some languid apparition, of half-sad, half-gay dances performed by charming spirits in a cemetery, in the rays of the moon and the shadows of tombs and ruins, this optical illusion was thoroughly successful. But especially touching and convincing was the appearance of Pavlova and Nijinsky, and their ethereal dance together, with its high noiseless flights, full of tender, slightly devitalized grace, gave a definite impression (and this in spite of the lack of any story) of a strange, phantasmal romance, a hopeless infatuation of disembodied beings, who know neither fiery embraces nor sweet kisses, and for whom all that is bacchic or passionate has been replaced by a sad tenderness, by the merest fluttering suspicion of physical contact."

It is difficult to give a more graphic and precise definition of the meaning of the ballet *Les Sylphides* than Benois gives in these words. The whole production is filled with the sentimental and spiritual romanticism of the 1830's, with all its conventions—the moon, tombs, hopeless love, etc.

As *Le Pavillon d'Armide* was the reincarnation of eighteenth-century France, so *Les Sylphides* was a return to the thirties of last century, a faithful return, in which even the accurate detail of the long *tutu Taglioni* was not omitted.

About the third main creation of the 1909 *Ballets-Russes*, *Cléopâtre*, Benois wrote:

101

"*Cléopâtre* made most money. They even started to give it at the end of the opera, as a bait for *Ivan the Terrible* (*Pskovitianka*). . . . The fascination was greatest for the dance of Nijinsky and Karsavina, Cléopâtre's two favourite slaves. They were such tender and carefree creatures, who, growing up on the steps of the terrible Queen's throne, were absolutely devoted to her. As children they played with her shawl woven of gold, tossing it to each other, running and jumping high in the air, unfolding it, and winding themselves into it. The climax of the performance was not so much the scene with Cléopâtre as the 'Bacchanal,' which always produced such enthusiasm that the orchestra had to stop playing and the artistes could not continue for several minutes. And it was the 'Bacchanal' alone which explains the overwhelming and unpredictable success of the ballet. . . . Bakst's scenery was rather hurriedly and sketchily executed, but the conception was good and the colour, rose-granite and dark violet, was beautiful. Against this weird, truly southern, oppressively warm background the purple costumes glistened richly, the plaited wigs stood out sombrely, the coffin-like, hieroglyph-decorated couch of Cléopâtre moved like a menace."

If *Le Pavillon d'Armide* was the essence of rococo, if *Les Sylphides* was the essence of romanticism, then *Cléopâtre* was something quite different. Although the theme was chosen from the remote history of Egypt, this ballet had less relation to the past than the other two. *Cléopâtre* was primarily a spectacle; the period was little more than a pretext for the real purpose, which was the presentation of a pleasing spectacle of colour and rhythm. The purely spectacular quality of ballet, its possibilities as an art apart from emotion or psychology, were brought out with special emphasis in *Cléopâtre*.

*Le Festin*, the first creative effort of the Diaghilevians in Russian folk-lore material, attracted less attention. It was admittedly the least successful ballet. Patched together from a miscellaneous collection of dances and tunes it is far removed in artistic achievement from similar future attempts of the friends. It gave no promise of such great things to come as *L'Oiseau de Feu*, and especially *Petrushka*.

The success of the *Prince Igor* dances was enormous, but this ballet cannot be considered original in the same sense as the other productions of 1909. Borodin's opera *Prince Igor* had been on the Russian stage for many years, and the "Polovetz" dance was no novelty. The originality here was the work of Fokine, who created quite a new, daring, and striking choreography.

These first ballet productions of 1909 already determined most of the directions which Diaghileff's future work was to take. *Les Sylphides* can be considered the original of all the romantic ballets of the Diaghilevians. It was the forerunner of such future productions as *Carnaval* and *Le Spectre de la Rose*. *Cléopâtre* was the commencement of the spectacular productions. This vein later produced such ballets as *Sheherazade*, *Le Dieu Bleu*, and *Thamar*. *Le Festin*, as I mentioned before, began the succession of national ballets which ended with the pre-War production in 1914 of Rimsky-Korsakov's opera, *Le Coq d'Or*. Finally, the *Prince Igor* scene, with the wildness, the primitiveness almost, of its choreography, already foreshadowed the 1913 production, *Le Sacre du Printemps*.

\* \* \*

On the days when there was no ballet performance at the Châtelet the Diaghilevians, and occasionally their intimate friends, arranged evenings in honour of the company. Valz gave a grand and very gay dinner at the Restaurant Le Doyen in the Champs Elysées. There were about twenty guests, nearly all ballet performers—even Diaghileff was not invited. The old Don Juan had a little money, and liked to play the part of Amphitryon.

Briand gave a big party in the Ministry of Foreign Affairs. Diaghileff was on good terms with him, and probably offered to bring along his company. Nearly the whole cast was invited, and the evening came to an end with a performance of Russian dances and a lavish supper.

Nearly always on the evening after a performance Diaghileff collected his own group in the Restaurant Viel on the Boulevard de la Madeleine. A long table on the left, occupying nearly the whole length of the wall, was always reserved for him. Diaghileff presided in the middle of the settee with his colleagues on either side of him. This was the resurrection of the old "Pickwickians." The ballet dancers did not take part in these evenings. The friends usually sat till two or three in the morning, drinking champagne and thoroughly enjoying themselves. Diaghileff paid for everything. He was the host, and was terribly angry if any of his intimates missed any of his gatherings. The evening was always lively and jolly.

Soon Nijinsky began to appear at these evening suppers. That he alone of the ballet dancers should be present was significant, and did not pass without remark.

At this time there were misunderstandings between Diaghileff and his secretary. There were several scenes, and the secretary was given money to leave Paris. Having reached Cologne, he changed his mind and returned. It turned out that he had been having an affair with one of the ballerinas. After running around Paris for a short time, keeping out of Diaghileff's sight, he left again, but this time was accompanied by the object of his affections. The era of Nijinsky had begun.

The company's last days in Paris had a tinge of melancholy. They all had little or no money, and the feeling that things were drawing to an end was painful. This feeling became still more acute when they returned to Russia, where they arrived in the middle of the silly season. Life seemed quite empty. The vacation ended and reaction set in. The great excitement which everyone had felt for a whole month in Paris gave way to a feeling of flatness, staleness, and depression. Life was boring and uninteresting.

# 7

AS has been said already, Diaghileff's enterprise was criticized in the French Press for its lack of national atmosphere. The French desired a folk-lore element, expected a special, almost exotic flavour in the performances. In short, they wanted what they, as Frenchmen, understood to be "du vrai Russe."

The search for a national ballet of this kind kept Diaghileff busy even in 1909. On September 4th of that year, whilst on the Lido, where he was spending a holiday, accompanied already by Nijinsky, he wrote to the Russian composer Liadov:

"I want a ballet, and a *Russian* one; there has never been such a ballet before. It is imperative that I present one in May 1910 in the Paris Grand Opera and at Drury Lane in London. We all consider you now as our leading composer with the freshest and most interesting talent."

Fokine already had a complete libretto. This was the beginning of *L'Oiseau de Feu*. The libretto was put together in a haphazard way. Hunting for folk tales, they sought information from the fashionable expert in this line, Remizov. Many people must remember him; a little, odd, extremely ugly man, resembling an overgrown sparrow and for ever muffled in warm clothes. For a long time he bewildered the friends with various tales, incomprehensible, strange-sounding improvisations at which he was a master.

"There are also 'Bellyboshkies,' " he would say, "evil sort of creatures, some with tails and some without." What Bellyboshkies were nobody could make out, but this nonsensical word sounded so attractive that the "Dance of the Bellyboshkies" in the train of the wicked sorcerer was produced. This, however, was the limit of Remizov's contribution to *L'Oiseau de Feu*.

The ballet was jumbled together from rags of various classical Russian fairy tales. The resulting patchwork, although colourful, was not convincing for a Russian. It was as if Alice of *Alice in Wonderland* were partnered with Falstaff in a Scotch jig.

At first things did not go right with the music. Liadov, a slow worker, was busy thinking out the ballet, but did not compose a note. They fell back on Tcherepnin, but the sketches composed by him were not satisfactory. Quite by accident, at a symphonic concert, the friends heard a short symphonic poem by a young composer. This composition was called *Fireworks*, and the name of the composer was Igor Stravinsky. Diaghileff went into raptures.

"That's the man we want for our ballet!" he bellowed. "It's wonderful! It's just what we want."

Before a day had passed Diaghileff made the young composer's acquaintance, and the proposal was discussed. Stravinsky took up the idea with enthusiasm, and composed the music with great speed. Soon Stravinsky appeared at Benois's also. The usual gatherings, discussions, and conferences followed. Stravinsky was accepted in the circle as one of "themselves." He was then still very young and modest and slightly flattered by his acceptance in such august company.

Diaghileff, with his usual flair, had made no mistake. Stravinsky proved one of the most important forces in the creation of future ballets. His extraordinarily fine rhythmic sense and great rhythmic inventiveness, his powerful, dynamic temperament and mastery of orchestration were qualities which made him extremely suitable for Diaghileff's requirements. Deficiency in thematic imagination and weakness of melodic line were unimportant. His music was interesting, brilliant, and full of daring novelty. It must be said that the marvellous score alone saved *L'Oiseau de Feu*. Except for the effective entrance of the Evil Spirits and the actual "Dance of the Firebird," the ballet cannot be considered very successful in comparison with others. Even in the second of the above dances the orchestral scoring is mainly responsible for the successful impression of the number. The orchestration was so novel and successful that some of the effects could not be understood. People seemed to want to rise and peer into the orchestra-pit, inquiring, "Who made those strange noises?"

As before, the rehearsals took place in the Ekaterinsky Hall. There was great difficulty in staging the passing of the two horsemen, Night and Day, by the footlights. It could not be managed at all, though the music was very appropriate with the suggestion of the mysterious stamping of hoofs. In the end the horsemen had to go on foot, pacing slowly across the stage to this "equestrian" music. Fokine himself danced Prince Ivan and Tamara Karsavina, for whom Bakst designed a charming flame-coloured costume, the "Firebird." Karsavina was understudied in the part by Lydia Lopokova, a young ballerina who had just joined the company.

The climax was a failure. The jubilant, triumphant procession of resurrected knights after the death of Kashei, whose heart was contained in the broken egg-shell, produced no effect. It was a straggling affair. Even the red flags which Diaghileff made them hold in their hands for the Paris presentation did not help. It had the savour of a synthetic folk tale.

The scenery by Golovin, the Moscow artist, was very fine, vivid, and effective, with the golden apples shining brightly on the tree.

*　*　*

At a charity performance, the so-called Academic Ball, during Lent 1910, Fokine first produced *Carnaval*. At one of the friends' conferences Fokine and Bakst were seen to whisper aside to each other. It turned out that Fokine was to stage the ballet, and Bakst was to do the costumes, which were to be made of ordinary calico. The ballet was danced on the empty stage without any scenery at all. The idea had been Fokine's, and Bakst, a great admirer of Schumann, adopted it enthusiastically.

Diaghileff decided to include this ballet in his repertoire. Work went with a swing. Bakst designed blue hangings with a frieze, very fine in their simplicity and distinction. He also made a whole series of charming costume designs. The whole production was kept true to the style of Biedermeyer. The hangings constituted almost the whole décor. Slightly to the left and at the back of the stage stood a settee, and nothing more.

*Carnaval* proved one of the most successful productions of the *Ballets-Russes*. Schumann's music was delightful, and the orchestration by Russian musicians did not destroy its charm.

The simplicity and severity of this ballet are wonderful. There is no striving after effect, no unevenness in it. It is simple, tuneful, devoid of tricks, and yet produces a vivid impression. In it Fokine demonstrated that he was capable not only of expressing dynamic force, as in the "Polovetz" dances, but also of great artistic subtlety. Briefly, the ballet might be described as a lengthy *pas d'action*. Each scene, each dance, has not only a choreographical but also an emotional and dramatic content.

The entrance of Columbine (Karsavina) and Harlequin (Nijinsky) is unforgettable. The Harlequin, tenderly embracing Columbine, leaps gracefully with her round the stage, parts from her and rejoins her, all to Schumann's charming music. In this ballet every part was perfectly cast. It was as if the dancers had been born in their rôles. Nijinsky's sister, Bronislava, made her first appearance before the public in this ballet in the part of Papillon.

Simultaneously with the preparation of *Carnaval* work was also being done on *Giselle,* which they had also decided to take to Paris. Although this ballet had no decisive importance for the future of *Ballets-Russes,* it deserves a certain amount of attention. *Giselle* was an old ballet. Adam's old-fashioned, touching music of the forties was still fresh and charming, and Théophile Gautier's romantic story was delightful. Enthusiasm for the romanticism of last century was very marked in Benois and the other friends. In France itself it did not become apparent until about 1930—the centenary of romanticism. In their youth the Diaghileff group had worshipped *Giselle*, fascinated by the extraordinary freshness and poetry which the ballet still retained.

The theme of the ballet is briefly as follows: A young peasant woman who loves dancing lives in a village with her parents. A prince (Albrecht) falls in love with her, disguises himself, and goes to live near her. The wicked forester is jealous on account of Giselle. He finds a valuable sword at Albrecht's cottage, and decides that the latter is a thief. The duke is hunting in the neighbourhood, accompanied by Albrecht's betrothed. Through the intervention of the wicked forester everything comes to light. Poor Giselle goes out of her mind, and the first act concludes with a dance, at the end of which she dies. The scene of the second act is a cemetery, where dwell the so-called wilis with their queen. At night they leave their graves and, dancing, lure to their death anyone who wanders in the cemetery. In this way the wicked forester is drowned in a marsh. The prince comes to the cemetery, and the wilis are foiled in their attempt to lure him to his death by Giselle. A love scene follows between Albrecht and Giselle, who forget everything else. Suddenly the cock crows. Giselle, late in returning to her grave, melts from Albrecht's arms and disappears, leaving him utterly grief-stricken.

Gautier's masterly pen is evident in this sentimental, romantic tale. In spite of its suggestion of absurdity, it is fresh and moving, and this ever-young ballet deserves the appreciation which it is given.[1] The acquaintance of Benois

[1] Tchaikovsky's favourite ballet was *Giselle*, "this pearl of poesy, music, and choreography." (*Life of P. I. Tchaikovsky*, by M. Tchaikovsky, vol. i, p. 116.)

in his younger days with this ballet partly explains the tendency of his later creations towards the romanticism of the thirties and his constancy to the theme of sentimental elegy.

The rôles of Giselle and Albrecht provided opportunities for the performers of displaying every side of their art. They required dramátic expression as well as technique. Fokine had faithfully revived the old Paris Saint Léon production. Benois, who designed the costumes and décor, wanted at first to use the ultra-romantic costumes of the forties in the troubadour style, but his courage failed in the end and his final designs omitted the more ridiculous elements of that style. The scenery had deep perspective and was quite dark in colouring.

Giselle was to have been danced by Pavlova, but she again let them down and did not come. Diaghileff's impression that Pavlova did not want to join forces with him openly and straightforwardly was gradually confirmed. It seemed that even in 1909 she could have arranged to arrive in time, but had not wanted to. Pavlova apparently did not wholly believe in the enterprise. She preferred not to appear until its success was less doubtful. She had many personal engagements which she valued as the source of a dependable income. She never considered where and in what conditions she was to appear, and danced quite frequently in music-halls and second-rate theatres.

Karsavina was given the part of Giselle. This met with the disapproval of Fokine, who, as it were, washed his hands of Karsavina, seeming to indicate that she would amount to nothing. Karsavina, however, passed this difficult test with flying colours. In this, her first big part, she proved not only a dancer of charm but of intelligence and emotional power, and revealed her deeper culture and more profound art. She was more highly cultured than the average ballerina. Unlike Pavlova, with whom one could not talk except in a half-coquettish ballet fashion, Karsavina was capable of sustaining a serious conversation.

In this production of *Giselle* Nijinsky had his first big part (Albrecht). It is hardly necessary to say that he proved equal to the task. His performance, besides being inspired, was even and sustained.

In his search for first-class music which could be adapted for ballet, Diaghileff hit upon the idea of producing a ballet to Rimsky-Korsakov's symphonic poem, *Sheherazade*. He proposed this suggestion to the friends.

As a youth Benois had heard and enjoyed this music, and for some reason he had associated it in his imagination with the prologue to the *Arabian Nights*, with the story of Shahryar and Shahzaman. He had even imagined tableaux corresponding to the music. I say "for some reason," because Rimsky-Korsakov's music was written to quite a different programme. It was inspired by several tales of Sheherazade, including the adventures of Sinbad the Sailor. Accordingly, in Rimsky-Korsakov's view, the music for the most part suggested seascapes. But youthful associations are evidently strong, and Benois continued to find in *Sheherazade* the atmosphere not of the sea but of the harem.

The conferences of the friends about the ballet generally followed these lines: the music was played until it had induced in the listeners some plastic image. Generally it was Benois who was the first to receive these impressions.

He would fall into a sort of trance, shout to the others to keep quiet, and begin abruptly, accompanied by the music, to relate the appropriate action. The oracle spoke, and the others listened. Bakst, too, was present, but as usual he was silent. In this manner the book of the ballet *Sheherazade* was composed. Sinbad the Sailor was replaced by Shahryar, with whose story the whole action of the ballet was concerned.

When the libretto was completely finished Benois wrote it down on the spot in Diaghileff's score.

On one of these evenings Benois for some reason had another quarrel with Diaghileff. (This happened about five times a year.) He went away offended. Diaghileff immediately delegated Prince Argoutinsky to follow Benois, appease him, and bring him back. Argoutinsky, catching up the long-striding Benois with difficulty, pulled him up and brought him back. Speaking on the way about *Sheherazade* and recalling his lack of recognition in *Cléopâtre*, Benois said to Argoutinsky:

"This time I have taken my precautions. I have written down everything with my own hand on the score, so that it can't be said later that anyone but I did it."

As will be seen later, this precaution did not save Benois from great annoyance.

Fokine did his part of the work very quickly. He produced *Sheherazade* with great fire and inspiration. As before, the rehearsals took place in the Ekaterinsky Hall, which they knew and liked. At rehearsal Benois was delighted with the three *almehs*, who sat on the ground making plastic movements with their arms. This new seated mode of dance greatly pleased him.

Originally the scenery was to be designed by Anisfeldt, but his sketches, seeming vulgar, did not suit. The work was given to Bakst. He brought many designs to the conferences. They were all discussed and rejected as not up to standard. After several attempts, one scheme was finally accepted. Soft, brightly coloured hangings draped the interior of a huge hall occupying the whole stage. The cushions and covered couches were also of soft material. The bright multi-coloured surroundings exuded an Eastern languor. The costume designs were even more gorgeous, fantastic, and picturesque in their exotic daring.

\* \* \*

Financial considerations and difficulties began even at this early stage to disturb Diaghileff. He went to Paris at Easter to try to arrange these matters. Nothing materialized. Diaghileff met with refusal everywhere. From Paris alarming telegrams showered on St. Petersburg. It seemed as if the season was doomed. The tone of Diaghileff's telegrams became so desperate that the friends were seriously upset about him, alarmed in case he committed suicide there.

Finally, something turned up in St. Petersburg. The Prime Minister, Count Kokovzov, informed the Tsar of the advisability of making Diaghileff a grant of £1,000. This sum was urgently required to purchase the tickets for the departure of the company. The Tsar signed the Minister's report. News of this became known about three o'clock in the afternoon, and Diaghileff went hurriedly to a banker of his acquaintance, and on this surety borrowed £1,000 for a few days. The tickets were bought. They could go.

At the last moment things again collapsed in tragic fashion.

It is thought that the Grand Duke Serge Michaïlovitch went to the Tsar with the story from his side; "this is not ballet, but heaven knows what! Some kind of decadent spectacle, discreditable to Russian art abroad . . ." and so on and so on. The Tsar stopped the money and refused the grant. The position was critical. The money had to be repaid to the banker, and it was already spent. Again the position was rescued. Prince Argoutinsky and Ratkoff-Rognoff signed a short bill for the requisite sum. Later this money was repaid out of the theatre receipts in Paris.

The scandal did not end there, however. The Tsar was persuaded to command all Russian embassies to refuse any support to the Diaghileff enterprise. The embassies were circularized to this effect. In this way it came about that Diaghileff met not only with no support but rather with opposition from the official representatives of Russia abroad.

It was the custom in the embassy to "sniff" at the *Ballets-Russes*. "What kind of ballets are they? There is ballet in the Maryinsky Theatre, but heaven knows what this is!"

Prince Argoutinsky, who was serving at the time in the Russian Embassy in Paris, remained their faithful friend, but his Foreign Office colleagues began to look askance at him.

On May 1st, a cold and rainy day, the company left for Paris. The 1910 season had been promoted from the private Théâtre du Châtelet to the Grand Opera. The ballet was eagerly awaited. The previous year's success had already made of the Diaghileff enterprise a great event. The greater part of the artistic select was already converted, and the snobbish social world was on its knees. It was already fashionable to enthuse about the ballet. Diaghileff could have no doubt of his success.

The purely financial success proved greater than in the previous season. In 1909 it was only towards the end of the season that they were drawing full houses. In 1910 it was already difficult to buy a seat. There was a full house every evening. The attendance was helped by the fact that there was nothing but ballet in the programme. The absence of opera not only helped to draw bigger audiences but saved enormous staging expenses.

This year, however, the ballet was less sensationally received. Instead of the furore of the first season, there was an even glow of admiration.

*Sheherazade* proved the high-water mark of the season. The whole atmosphere of this bright, exotic ballet astonished the public by its originality and verve. Nijinsky was superb. His final leap, a tragic death convulsion through the air, was breath-taking. Ida Rubinstein also shone to advantage. Her strange, youthful, exotic figure and her Eastern profile were again very appropriate to her part. Fokine's plastic imagery was splendid, but the main attraction of the ballet was due, of course, to Bakst. His scenery and costumes were truly magnificent, his greatest achievement. His style was particularly suitable just because it was personal and not purely Russian. A born cosmopolitan, he hit upon exactly the right note for Paris, he gave a rendering of the exotic as it appeared to Western eyes.

The influence of his style was felt far beyond the confines

of the theatre. The dress designers of Paris incorporated it in their fashions. Poiret and Callot began to model gowns inspired by Bakst's painting. Turbans and cushions "Ballets-Russes" came into fashion; dress material, even, began to be manufactured in the same style.

The protests of Rimsky-Korsakov's widow sounded vain and academic. She complained that serious symphonic concert music should not be danced to, and protested against the cuts which had been made. In the success of the ballet these protests were not heard.

*L'Oiseau de Feu* was successful mainly with musicians. Stravinsky's orchestration deservedly made a great impression. The ballet itself, though pleasing people by its colour and novelty, was not a sensational success. The book of this ballet, badly constructed even in Russian eyes, was quite incomprehensible to foreigners.

The success of *Carnaval* was of a special type. It also produced no sensation, but its charm and delicacy delighted people. It proved to be one of the most securely established and enduring features of the *Ballets-Russes*. When such productions as *Le Festin*, *Giselle*, and *Narcisse* were merely memories *Carnaval* was still being played, and its capacity for survival proved very great. *Carnaval* is one of the most perfect creations of Fokine. The smallest detail in it is planned and developed with purpose, and, seeing it performed, one has that sensation of perfection and finality which only a great work of art gives. Apart from this, the ballet was very well produced. The dancers could not have been bettered in their parts, and Fokine's treatment and Bakst's scenery, in their essential simplicity, brought out the personal qualities of each artiste.

118

Paris gave *Giselle* only a luke-warm reception. The snobbish, sensation-seeking public found nothing to satisfy its expectations in this ballet. The dated story and the old-fashioned music aroused no interest. This attempt to revive romanticism proved premature. Apparently it was not old enough to be new again. There were, however, some individual exceptions; Jean Louis Vaudoyer was enraptured with it.

Ida Rubinstein's personal success in the capital was even greater than in the previous season. Jacques Émile Blanche painted a large portrait of her lying on a couch dressed in her *Sheherazade* costume. One of the most gifted Russian painters—Serov, a Moscow friend—also made a portrait of her, lying on a couch in the nude. The sittings for these portraits, oddly enough, took place in a building in the Boulevard des Invalides which had once been a monastery. She posed in the apartment which had previously been a chapel. At this period Gabriele D'Annunzio appeared in Paris, and immediately became Ida Rubinstein's devoted admirer. She emphasized in every possible way her peculiar, exotic, eccentric style, and even procured a black panther. Apparently her main aim was to attract people's notice, and the question of good taste did not trouble her.

Presently a misunderstanding occurred which caused a definite break between her and Diaghileff. Apparently Ida Rubinstein became tired of being given only miming rôles. She became bored by plastic movements, caresses, embraces, and stabbing herself. She wanted to dance. Diaghileff, who knew perfectly well that she was no good as a dancer, gave her a decisive rebuff, at which she took offence. She realized that a dancing career with Diaghileff was closed to her for ever. Relations between them were severed, and she never forgave Diaghileff for turning her down. In the following year she began to give productions of her own. *St. Sebastian* was one of these. In spite of the collaboration of such great powers as D'Annunzio, Debussy, and Bakst, nothing but a cold, academic success was achieved.

Arising through Bakst's collaboration in this there began one of the first quarrels between him and Diaghileff. Later these quarrels became more frequent and more complex, but in this first quarrel Diaghileff, I think, was in the wrong. Bakst's connection with Ida Rubinstein was not a casual one. It was partly through him that she had been discovered, and he always supported her. One could not expect him to refuse her his help.

In *L'Oiseau de Feu* Lydia Lopokova met with great and perhaps surprising success. She was a splendid dancer with good *élévation,* and possessing on the stage a certain lyrical charm. The company considered that she was not to be compared with such powers as Pavlova and Karsavina, but she had nevertheless a great success, and this period marks the beginning of her fine world-wide career.

The prima ballerina of the Moscow Grand Theatre, Katerine Geltzer, had also been invited to take part in this Paris season. Partnered by Volinin, she danced the Russian dance in *Le Festin.* She possessed the technique of a virtuoso, but was absolutely devoid of talent and was very vulgar. When she appeared on the stage in her cheap Russian costume, with its "kokoshnik," one felt ashamed on her behalf. She met with no success whatsoever. She had been invited for some reason of "diplomacy," and after this season never again took part in the *Ballets-Russes.*

PLATE VIII

COSTUME FOR "SHEHERAZADE"

*By L. Bakst*

PLATE IX

COSTUME FOR "L'OISEAU DE FEU"
*By L. Bakst*

Nearly all the old friends of the ballet were present, and several new friends were added. André Saglio (Dresa), the Director of Fine Arts in charge of French exhibitions abroad, and the painters Barbier and René Piot became intimate with the Russians. They, and some of the old friends, were the first French painters to work for the theatre. Later their activity in this direction became considerable.

During this season there appeared in the ballet circle Jean Cocteau, then little more than a boy. He was not yet the arbiter of taste which he later became and took no actual part in the work of the circle. He was a rather charming person, already sparkling with wit and audacity. People used to play practical jokes on him. On one occasion Diaghileff, who after a celebration was taking him back in a taxi, got out at the Hôtel Mirabeau, and ordered the driver to take Cocteau, who was still inside, to the Hôtel des Réservoirs at Versailles. Cocteau could never understand how he came to be there.

On the day on which the company left Russia for Paris Benois had met with an accident. It appeared that his passport had not been prepared, and he was unable to travel with the company. Thoroughly infuriated, he returned home, and in his anger broke a window-pane with his fist. The blood spurted freely from an artery, and could be stopped only with difficulty. It was evident that the healing would be a slow process, and the hand, after three weeks in plaster and bandages, could not be moved. Benois was very downcast; for a painter to lose the use of his right hand is a tragedy. He gave up all intention of going to Paris, and to complete his convalescence went to Montagnola, a charming, poetical little spot near Lugano. Fortunately, he was able before long to move his hand and scribble with it.

Meanwhile he was receiving by every post from Paris urgent letters demanding his immediate presence there. At length he decided, towards the close of the season, to go.

On the evening of his arrival he went to the Grand Opera to see the ballet. He found his way to his seat, sat down, and turned over the pages of the programme. At first he could not believe his eyes. There it was: "*Sheherazade*, Ballet by Léon Bakst." He thought there must be some mistake. The precaution he had taken in St. Petersburg of himself writing the libretto he had created in Diaghileff's score had not benefited him. His name was not even mentioned anywhere. All there was was "Ballet by Léon Bakst"! Deeply indignant, Benois went to Diaghileff to ask for an explanation. To all his excited protests Diaghileff calmly answered:

"What about it? These things do happen. Bakst had to have a ballet. You have *Le Pavillon d'Armide*. And now Bakst has *Sheherazade*."

Offended and hurt, and having achieved nothing, Benois left Paris in three days and returned to Switzerland.

It must be explained that there was no monetary consideration behind this quarrel. At this time the friends had an extremely naïve business outlook. Benois did not even know that his authorship entitled him to royalties. He had received nothing for *Le Pavillon d'Armide*. It was not till 1911, when Stravinsky took him to the Société des Auteurs, that Benois learned how to secure his rights in *Le Pavillon d'Armide* and *Petrushka*. The quarrel was purely on grounds of artistic etiquette and on a matter of principle. It was, however, none the less serious on that account. From Montagnola Benois wrote Diaghileff a letter, quite friendly in tone but refusing point-blank to collaborate with him further.

Shortly after this the season in Paris came to an end, and Diaghileff, accompanied by Stravinsky and Nijinsky, came to Montagnola to make his peace. Diaghileff was wonderfully adept at conducting peace-making discussions. His appearance of embarrassment made one feel sorry for him. He was a master at touching the sentimental chords of friendship, and even shed real tears, with the result that it appeared that the offended and insulted party was Diaghileff and not the other person. In this case, however, he failed in his object. Benois stood firmly by his decision not to collaborate with him further. They remained for a week, and after friendly confidences, kisses, and embraces left without having won Benois over.

Benois, of course, did not turn into an enemy of Diaghileff, and their personal relationship did not suffer in any way. At Montagnola Benois wrote two long articles on the ballet, one of which was a sort of panegyric to *Sheherazade*. Here is part of an article in the Russian newspaper *Rech*, written by the "offended" Benois:

"To Bakst really belongs the credit of creating *Sheherazade* as a spectacle and an astonishing, I should say, unique spectacle. When the curtain rises on this impressive green 'alcove' you immediately enter a world of special sensations, similar to those you enjoy in reading the *Arabian Nights*. The emerald shades of these awnings, hangings, walls and throne, the deepness of the night which pierces the barred windows opening on the oppressive harem garden, these piles of embroidered cushions and mattresses, and, in these grandly conceived surroundings, these half-naked dancers entertaining the sultan with their sinuous, strictly symmetrical movements, all these things produce a complete and instantaneous charm. From the stage there seems to pour spicy, sensuous aromas and the soul is filled with alarm, as you realize that here, following the festival, behind these extraordinarily sweet images, must flow rivers of scarlet blood. It is difficult to imagine a finer, more relevant and less obtrusive dramatic exposition than is contained in these scenes of Bakst. I have never before seen such a harmony of colour on the stage, such a fine and complex orchestration of colour. And that is not all. Bakst knew how to transform the artistes in some way, how to make them creations of his own. Although I knew every performer well, I could recognize none of them in this performance—and this not only from the distance of the auditorium, but also from the proximity of the stage—so fine and appropriate, without the slightest compromise, was the invention of these costumes, all in the same spirit of fairy tale. Two such masters as Bakst and Fokine have created in this ballet the impression of a wonderful creation of pure art."

It is amusing to read what Benois wrote at the same time about another of this season's productions, *L'Oiseau de Feu*:

"A young composer, I. F. Stravinsky, a pupil of Rimsky-Korsakov and the son of a well-known opera singer, agreed to compose the music for this wonderful ballet, and it must be admitted that Diaghileff's courage,

124

in entrusting blindly such a precarious matter to a composer who had not yet anything serious to show, proved extremely happy. If in all other respects *L'Oiseau de Feu* was not quite what we had anticipated, the music at least achieved immediate perfection. One cannot imagine music more poetical, more expressive in every movement, more beautiful, and with more of the spirit of fantasy."

Few people nowadays, I think, know that the father of the famous composer Stravinsky once sang on the boards of the Maryinsky Theatre, but in 1909 the Russian public had to mention the father in order to make clear who this unknown young man was. The production of *L'Oiseau de Feu* at the Grand Opera in Paris transformed for ever this young nonentity into the world-renowned composer, Stravinsky.

Success among the wider public, the possibility of which had revealed itself in the 1909 season, was definitely achieved in the second season of ballet. The influence of the *Ballets-Russes* spread far beyond the confines of the Paris *élite* and exerted itself on the wide masses of the population, affecting even the man in the street. This was mainly the result of the enormous success of *Sheherazade*, and particularly those aspects of it which were the work of Bakst.

How great this influence was may be judged by the following extract from an article, "Painters and the *Ballets-Russes*," by the French author and critic, André Varnod.

"In any case, it was a perfect enthusiasm which, sweeping away the artistic, literary and social worlds, reached the man in the street, the wide public, the gown-shops and stores. The fashion in everything was *Ballets-Russes*. There was not a middle-class home without its green and orange cushions on a black carpet. Women dressed in the loudest colours, and the *bibelots* were all striped. This was not always in the best taste, however. Soon house-decorating, shops, brasseries and cafés followed suit, post-War dance-halls were directly inspired by them, and the 1923 exhibition showed many traces of their influence."

The popular success of Diaghileff's enterprise was, however, a purely local and Parisian one. There it was established; there were full houses from the first to the last performance. There was a brisk trade in tickets, and sometimes even a fight for them. The next step, international renown, was to be attained by the Diaghilevians in the following season, 1911.

On their return to Russia, during the winter at the end of January 1911, an incident occurred in the Maryinsky Theatre which had a considerable effect on the *Ballets-Russes*. Vazlav Nijinsky was "expelled" from the Imperial Theatres.

There are many versions of this, so to speak, famous scandal. The version based on a remark of the Empress Maria Feodorovna, who was present with her grand-daughters, the daughters of the Tsar, is of course untrue. For one thing, she herself denied it later in conversation with Lady Ripon, and for another, even if she had noticed any indecency, it is extremely unlikely that she should have mentioned it to anyone. She would undoubtedly have taken the view that she should see nothing. She answered plainly to this effect when Baron Frederix, the Minister of the Imperial Household, and Teliakovsky, the Director of the Imperial Theatres, called upon her to present their apologies for the incident.

The story that Nijinsky's tightly fitting loin-cloth, without a suspensory bandage, revealed some of the usually concealed parts of his anatomy is also untrue. Male dancers invariably wear a special *cache-sexe* which renders this impossible. This is not a matter of decency but of dancing practice.

I shall give the version told me by Benois.

A performance of *Giselle* was being given, and Nijinsky had to appear in the first act in the costume which Benois had already designed for the Paris production. It must be said that at that time skin-tight costumes in general were considered rather improper. In this case Diaghileff cut away the greater part of the jacket which Nijinsky was to wear. The loin-cloth became in consequence too prominently visible, and Bakst, Diaghileff's constant companion, advised that it should be taken off. When this was done the lower half of Nijinsky's trunk, which was developed out of all proportion to the upper half, drew attention to itself. When he appeared on the stage, and the Director, Telia-kovsky, saw from his box *ces rotondités complètement impudiques*, he was infuriated. The presence of the Empress in the theatre added to the scandal. During the interval the Director rushed behind the scenes and "told off" the indecent offender. On the following day Nijinsky was expelled from the Imperial Theatres company.[1]

At that time the Empress knew nothing of what was happening. As is clear from her conversation with Lady

[1] Romola Nijinska's story that he was merely suspended, resigned voluntarily, and was begged to come back, is fantastic.

Ripon, she even regretted Nijinsky's expulsion. The Directorate simply showed an excess of zeal and loyalty. Perhaps also there was a desire on the part of the Directorate to make things difficult for Diaghileff, who was certainly strongly disliked in the Imperial Theatres. If this is so, they made a great mistake.

Actually this incident was playing into Diaghileff's hands. Diaghileff loved the atmosphere of conflict, scandal, and quarrelling. He made a great story of it in which the Directorate did not appear in a good light. But what was more important and more beneficent to Diaghileff was that Nijinsky's expulsion placed the dancer wholly in his hands. The man whom Diaghileff not only loved, but who was the trump card of his ballet, was put in a position of complete dependability on him.

The possibility of the whole scandal being a clever tactical manœuvre of Diaghileff is not to be ignored. Perhaps in shortening Nijinsky's jacket Diaghileff really foresaw the possible results of his action. Diaghileff had a faculty for creating scandals. This will be seen later in connection with the productions *L'Après-midi d'un Faune* and *Le Sacre du Printemps*. In an atmosphere of uproar he knew better than anyone how to emerge with credit. Of course, this is merely a supposition. There are no facts to go upon—and there could be no facts. But, knowing Diaghileff, one finds difficulty in believing that he did not know what he was doing when he altered Nijinsky's costume.

This occurrence had great importance for the *Ballets-Russes*. From the day of Nijinsky's expulsion from the Imperial stage the *Ballets-Russes* gradually began to be

PLATE X

NIJINSKY'S OFFENDING COSTUME, "GISELLE"

*Drawing by A. Benois*

BALLET PETRUSHKA
*Design by Alexandre Benois*

transformed from a temporary affair of a season into a permanent independent company. Before long tours of the whole of Europe began with their seasons occupying always greater parts of the year, and a nucleus of permanent, loyal performers was formed. In addition to Nijinsky and his sister Bronislava, Diaghileff was joined by Fokine,[1] Vera Fokina, Bolm, Karsavina, Ludmila Schollar, the producer Grigorieff, the Baranovitch twins, Lubov Tchernicheva, Kandina, Nesterovskaya, and others. This formed the core of the future permanent company. Some of them continued their relations with the Maryinsky company, but at heart they were with Diaghileff, and he could count on their allegiance.

In another direction the Nijinsky incident widened the gulf which was growing every year between Diaghileff and Russia. The complete break with the fatherland occurred later, after the War and the Revolution. When the Bolsheviks came into power the *Ballets-Russes* even became the *Ballets Serge de Diaghileff*, and the last link was severed. But already, in the beginning of 1911, after many disappointments and failures in Russia, this final break could be foreseen.

[1] In St. Petersburg Fokine was looked at askance for political reasons—he was in the 1905 revolt.

# 8

## PETRUSHKA

INCLUDED in the programme of Diaghileff's 1911 season in Paris was the ballet *Petrushka*, created jointly by I. Stravinsky and A. Benois to Stravinsky's music.

I should like to separate this ballet from the joint work of the season and talk about it specially. This ballet is the greatest achievement of the friends; the spirit of their work shines there with special clarity, and their creative enthusiasm is particularly evident. By studying the history of the creation of *Petrushka* one can more easily understand their general method of collective creation, the normal genesis of *Ballets-Russes*.

There are certain undertakings which seem to be conceived, to grow and mature under the guidance of some special providence; everything seems to succeed, every element to merge in one beautiful whole. Such a special providence seemed to watch over the creation of *Petrushka*.

It is difficult for me to write objectively about this ballet without an inward tremor. I had never had the good fortune to see on a stage before such a unified, such an integrated spectacle, satisfying simultaneously eye, ear, and mind in one great artistic expression. The décor, the costumes, Stravinsky's truly magnificent score, the actual theme with its suggestion of terrifying Hoffmannesque

fantasy, the brilliant choreography, and the inspired performance—in short, every single element seemed to be
organically connected in a strange, rather terrifying and
yet pleasing entity.

It is difficult to believe from seeing and hearing *Petrushka*
that this ballet was the result of a collective creative impulse.
Rather does it seem as if a single super-genius, equally
gifted in music, art, painting, and choreography, had conceived, devised, and staged this ballet. It is, of course, the
greatest achievement of the *Ballets-Russes*, their admitted
masterpiece. It is not new now, it has been in existence for
a quarter of a century, and possibly it does not strike a
modern spectator by its novelty and daring as forcibly as
it struck us at the time. But the balletomane to-day will
assuredly receive as irresistible an artistic impression, and
I cannot imagine any spectator who does not feel after
experiencing *Petrushka* that mood of exalted satisfaction
which can be given only by a great complete work
of art.

The story and the setting are well known, but I shall,
nevertheless, recapitulate them briefly.

The scene is that of a crowded holiday fair during
Carnival in St. Petersburg in the thirties of last century.
There is, among other stalls, one belonging to a Charlatan,
who has three dolls, the Dancer, Petrushka, and a Blackamoor. These dolls dance gaily and half mechanically
among the crowd, to the general amusement. But the
heartless Charlatan had endowed these marionettes with
the faculties of living beings, and through this had thrown
them into the abyss of human suffering. Alone and unseen
in their cubicles they play out a living human drama.

Petrushka suffers the torments of jealousy. He is in love with the Dancer, who is dazzled by the Blackamoor, while he is absorbed in himself. The gaudy Blackamoor starts to play with a coco-nut, then prays to it, and finally smashes it to discover what is inside, what he has been praying to. The Dancer enters and commences a flirtation with him. Then Petrushka rushes in. The drama grows and develops, and finally the dolls, out of control, rush from their cubicles into the square. The Blackamoor pursues Petrushka and, in the midst of the crowds, stabs him with his sword. The agitated crowd gathers round the dying Petrushka. A policeman drags the Charlatan, probably from the neighbouring public-house, to the scene of the tragedy. The Charlatan explains that it is all a mistake, that the figure on the ground is only a doll. The mob of people disperses, and the Charlatan strolls back to his booth carrying under his arm the doll, from which the sawdust drops out. He intends to repair the doll and give it back its life, when suddenly above the booth appears the spirit of Petrushka, making passionate gestures in accusation of the Charlatan's cruelty.

Benois was often asked about the inner meaning of *Petrushka* and questioned as to what he really intended to say. He always refused to answer such questions, and, in my opinion, he is profoundly right to do so.

The desire to seek, at any cost, in a work of art for something different, something moral or philosophic, only indicates, I think, an incapacity to be absorbed by and satisfied with the essential art of the work. It is possible, of course, to debate whether *La Gioconda's* half-smile conceals a sarcastic disdain for the world or expresses her awareness of a mystery which she alone has solved. One can—but to what end? *La Gioconda* is a great painting, and anyone who seeks something beyond is probably incapable of appreciating painting. The whole meaning, the whole value of *La Gioconda* consists in the inspired canvas of the painter, and no philosophic theory can improve on it.

It is possible also to philosophize about *Petrushka*, to argue that it is an eternal tragedy of the clash between a true and simple love and the feminine incapacity of understanding it, the feminine weakness for cheap glitter as represented by the bedizened Blackamoor. Or one can say that *Petrushka* expresses the bewitchment of human life, the tragedy of human impotence. In short, a great deal can be said, but to no purpose. One must know how to appreciate the complete artistic impression of this marvellous spectacle, to delight in its artistic essence, and to understand that its whole meaning consists in this, and that no philosophizing can add anything further to this meaning. Certain German producers tried to solve the "secret" of *Petrushka*, and presented it as a sublimated "Weltschmerz" in a kind of Greek robe. But then I have seen Shakespeare's *Hamlet* played in dinner-jackets. Such people do exist. Peace be with them! Generally speaking, all this philosophizing about art is a sure sign of a lack of talent, the result of inability to delight in a created work of art. And delight is the only true approach to art, the only proper reaction to it, and therefore the only way to understand it. As there are creators without talent, so there are spectators without talent—spectators who simply do not know how to respond emotionally to art, how to delight in it, but try instead to philosophize about it in an effort to persuade themselves and others that they do understand it.

The story of the creation of *Petrushka* does not lend itself to smooth consecutive treatment. Under the guiding influence of Benois, the collective collaboration was so closely fused that the separate contributions cannot be clearly disentangled. Several greatly talented persons worked together as an enthusiastic team, improving, inventing continuously something new, adding details, corresponding with each other, meeting together and discussing. Despite being separated sometimes by great distances and despite lapses of time, the collaborators were, by some miracle, attuned in complete artistic harmony in producing this beautiful, coherent, and homogeneous creation.

The story begins with a letter of Diaghileff from abroad to Benois, who was then in St. Petersburg. The letter contained a friendly admonishment: "Enough of sulking. Put aside old grievances. You must make the ballet which Igor Stravinsky and I have in mind. Yesterday I heard the music of the Russian Dance and Petrushka's shrieks which he has just composed. It is such a work of genius that one cannot contemplate anything beyond it. You alone can do it. . . ." And so on. The tone of the letter resembled that of a patriotic appeal, something in the nature of "England needs you."

In spite of the quarrel three months previously over *Sheherazade*, Benois responded, with full and complete agreement. He was induced not only by the fact that the offence had grown cold with time, but mainly by the extraordinary attractiveness of the theme. From childhood

Benois had loved Petrushka, the Russian Punch and Judy. As a child he had several guignol theatres, for which he wrote plays. His puppets were very splendid, and he even sometimes made them himself, making the heads out of potatoes and painting them elaborately.

However, the traditional Russian guignol Petrushka was different from the Petrushka of the ballet. He was a gay and dashing roysterer who was always having adventures. He killed someone, and mocked and beat his wife. He played cruel tricks on the watchman and the policeman. Part of the time he had a soldier's close-cropped hair. He marched up and down, "One, two, one, two, three . . ." and killed his officer. But he, too, met with misfortune. A fluffy, woolly lamb appeared on the scene, and Petrushka was delighted. He caressed it, called it "Sly little darling," sat astride of it, and pranced round. After two turns round the stage the lamb suddenly stood erect, was transformed into the Devil, and hauled Petrushka off to the lower regions in quite a terrifying fashion.

The action of Petrushka was interspersed with a mocking dialogue between him and the organ-grinder, who warns him, "Look out! You'll get into hot water." Petrushka only laughs, shrieking out, "He, he, he!" in his piercing voice. For the rôle of Petrushka the operator put in his mouth a little contrivance which gave a nasal tone to the voice. It was these weird shrieks which inspired the piercing dissonance of the shrieks in Stravinsky's score for the ballet *Petrushka*.

In the Russian guignol there was an interlude which seemed to have no connection with the rest of the performance. This consisted in the appearance of two gor-

135

geously dressed Blackamoors ("Arap") with plumes in their hair. The black, wooden, roughly shaped heads with their glittering golden features were terrifying. The Blackamoors played about on the stage, throwing sticks at one another. Probably they were the survival of a very old tradition; there was something eighteenth century about them.[1]

From his childhood days Benois had a feeling of affection mingled with terror for these "Araps." In the alphabet which he later designed for his children the "Arap" has a big part: he begins and ends the book and embellishes the cover in all his terrifying and gaudy fascination.

The Russian guignol was presented, as elsewhere, from behind screens. The marionettes were worked by a concealed operator. They moved about and spoke, though their empty, shrunken legs dangled lifelessly over the edge of the stage.

It appears that Diaghileff and Stravinsky had this guignol theatre in mind at the start.

Before long Diaghileff returned to St. Petersburg, and immediately called upon Benois.

"Well," he asked, "how do you see it? Have you thought anything out?"

Benois was already in the throes of creation.

[1] The Russian word *Arap* (Blackamoor) formerly meant an Abyssinian, that is an African Semite and not a negro, as understood to-day. Peter the Great's famous *Arap*, Pushkin's ancestor, was an Abyssinian. The custom of having *Arap* attendants was prevalent for a long time not only at Court but in the houses of the aristocracy. Until the revolution of March 1917 two gorgeously dressed Abyssinians stood outside the door of the Emperor's chamber. They had no other function than a decorative one. As regards the aristocracy, the custom ceased to be observed about the middle of the nineteenth century.

PLATE XI

DÉCOR FOR FIRST TABLEAU OF "PETRUSHKA"

*By A. Benois*

PLATE XII

COSTUMES DESIGNED FOR "PETRUSHKA"

*By A. Benois*

"Petrushka," he replied, "Petrushka—by all means. Shrieks—yes, certainly. But screams—no! It must be done in a different way. Petrushka must be brought from behind the screens to the stage. Their legs must move, of course, so that they can dance. They must be changed from guignol figures into dolls, dummies, half-human beings."

Benois had already three figures in mind: Petrushka, the Dancer, and the Blackamoor. He was now occupied with the question of the surroundings for the action.

"Do you know what we will do?" he exclaimed. "We'll turn it into a Fair."

These fairs were also one of his cherished childhood memories. During Lent in St. Petersburg it was an old-established custom to hold an amusement fair with booths and stalls. In the thirties these were held in Admiralty Square. Later the Fair was moved to the Winter Palace Square, and towards the end of last century to the Field of Mars. At the commencement of the last reign these fairs were "banished" to the out-of-the-way Semenovsky Field, and there, unfortunately, this gay and motley amusement fair gradually died out.

Having decided upon the Amusement Fair as a setting, Benois proceeded to invest it with his favourite Hoffmannesque atmosphere.

The evil Charlatan was invented. He creates the dolls in mocking travesty of mankind, making them half-human beings who remain under his domination. Through this arise the sufferings of Petrushka. The shrieks of Stravinsky's music already expressed not so much the cries of Petrushka's voice as the sufferings of his soul. Now the conception of Petrushka's character was changed. Instead of a rowdy

137

Russian adventurer he became something in the style of Pierrot, with his simplicity, *naïveté*, and suffering. Gradually the theme began to crystallize into something simple, half fantastic, and tragic.

Correspondence between Benois and Stravinsky had already begun, and now became regular and frequent. Benois was in St. Petersburg, Stravinsky first in Paris, later at Morges in Switzerland. There went backwards and forwards long, detailed, enthusiastic letters in which everything was discussed, new ideas suggested, progress announced. Stravinsky's first letter said how glad he was at the prospect of working together. Finally, in December he informed Benois of his coming visit to St. Petersburg. During the week of Stravinsky's stay in Russia Benois saw him nearly every day. From their joint discussions the action of the Fair scene began to take shape. Stravinsky played the sketches of his music, and Benois approved of them with delight. Stravinsky was the only one who could play the music. Apart from the fact that nobody could make out the scribbled score, the extraordinarily complex execution demanded was puzzling.

The jostling crowds, the thronged streets, the booths— all began to take concrete form. Stravinsky hit upon the idea of the two organ-grinders and the drunkards with the accordion. In this connection a rather curious incident is worth mentioning. For the accordion music Stravinsky chose several themes from well-known popular songs of the day. He was guided in his choice, evidently, mainly by the vulgarity and plebeian coarseness of the songs. Later, in Paris, it turned out that the author of one of these songs was still alive. He began to protest and make

138

an outcry about plagiarism, demanding royalties from the receipts of *Petrushka* on his song, "She had a wooden leg." The affair was settled, and apparently the author got his royalties. I have even heard that he earned a pension for life in this way. I cannot vouch for the truth of the story, but it is certain that in the Fair scene Stravinsky faithfully reproduced the melody of "She had a wooden leg," and that, as he developed it, it produced a lively, bright, and colourful impression.

Stravinsky only stayed in St. Petersburg for a week, and after his departure the regular correspondence commenced again. Some of the details incorporated were discovered almost accidentally. Benois, for example, at a recital of folk-songs by Plevitskaya, was greatly attracted by a song about a gay merchant. He wrote of this to Stravinsky, who immediately composed the music, and the character was introduced into the action. The coachmen and grooms were Diaghileff's suggestions. He demonstrated to Benois the gestures of drivers beating their hands on their sides to keep themselves warm. Benois added to these the character of the Court coachman. It was also Benois who invented the gipsies and mummers. Stravinsky proposed the wet-nurses. In short, the whole structure of the crowd at the Fair, so compact and complete in appearance, was improvised by several people and by correspondence at a distance of thousands of miles.

The Blackamoor scene was first drafted as a scenario and the music was composed later. Benois's first idea was to retain the poles of the traditional Russian interlude. Later he substituted the coco-nut for these poles. Gradually the religious significance of the coco-nut took shape, and

139

THE BIRTH OF BALLETS-RUSSES

finally the Blackamoor's fury was invented, his wild desire to discover the secret of his idol, to look inside the nut. The Dancer's entrance and the development of the drama between the three dolls was then worked out. Benois kept Stravinsky informed of all these developments by letter, and Stravinsky replied in delighted agreement that he had set to work composing the music.

During the whole of this winter Benois was busy making designs for the scenery and costumes. The Square, with its merry-go-rounds and booths, was bright and colourful. Petrushka's cell was black, dotted with stars. The Blackamoor had a red cubicle with palms, tigers, and other exotic motifs. The curtain represented the Charlatan surrounded with clouds and with a flute in his hands. For subsequent versions of *Petrushka* Benois replaced this curtain by one representing a night sky across which flew various evil spirits. The reason for this change is not known. Benois does not care to speak about the subject. It cannot even be explained by the failure of the first attempt, since it was more beautiful than the following one.

In order not to be disturbed in his work, Benois found modest lodgings not far from his St. Petersburg apartments. He retired there and designed an immense number of costumes for the Fair scene—holiday-makers, wet-nurses, and so on. What was his surprise one day when from the premises below his quiet retreat he heard sounds of loud revelry, the strains of accordions and balalaika, the stamping of feet, women's screams. . . . It proved that beneath him were the quarters of Count Bobrinsky's coachmen, who were entertaining their women in dance and debauch. Benois says that he had the unique experience of finding

140

that the near-by "music" not only did not interfere with his work but, on the contrary, actually gave him additional inspiration. Amid the sounds of their gay revelry and the noisy stamping of their dances he designed with ease the costumes of the holiday-makers, the booths, and the merry-go-rounds.

For the first version of *Petrushka* an interlude scene was considered for inclusion. They had the idea of depicting Admiralty Square by night, with the moon lighting up the deserted booths and stalls. Unfortunately, in the further development of the ballet, the dramatic action took such a firm control of the production that this scene was omitted. Benois has regretted it ever since.

Towards spring the friends met in Rome, where a World Exhibition was being held. The *Ballets-Russes* were invited to give several performances at the Teatro Costanza. *Petrushka* was far from finished; much had still to be done to it. Only six weeks remained before the Paris *première*, and the conclusion of the ballet was still dim to the creators. Benois and Stravinsky put up together at the Hôtel d'Italie. Benois could hear Stravinsky working in his room composing the music. The scene in Petrushka's cubicle was completed in Rome. It was constructed to the music which Stravinsky had already composed on the theme of Petrushka's shrieks. In this instance Benois fitted the action to the music, and with brilliant results. It is difficult now to believe that the creation was invented for the music and not the music to represent the action.

For a long time the end of the ballet presented difficulties. At last, working together, they planned the agony and death of Petrushka, the Charlatan strolling back with the doll under his arm, the appearance above the booth of Petrushka's spirit, and Stravinsky finished the ballet with an unfinished suspended phrase from the orchestra. All this having been done, they came into collision with Diaghileff.

"It can't be ended like that," he said. "A major final chord is wanted."

He had to be argued with for a long time, but Stravinsky persisted in having his way, and the acidulent unfinished phrase terminated the ballet like a mark of interrogation.

In the final phase of the creation of *Petrushka* it is almost impossible to dissociate Benois's contribution from Stravinsky's. There was a creative ferment in which each shared, and the work was carried on jointly in a spirit of friendly enthusiasm. This period was the consummation of the fire of inspiration which created the *Ballets-Russes*. It was this fire which for many years later illuminated the path of ballet-workers and which even now has not lost its invigorating strength.

The rehearsals of *Petrushka* took place in the buffet of the Teatro Costanza, which was situated in the basement. On a dirty red spotted carpet in these shabby, stuffy premises, and in an atmosphere of terrible heat, Fokine staged the dances, while Stravinsky played the music without sparing himself. The music of *Petrushka* did not at first altogether please Fokine. It seems that these strange piercing sounds, which were such a striking novelty, affected him disagreeably. To-day we can scarcely understand such an attitude to Stravinsky's marvellous score, especially on the part of so musically cultured a man as

## PLATE XIII

IGOR STRAVINSKY AT REHEARSAL IN ROME, 1911

*Drawing by A. Benois*

PLATE XIV

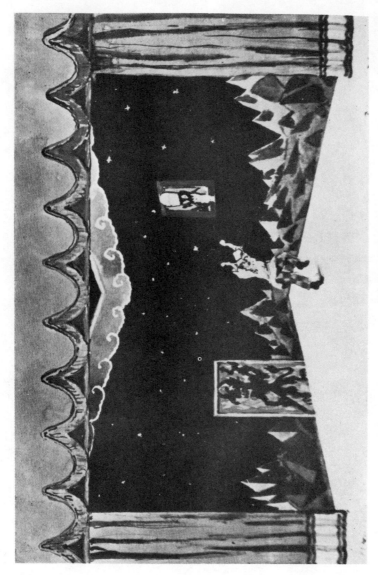

DÉCOR FOR SECOND TABLEAU OF "PETRUSHKA"

By A. Benois

Fokine. We have forgotten what a startling impression it produced in 1911. Much water has flown under the bridges since then; the sharp, venomous "harmonics" of contemporary music have made our sense of hearing callous. The orchestration of *Petrushka* already seems to us simple, almost classical. After the world-wide orgies of jazz, Stravinsky's rhythm does not astonish us; we accept it calmly, without protest.

In those days it was a different matter. One has only to remember that the members of the orchestra, rehearsing *Petrushka* at the Châtelet, burst into loud laughter. The conductor, Monteux, who admired the score, had the greatest difficulty in restraining them. In Russia certain circles of cultured music-lovers were a long time in appreciating Stravinsky's music. In St. Petersburg, during the winter following the Paris production, Benois invited such an enlightened circle of music-lovers to hear the piano score of the ballet. The result was a complete failure. People did not understand. Benois swore that it was excellent music, marvellous music, begged them to take his word for it. The music-lovers were simply puzzled.

Benois was not quite satisfied with the staging of the Revellers' scenes. He argued, criticized, approved of one point and disapproved of another. He considered the entrance of the Gay Merchant a success, but was displeased with the treatment of the wet-nurses. He wanted to avoid completely a normal ballet treatment of the jostling crowds. He aimed at the fusion of the ballet element with the dramatic, realistic handling of the scene. *Petrushka* is probably the ballet in which the influence of the decorator on the character of the choreography was most marked.

Benois's collaboration with Fokine was both close and practical.

The success of *Petrushka* in Paris was enormous. Although most of the spectators did not understand Stravinsky's daring and original music, the ballet gripped them. The members of the orchestra might laugh at rehearsal, the music-lover might throw his hands in the air at the piano score, but the music had a better reception from ballet audiences. The truth is that one of the chief merits of the musical score is its illustrative qualities. If it was difficult to appreciate at that date the purely musical qualities of Stravinsky's composition, the same music combined with the visual stimulus of the ballet produced a powerful and direct impression. Whether as the result of the closeness of the collaboration or purely by chance, the music of *Petrushka* identically fits the action, and the congruity of visual and auditory images attains perfection. For this reason the Châtelet public accepted this music, though perhaps unconsciously, without the astonishment and protests which one might have expected.

The public was also, of course, greatly struck by the dramatic character of the ballet. In the whole history of ballet, *Petrushka* seems to have been the first instance of a fundamental, compelling tragedy. The ballet is so constructed that the centre of interest lies in the tragic nature of the action and not in the dances themselves. *Petrushka* is not a ballet with a dramatic theme, but a choreographic tragedy. In this sense it was a complete novelty and naturally carried away the public.

A large part of the success of *Petrushka* was due also to

the convincing and authentic nature of the "folk" scenes. The costumes of the revellers at the Fair were extremely successful in colouring and style. They seemed both strange and picturesque. The St. Petersburg of the thirties, with its wet-nurses wearing gaudy-coloured necklaces, its coachmen in wide *caftans* and high-crowned hard hats, and its long-bearded peasants, seemed to Paris something exotic, remote, and picturesque.

The choreography of the ballet was also novel and surprising. Instead of the customary light, fluttering movements, the spectator was presented with angular, doll-like, *terre-à-terre* dancing, full of rhythmic accent, a drunken "Prisiadka"[1] by coachmen, and the smooth gestures of Russian peasant women.

The choreographic theme of a doll coming to life was not an original idea, but the manner of treating it was. In previous ballets, for example in *Coppelia*, the introduction of dolls was little more than a pretext, and the ballerina danced her invariable *pas seul* with the same classical *entrechats* and *battements* as in any other classical ballet. In *Petrushka*, on the other hand, the doll-movements were present throughout. The whole character of the dancing, the poses of the figures, the angular movements and gestures, the doll-like immobility of facial expression, the strange jerkiness of the positions, were not normal ballet and had never been seen before.

I need hardly say that the brilliant execution of the dances had a great deal to do with the success of the ballet. Petrushka was always Nijinsky's favourite part. There is a curious correlation between the rôle of Petrushka and

[1] *Prisiadka*—a squatting dance of peasant origin.

the personality of Vazlav Nijinsky himself. This dancer of genius seemed scarcely to exist in private life. Silent, un-remarkable, helpless, apparently semi-conscious, he seemed to be scarcely alive off the stage, seemed at best to be living some doll's life of his own. And, at the same time, this strange, doll-like personality concealed a tragedy of spiritual death, and Nijinsky could, perhaps, have leant over the footlights and demanded passionately of his conjuror Diaghileff, "What have you done to my im-mortal soul?"

Nijinsky danced this part with genius. He knew how to combine angular doll-movements with complete natural-ness. The frozen, mask-like immobility of his features was deeply tragic, only emphasizing the dramatic terror of the half-human doll. The whole dramatic image of Petrushka was complete and seemed to be profoundly thought out. I say "seemed," because the impossibility of anything "thought out," of any conscious directing intelligence behind that apparently fogged mind, must be evident to anyone who knew Nijinsky. Nijinsky understood by instinct, by intuitive genius, and not by rational analysis. His unerring creative sense enabled him, in spite of his lack of rational intelligence, to create profound and com-pletely satisfying dramatic images. And perhaps the most powerful and satisfying of all his parts was Petrushka. From the first moment of his appearance on the stage one felt that here was neither doll nor man, but a strange and terrifying mixture of both, and one was overcome by the pathos of his helpless, bewitched suffering. The contrast between the vigorous animation of his quick muscular movements and the pitiful appeal of his tormented soul with its petrified mask was breath-taking. Nijinsky's Petrushka is one of the most vivid and unforgettable impressions I have ever experienced.

Karsavina—the Dancer—was quite on the level of her wonderful partner. Her physical appearance was a great aid in this. She was a beautiful woman, and, by the use of make-up, her charming face was changed into the soulless plaster mask of a doll. Her technique and lightness of movement were perfect. She was the complete image of an empty, stupid, beautiful woman—a soulless, thoughtless doll. Karsavina's strength never lay in her temperament, and her classical style of dancing suited this part to perfection. The clarity, the plastic beauty and airy lightness of her movements gave her dance great freshness and a charming unreality.

The Blackamoor, played by Orlov, was also splendid. His dark-skinned, gaudy figure, surmounted with glittering plumes, was primitively terrifying. Of course, this part was an easier one than the other two. The greater part of the impression was created by the glittering costume and the brutal and exotic appearance. But Orlov, both in dancing and dramatic power, was equal to his partners.

Though all these separate factors contributed to the success of the ballet, it seems to me that the chief factor of all was the unity of the whole artistic impression. The merging of arts is a difficult task which rarely succeeds. The unity of impression is almost always damaged by something, sometimes by a trifle, sometimes by an important incongruity; and a real work of art should be always finished to the last detail. It seems to me that the main

147

function of a ballet performance is to create just such a unity. Music, drama, and spectacle attain organic fusion only when combined in ballet form. Drama alone, of course, can give an impression of totality, but it dispenses with music. Opera, in spite of many attempts, notably Wagner's, does not in my opinion achieve this fusion. It is hampered by many obstacles, and the obstacles are, perhaps, impossible to overcome. Music is irrational, and words can never be absolutely divorced from their rational meaning. Thus recitatives are eternally condemned either to fail to be music or to fail in making sense. On the other hand, to change from song to talk always grates on the listener's ear. Besides, and this is not unimportant, it is hard to demand from singers, in addition to voice, a suitable figure and acting skill. Felia Litvin was a wonderful singer, but she was so tall and stout that she was called "The whale who swallowed the nightingale." Her musical effect was superb, but her appearance was dramatically wrong. Apart from this, the singers are nearly always dependent upon the conductor's baton and the prompter's box. They are not free agents. I even prefer the old style of Italian opera. There the tenor, ducally dressed, walked without embarrassment to the footlights, stretched out his hand and took his note. This, at any rate, is consciously done, almost intentionally gauche, with no pretence of realism.

Opera, too, has given me at times great artistic pleasure. One has only to remember the genius of Chaliapine in his prime. But the impression has always been fragmentary; sometimes it was a singer, sometimes a particular scene which attracted me, but I have never seen or heard an opera which made a coherent whole, and I think that no self-conscious person ever can get such an impression from opera.

With ballet the case is different. One of its first essentials is that the performer should have a well-shaped body, and dramatic skill is indispensable. In ballet, too, the dancer is free from the conductor's baton and the prompter's box. No absurd conventions, no false pretence of realism govern ballet. The music, the dances, the costumes and décor, are equally removed from the rational plane, and can thus easily be fused to create a single complex impression. Moreover, the origin of ballet is more essentially theatrical than the other arts of the stage. Ballet is primarily a spectacle, and this essential requisite of the stage seems to have been forgotten by the other arts. The centre of gravity in drama lies in the emotions, in the ideas, and sometimes in the wit. Opera has no meaning apart from the dramatic and lyrical expressiveness of the music. But ballet is above everything an artistic spectacle; in other words, ballet is of the essence of theatre. We can read a drama in the study, listen to an opera with closed eyes, but ballet cannot possibly be detached from the vision. In this connection ballet has a distant and rather humble relation—revue. This relation has turned out badly. It has been seduced by the easy money to be gained by indulging in cheap luxury and tinsel and by pandering to popular taste. It is not concerned with its main theatrical function—art. It is a spectacle, but it has ceased to be artistic. The responsibility for this lies with that disease which is fatal to all art—box-office dictatorship.

In connection with *Petrushka* two incidents come to

mind which are characteristic of the prevailing atmosphere in which the friends' work was carried on. The first of these incidents indicates the friendly nature of the collaboration.

Benois, sitting in the Châtelet buffet, was approached by Stravinsky, who said:

"Well, now that the ballet is finished, we must decide under whose name to register it."

"Well, who is the author of the ballet?" asked Benois.

"In my opinion *you* are," said Stravinsky.

"Oh, no," retorted Benois, "*you* are."

"I? Nonsense! It was you who invented it all."

"But you had the idea first."

The friends argued for a long time, each giving the credit to the other. Finally it was decided that the ballet should be attributed to both jointly. Benois so far prevailed, however, that the alphabetical order was disregarded and Stravinsky's name put first.

There can be no doubt that the author of *Petrushka* was mainly Benois; but the collaboration was so close and friendly that the participants themselves could not tell their own particular share. Stravinsky once more sealed the pact of friendly collaboration with Benois by inscribing on his marvellous score, "Dédié à M. Alexandre Benois."

The second incident reveals the nervous tension during the production of the ballet.

Shortly before the dress rehearsal of *Petrushka* Benois had an abscess on his right elbow which prevented him from moving his arm. The scenery which Benois had designed, and which was painted by Anisfeldt in St. Petersburg, arrived in Paris. Something went wrong with the scene of Petrushka's cubicle. Benois was informed that the Charlatan's portrait in the set had been damaged, either by being torn or in some other way.

Bakst called on Benois and explained with embarrassment that he had "repaired a little bit, made a tiny alteration." Actually Bakst, probably at the instigation of Diaghileff, who disliked this portrait, had made quite a different design, which did not at all correspond to Benois's conception.

When Benois saw Bakst's new design at the dress-rehearsal he promptly flared up, began to shout, threw the portfolio he carried on the floor, scattering its contents, and dashed out of the theatre. Once outside, he went to the Café Zimmer and had a long drink to cool himself. He did not want to return to the theatre, but he also did not want to go away without knowing the upshot of the matter. He waited at the exit for his wife and Prince Argoutinsky, who were unable to pacify him.

On the following day Serov came to appease him. Benois, still indignant, yelled at him also. He could not reconcile himself to the fact that, under the guise of a friendly service, he had been played a mean trick. Serov took offence, and went to Argoutinsky to complain, but this did not prevent him from offering to restore the Charlatan's portrait, following Benois's design. This he undertook and executed beautifully.

All the same, it was a long time before Benois came round. He did not easily overlook such questions of principle and art. He wrote to Diaghileff refusing to be Art Director of the *Ballets-Russes*, and, having finished the designs of the costumes for Covent Garden, left for Lugano.

151

To understand this incident clearly it is necessary to imagine the state of everyone's nerves at the end of the season. The heightened mood of continuous creation over a period of months, together with thousands of irritations and slights, often quite petty, preyed upon the nerves. Many of the participants became quite hysterical. On one occasion, for example, I have heard that Fokine, on account of some delay in receiving money from Diaghileff, wanted to throw himself out of the hotel window. Benois's nerves could not have been anything but frayed. The creative impulse must be paid for, especially when it takes the shape of a continuous inward fire, a quenchless enthusiasm. And that was how *Petrushka* was created. The fury of creation required a heightened nervous tension, and Benois, living on this different plane during the whole period of creative activity, even with his enormous energy could not help being fatigued.

Before finishing this chapter on *Petrushka* I should like to say a few words about the art of ballet and people's attitude to it.

Madame d'Agoult, the friend of Liszt, in her diary for 1839 wrote: "Since David's time, the art of dancing has been discredited. I have always considered dancing a very serious, even a very religious, art."

A disdainful attitude towards ballet was prevalent for long. Even to-day it can be met with among the professionals of other arts. People seem not to want to understand that there is no art that is "superior" or "inferior" to its sister arts. Once art exists, once the spirit of mankind exercises itself creatively, there can be no dispute about

PETRUSHKA

the relevant value of the particular sphere in which this creative activity manifests itself. One can speak of great or small achievements in art, but not of one art as greater than another. During the whole nineteenth century there prevailed in Europe the mistaken attitude to the living plastic art, as if Terpsichore was not one of the Muses, as if dance was not one of the chief original arts, connected from time immemorial with that other, that first of all arts—music.

The task of rehabilitating the art of ballet was the function of the *Ballets-Russes*. After their appearance every cultured person was forced to admit that ballet was on an equal footing with the other arts. Its natural birthright was restored to ballet.

The Diaghilevians accomplished this finally in 1911. During this season their earlier success was consolidated, was placed beyond controversy, and one of the chief factors in establishing this was *Petrushka*. The very character of the *Ballets-Russes* altered the popular attitude to the ballet. Hearing and seeing *Petrushka*, it was unthinkable to mention *"divertissement,"* "entertainment," "soothing music," or "pretty women." There could not remain the slightest doubt in the spectator's mind that he found himself in the presence of an art, of a great, complete, important manifestation of the creative spirit of man.

# 9

## 1911

IN 1911 Benois was Art Director of the *Ballets-Russes*, and for this reason he had to leave St. Petersburg in early spring for Monte Carlo, where there was a season of ballet. He spent part of March and April there with the company, carrying out his complicated and exacting duties.

Although Stravinsky was living quite near by in Beaulieu, no work was done on *Petrushka*. Benois had finished the artistic side of the preparation in St. Petersburg, and in Monte Carlo there was a great deal of other work to do.

*Narcisse* was in the course of production, and the work was not progressing very well. The theme was not very adaptable to ballet purposes. Narcissus, self-intoxicated and rooted to one spot in admiration of his reflection in the water, was difficult to fit into an animated ballet movement. Bakst designed very effective bright green scenery and beautiful costumes. His violet and silver costume for Echo (Karsavina) was particularly successful. There were many choreographical difficulties, however. Nijinsky's entrance was a failure. He appeared on the stage with a positively tremendous leap, and the tense strain of this almost record-breaking jump destroyed the impression of airiness and freedom upon which mainly depended the illusion of Nijinsky's *élévation*. Also the crash of his landing, almost in the centre of the stage, was heard

154

throughout the entire house and made a bad impression. Nijinsky had a similar enormous leap in another ballet, *Le Spectre de la Rose*, where he flew from the stage through a window. But in this case his back was to the audience, the tenseness was not remarked, and he landed on a mattress concealed from the spectators behind the wings. Here the illusion of airy flight was completely convincing.

Karsavina was very suitable for the part of Echo. Fokine was perfectly successful in inventing for her movements which, repeating those of Narcissus, seemed a sad reflection of his dance, and Karsavina was at her most charming in this rôle.

A disagreeable effect was produced on me by a seeming trifle in *Narcisse*. At the end of this ballet, from the spot where Narcissus had disappeared, there grows through a trap-door a papier mâché flower. This shabby, ragged imitation narcissus seems to me to demonstrate the great importance which the smallest details have when worked out on the stage. These trifles, as they appear to some people, often ruin the general artistic impression of a production.

In this connection I remember the bad impression produced on me by the boot-soles of a fine Swedish actor in Stockholm Royal Theatre. He was playing the part of a Protestant reformer, and when he knelt with his back to the audience he revealed a clean pair of soles, fresh from the shoe-shop. They were an eyesore, destroying one's belief in the theatrical illusion. In another performance at the same theatre a bush was lit up fitfully to produce the impression of a windy, cloudy, moonlit night. But here, in the same scene, the lighting of the façade of the house never varied throughout. In painstaking productions, not to mention first-class productions, such things ought not to happen. There is no place in art for the slipshod. No painter permits himself to be careless in painting a tree because it happens to be in the background of his picture; no composer is negligent about the score for the second trombone because it is not the vocal solo. Either the stage is not an art and is allowed a latitude which true art does not desire, or it is an art and must take pains with every detail.

The production of *Narcisse* in 1911 was the result of various disconnected causes. A ballet on the theme of Longus's *Daphnis and Chloë* with music by Ravel had been contemplated for this season. The scenario, which Fokine had composed in 1904, did not satisfy Diaghileff. The ballet had to "feature" Nijinsky, had to be "his" ballet. In the story, however, the parts of Daphnis and Chloë were exactly parallel and of equal dramatic importance. Diaghileff started to look for different material. Bakst was at this time greatly interested in archaic Greek art, enthused about it, and dreamed of staging a ballet on some mythological theme. The Narcissus story which he suggested seemed suitable for the purpose. The part of Narcissus was central, and round it was built the whole story. Tcherepnin's music also turned out quite well, and the production was decided upon. The Daphnis and Chloë theme was postponed till the following season.

The ballet *Narcisse* proves how the expectations of even the most talented creators may be misjudged.

*Narcisse* had some success and was quite well received by the Press and public, but it was neither a sensational success nor a triumph for Nijinsky. Finally the ballet did not for long retain its place in the repertoire.

In 1911 another short ballet was in preparation. Diaghileff and his friends did not take this very seriously, regarding it rather as a "stop-gap" in the repertoire. No special attention and no great effort were devoted to this ballet, which was called *Le Spectre de la Rose*, and which proved to be just that unquestionable and lasting "triumph of Nijinsky" which Diaghileff had vainly sought in *Narcisse*.

In the previous year, 1910, Jean Louis Vaudoyer, then still a young and unestablished man of letters, had suggested to Diaghileff the staging of a ballet on the theme of Théophile Gautier's *Loin du Bal*, from which he quoted the couplet:

> Je suis le spectre de la rose
> Que tu portais hier au bal.

At the time this suggestion did not seriously attract the attention of the friends, and they almost forgot about it. However, in preparing the programme for 1911, they required a short one-act ballet, and Diaghileff recalled Vaudoyer's idea. Weber's music, "Invitation à la Danse," suggested by Vaudoyer, was admirably suited in period and spirit to the romantic style of Gautier's poem, and it was also of the required length.

They decided to produce the ballet.

"Why not support a talented young writer?" the friends asked themselves.

The designs for the scenery and costumes were entrusted to Bakst, and were brilliantly executed by him. The young girl's bedroom was charmingly simple and innocent. The colour scheme was blue and white, and there was an alcove draped with tulle hangings. On a table there lay a piece of embroidery where it had been left on the previous day. There were besides two or three simple pieces of furniture. The whole room was redolent of virginal freshness and tranquillity. Bakst was very eager to round off the picture by hanging a cage with a canary in it, but wherever he placed it it interfered with the dancers.

*Le Spectre de la Rose* was produced in haste in three or four rehearsals. It turned out to be one of Fokine's finest improvisations. Perhaps the very speed with which the work was done gave it that character of extraordinary freshness and unity. Fokine could sometimes do this, creating a ballet in a sudden rush of inspiration—with one stroke of the brush, as it were. This had been the case with the "Polovetz" dances, and now it happened also with *Le Spectre de la Rose*. It took the form of a *pas de deux* which fused together with the subject, scenery, and music in one poetical entity. There was nothing fragmentary in the movement, no suggestion of "numbers." The choreography was developed simply, fluently, and poetically, in keeping with the music and scenery.

Of course, Fokine had exceptional artistic material at his disposal—Nijinsky and Karsavina. Nijinsky as the "spirit of yesterday's rose" was at the height of his genius. His airy lightness, his faculty of flying through the air without appearing to touch the ground, produced a perfect illusion of something non-human, something apart from the earth and sex and life, the spirit not of a human being but of a flower. When with his final leap he floated through the window into the night, one was convinced that he

158

continued to fly higher, ever higher, into the depths of the sky, into infinity.

Karsavina was quite worthy of the genius of her partner. The expression of the "eternal feminine" was particularly congenial to the talent of this delightful ballerina. The image of girlhood created by her was graceful, innocent, and poetical. Her dream-dance had a quiet, virginal, romantic charm.

The theme of the ballet is simple and charming, as is everything which bears the stamp of Théophile Gautier.

A young girl, returning from her first ball, recalls in her bedroom the events of the evening, falls into a reverie, and kisses the rose given her at the dance. Tired and happy, she sits down in an armchair and falls quietly asleep. From the moonlit night there flies through the open window into her room the incarnation of the spirit of this rose. This is her dream. The spirit of the rose hovers about and floats through the room around the sleeping girl, approaches her, and finally draws her, still asleep, into aerial dance with him. The dance of the pair is the expression of a pure and virginal love. At the end of it the spirit of the rose gently sets the girl back in the armchair, and when she lies still, in quiet dream, he gives her a light, pure kiss and flies through the window into the moonlit night again. The vision is over. The girl wakes, and, as she remembers her dream, her face is lit by a serene smile, she lifts the fallen rose, presses it to her lips and—the curtain falls.

*Le Spectre de la Rose* was an improvisation in every respect. Even Nijinsky's costume was altered at the last moment. When the dressmaker brought it at the beginning of the dress-rehearsal it was quite useless. A council was hurriedly called and, amid Diaghileff's curses and with the help of the scenic decorator, O. Allegri, they began to alter the costume on the spot behind the scenes. Nijinsky was nervous and difficult to please—a rare occurrence with him. He stood there trembling and impatient, like a race-horse before the start of a race. Diaghileff, in top-hat, gloves, and cape, and Bakst were showing the dressmaker, Maria Stepanovna, where to sew the rose-petals to the tights. In this way, with Nijinsky already wearing the costume, it was completely altered at the very last moment.

The ballet had an amazing success. During the whole of Nijinsky's dance the audience sat enraptured. The ballet had to be given in its entirety a second time.

This short ballet, an improvisation and, in the eyes of the friends, a trifle, proved one of the greatest and most lasting triumphs of the *Ballets-Russes*. During the season of 1911 *Le Spectre de la Rose* was performed thirty times, and, in 1912, seventy-six. To-day it is still alive and, together with *Petrushka*, *Carnaval*, *Les Sylphides*, and *Sheherazade*, wins a place for itself in the ballet repertoire.

Although it is a quarter of a century since it was first created it is still as young, fresh, and delightful as in 1911.

The *premières* of *Narcisse* and *Le Spectre de la Rose* were given this year in Monte Carlo. This was an innovation. Diaghileff generally reserved his new productions for the opening of the Paris season in May, but this was his first season on Monaco—and quite a long one (sixteen performances were given). Besides, Diaghileff and his company received a very kind reception in Monte Carlo, and from this year began to visit it every spring for the preparatory work of the season. The patronage of Monaco Court circles meant much to Diaghileff and his circle both then and in later years, and in 1923 the invitation to Monte Carlo saved Diaghileff from desperate financial straits. The present-day *Ballets de Basil* was for a long time called the *Ballets-Russes de Monte Carlo*, and it is hard to determine whether Colonel de Basil, despite his unquestioned business talent, would have succeeded in reviving Russian choreography as brilliantly as he has done without the help of Monte Carlo.

For the 1911 season the production of still another ballet was in view. This was *Péri*, to the music by Paul Dukas. At that time Diaghileff already had a glimpse of the idea of transforming his *Ballets-Russes* into a world-wide artistic organization. This was the start of his aspiration towards internationalism, of his freedom from the "national" basis. Dukas was a prominent French composer, and Diaghileff commissioned the music for a ballet from him. Unfortunately, as it happened, Dukas was a patron of Nathalie Trouhanova, and made it a condition that she should dance Péri. The music was finished and the libretto prepared. Trouhanova, however, had no technique; she was a ballerina of an amateur type. Besides, she was rather stoutly built and was completely unsuitable for the part of the ethereal Péri. Diaghileff began to employ Fabian tactics. Rehearsals were continuously postponed. Dukas called almost daily at the theatre to ask when they would finally start. Diaghileff delegated one or other of the friends to talk him over, take him to the neighbouring café and calm him down. In the end Dukas lost patience. He wrote a letter to Diaghileff cancelling the production. In this way, although *Péri* was announced in the programmes for the season, it was not presented by the *Ballets-Russes*. Later *Péri* was produced at the Opéra Comique with Trouhanova and with scenery by Piot. It was a failure.

The fourth creation of the 1911 *Ballets-Russes* was the tableau of the under-sea kingdom from Rimsky-Korsakov's opera *Sadko*, with scenery and costumes by Boris Anisfeldt. The music was rearranged for the ballet. It began with the first strains of the overture and then, omitting the purely choral part of the act, passed directly to the ballet scene. The music for the singing during the dances, which were in the composer's score, was somehow glossed over. This ballet produced no great impression. Great success could not be anticipated; an act of an opera adapted for ballet is seldom successful. It is a compromise, and art scarcely admits of compromise. The success of the Polovetz scene from *Prince Igor* can be explained partly by the fact that no alterations were necessary in it. In the first instance the whole act of the opera complete with singers was given, and when, later, they gave only the "Polovetz" dances, it was as a special number written down in Borodin's opera.

In addition to the above-mentioned new ballets, there was included in the 1911 programme a symphonic *entr'acte*, "The Battle of Kerzhenez," from Rimsky-Korsakov's opera *Grad Kitezh*. Diaghileff had a high opinion of the music, and ordered a curtain for it from Rœrich, probably on account of his success with the scenery for the Polovetz scene. The symphonic *entr'acte* was played before this lowered curtain, which Rœrich executed in extraordinarily vivid colours. The striking red and green curtain, representing a battle between Slavs and Mongols, was quite dazzling to the eyes. Later the curtain was purchased for Russia, and, unless I am mistaken, decorates to-day one of the walls of the Kazansky railway station in Moscow.

Serov, their Moscow friend, had drawn a special curtain for the re-staging of *Sheherazade*. It was lowered before the beginning of the ballet while the orchestra played as an overture the first part of the symphonic poem which had previously been omitted. The curtain was a splendid piece of work. Designed in the style of Persian miniatures, it represented a hunt taking place over fantastic pink cliffs.

During a rehearsal of *Le Pavillon d'Armide* an accident occurred which depressed the whole company. During the scene of the coming to life of the Gobelin tapestry, while the orchestra was playing *fortissimo*, two trap-doors were open on the stage, through which rose little negro boys carrying white plumes. There had never been any trouble with this before, but unfortunately, on this occasion, the former singer Muratore, who was in charge of publicity, arrived at the theatre, walked on the stage, swept aside Cecchetti, who was guarding with outspread arms the open trap-doors, and fell into the basement. He was killed instantaneously. The impact was so severe that even the rings on his fingers had fallen off. Fortunately the negro boys were not in position at the time and were unhurt.

For the Rome presentation of *Le Pavillon d'Armide* female Italian dancers had to be engaged for the parts of the Awakening Hours. On the morning of the appointed day Benois and Fokine went to inspect the candidates. They found a row of appalling-looking, dishevelled old women sitting round the room waiting for them.

"Where are the dancers?" they asked.

"*Eccole*," was the reply.

In fact these really were the Italian ballerinas. Several of them had actually to be employed in the production. With the addition of five or six of their own company, Fokine managed to stage this scene of the "Awakening Hours."

The *Ballets-Russes* moved from Monte Carlo to Rome in April. They had been invited for a short season of nine performances by the committee of the World Exhibition which was being held there. It is possible that friction had occurred between the Costanza management and the Exhibition committee. In any case, many obstacles were put in the way of the Diaghilevians in the theatre. Even the active help of the courteous Director of the Exhibition, Count San Martino, could not overcome the inimical attitude of the theatre employees. The difficulties were so great that Diaghileff himself decided to take charge of the lighting for the *première*, and Benois was entrusted with the task of giving the signals. Diaghileff sat beneath the stage during the whole performance of *Le Pavillon d'Armide*. Benois avers that he was seldom so nervous in his life as when he was confronted with about fifteen different switches; the thought of making a mistake and giving the signal for opening a trap-door instead of for raising the curtain was rather terrifying. Nevertheless, everything went smoothly and there were no mishaps. After the first striking success of the ballets the theatre personnel changed its recalcitrance for goodwill, and matters proceeded peacefully and quietly.

1911 represents an important date in the history of the Diaghileff ballet. In this year the *Ballets-Russes* first begins to be transformed from Russian ballet artistes touring Europe into a permanent ballet organization, existing and appearing in Europe only, and gradually severing connections with Russia.

The first small cadre of a permanent troupe was formed. After Nijinsky's expulsion from the Imperial Theatres, his sister followed him, and wholeheartedly joined forces with Diaghileff, Bolm handed in his resignation and threw in his lot with the *Ballets-Russes*. Fokine, in spite of being officially reckoned as a member of the Maryinsky Theatre, in actual fact completely broke with it. In the Maryinsky Theatre he was entrusted with no productions and was looked at askance as a revolutionary in art and also, in some sense, in politics.

The *Ballets-Russes* seasons became longer, and Diaghileff began to sign contracts in other countries. Moreover, the success of his ballet was already firmly established. In Paris the *Ballets-Russes* became an annual event. The victory was won and the position had been consolidated. It was only this firmly established reputation which explains the invitation of the *Ballets-Russes* to take part in the Coronation performance at Covent Garden in London. In this connection certain friends had used their influence, but that alone would have been insufficient without the unquestionable success of the *Ballets-Russes* themselves.

The Coronation performance was a brilliant affair. The company was amazed by the extraordinary luxury of the auditorium. The brilliant uniforms, the fairy-tale costumes of the Indian rajahs, evening-dress covered with ribands and decorations, women glittering with precious jewels— this old-world luxury dazzled the Russians. The whole theatre was decorated with flowers. Over the royal box in huge floral letters was written "India" as a tribute to the largest and most wealthy possession of England. The performance was a mixed one. The *Ballets-Russes* only gave the scene of the revival of the Gobelin tapestry from *Le Pavillon d'Armide*. For this occasion Benois made, without regard for expense, special royal costumes, with huge plumes for the heralds, trumpeters, and slaves.

Owing to the established success of the *Ballets-Russes*, offers from various countries began to shower on Diaghileff. It was an *embarras de richesses*, and Diaghileff began to sign contracts for appearances in various European towns. In 1911 the ballet did not do a great deal of travelling— Monte Carlo, Rome, Paris, London in June and October, and Paris again in December. But already contracts were signed for appearances during the following year in twelve towns, including visits to Germany, Austria, and Hungary, as well as the usual round of Monte Carlo, Paris, and London.

Thus started the wandering of the *Ballets-Russes* over the world. Several causes led Diaghileff to this. In the first place, financial considerations were an inducement. Diaghileff was no money-grabber; he died a poor man, and he never knew, and perhaps did not want to know, how to niggle about money. The performers were paid punctually, but in order to do this money had continually to be found at the last moment. By the end of the season there usually remained only debts, and these pressing ones. This continuous need of money partly explains the signing of many contracts. Diaghileff made a sum in advance a condition of the contract, and these helped to cover the more urgent debts.

There were certainly other causes. Not the least of these was that Nijinsky, with the Imperial stage closed to him, could appear only with Diaghileff. Diaghileff's love for Nijinsky was strong, "*c'était la passion de sa vie,*" and he certainly made every effort in order that Nijinsky should make as many appearances as possible. As a general rule Diaghileff liked to advance his collaborators, and this was specially important in Nijinsky's case, all the more so because Nijinsky's genius and his overwhelming success completely justified his advancement.

In addition to these considerations, we have already seen that Diaghileff had begun to conceive the idea of transforming the *Ballets-Russes* into a world-wide artistic organization. He already saw his way clear to collaborate with other Russian artistes, and he had a vision of himself turning from an exporter of Russian art to a protagonist of the *avant-garde* of the world theatre. How far he succeeded in this and how far he was satisfied with the result he achieved will be seen later. Now all that need be said is that on 1911 lies the shadow, the first shadow, of the rupture of the *Ballets-Russes* with Russia.

The nomadic life of a wandering ballet troupe was a complicated and exacting business. To attend to the transport of truck-loads of scenery and crowds of performers demanded of the organizers a great deal of detailed work. Finding hotel accommodation for the company, the packing and unpacking of scenery, the adaptation of the sets to stages of various sizes with different technical equipment and in each new place a strange technical personnel, lighting difficulties, and so on—all these things irritated nerves that were already highly strung and created many minor difficulties which often seemed at the time catastrophic.

The same nervous exhaustion was evident in the performers. It is not easy to dance on a stage to which one is unaccustomed. The size of the stage and, consequently, the disposition of the properties are different. In order not to cause confusion, the dancer must judge in which direction to make a particular leap, in what position on the stage he will find himself after this or that figure. He must forget how he performed his evolutions on the Grand Opera stage and learn anew. On account of this nervous condition there occurred continually petty quarrels, misunderstandings, and offences which had to be cleared up and smoothed over.

\* \* \*

I have treated the year 1911 in such detail because it seems to me the culminating point in the creation of the *Ballets-Russes*. The "Polovetz" dances, *Les Sylphides, Carnaval, Sheherazade, L'Oiseau de Feu, Le Spectre de la Rose* and *Petrushka*—in a word, almost everything which was destined to remain alive for many years to come—are already created. The character of the *Ballets-Russes* is already determined, the new art is there, its individuality strikingly demonstrated. The revolution in choreographic and ballet art is brought to a successful conclusion. Until the present day ballet art has lived precisely on its inheritance from these first tumultuous creative years, from this, shall we say, romantic epoch of the *Ballets-Russes*.

This art was created without any break with tradition. The artistic and choreographic material was drawn from the enormous reserves of talent in Russia. Despite the appearance of revolt there was no rejection of the past; even the classical school of choreography was not discarded. It was expanded, it evolved, but the "classical" dance remained the basis of the new choreography. In all the ballets mentioned above you will find a basis of the old school, the heritage of Taglioni and Noverre.

In 1912 there appears the first sign of something new, a search for something different, a break with the whole past, a departure from all tradition. This tendency was not immediately evident, but gradually, as time goes on, it prevails, and in the post-War period, during the time of the *Ballets Serge de Diaghileff*, it is this tendency which is predominant.

Whether this trend was to the benefit of ballet art is another question. It appears that in the last few years of his life Diaghileff himself considered that he had taken a step in the wrong direction, but it required many years again before the grandchildren could remember and understand their grandparents.

In the present brilliant *Ballets de Basil* this return to the past is clear and evident.

# 10

1912

IN the winter of 1911–12 in St. Petersburg the ballet *Le Dieu Bleu* was prepared. Fokine rehearsed the choreography in the Ekaterinsky Hall. The French composer, Reynaldo Hahn, to whose music the ballet was set, arrived in Russia, and completely charmed all the friends by his delightful manner of playing and singing his own music. When he played it, the music seemed very fine, though actually it was a little flat, charming enough but lacking in interest and importance—India seen through the eyes of Massenet, sweet and insipid. Fokine completed nearly all the work in St. Petersburg, except for the part of Nijinsky, who was abroad at the time.

*Le Dieu Bleu* cannot be considered one of the highest ballet achievements. In spite of a very thorough study of India and its plastic art, in spite of visits to museums and the examination of many documents and much material, Fokine was unsuccessful in creating convincing Indians in this ballet. Western Europe had already been acquainted for a considerable time with Indian dances, and the execution of certain experts (Ruth St. Denis, to mention but one) was much more authentic in this direction than the *Ballets-Russes*. *Le Dieu Bleu* had no great success in spite of Bakst's wonderful scenery and costumes. It was staged only six times during the season in Paris.

*Daphnis and Chloë*, postponed from last year, was pro-

PLATE XV

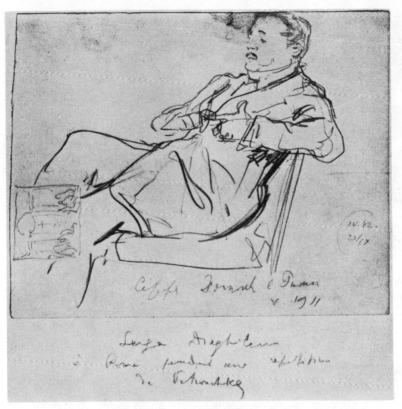

SERGE DE DIAGHILEFF, 1911
*Drawing by A. Benois*

PLATE XVI

DÉCOR FOR "THAMAR"

*By L. Bakst*

duced in 1912. Its preparation took place during the spring. The work was done in a hurry and the ballet was compressed. Very little of the original tale remained in Fokine's scenario. The procession in honour of Pan, the kidnapping of Chloë by the pirates, and her rescue by the mysterious shadow, were all that remained of the tale, but, nevertheless, Fokine seems to have understood the spirit of Longus's pastoral.

*Daphnis and Chloë* was written by the Greek Longus in the third century A.D. It is a pastoral in the pseudo-classic vein—in the style of the French eighteenth-century pastorals. A very unconvincing innocence is blended with the sensuality of an experienced libertine in this none the less charming work, which certainly belongs to a decadent period, possesses no authentic classicism, and is permeated throughout with sentimentality.

Ravel's music for this ballet is very fine, and the success of *Daphnis and Chloë* is mainly due to it—all the more so because this was the first occasion on which Diaghileff presented a ballet with music commissioned from a French composer. In Paris, where this ballet was given only twice at the end of the season, this innovation was hailed with great satisfaction both by Press and public.

Perhaps, of the new ballets, *Thamar* had the greatest success in 1912. It was given thirty-four times during the year—more than all the other new productions together. *Thamar* kept its place in the repertoire for many years, and is even given occasionally to-day.

The success of *Thamar* is not, I think, to be explained by its artistic importance. The one thing in it which is of real value is the music.

Balakirev's music is, unfortunately, far too little known in the West. Lovers of Russian music know him mainly as a leader and inspirer of the so-called "Big Five"[1] who created Russia's national music. Moussorgsky, Rimsky-Korsakov, Borodin, and others were Balakirev's "fledglings." His importance in the history of music is so great that one tends to forget his personal creative achievements. Listening to his music, one realizes how much these "fledglings" have borrowed from him. His symphonic poem *Tamara*, constructed on the programme of Lermontov's poem of the same title, is a beautiful piece of work. In its drama and expressiveness it could not be more suited for stage representation. The actual legend of the cruel Georgian Queen Tamara (twelfth century), who lured young men to her castle and killed them, is striking and dramatic. It is something in the nature of a Caucasian variation of the 1909 ballet *Cléopâtre*. The dramatic theme, illustrated by beautiful music, is heightened by the richness of Eastern costume and by the exotic Caucasian "local colour."

Bakst expressed this variety of colour quite successfully, though perhaps in this ballet he was not at the highest level of his powers (*Sheherazade* and *Carnaval*). The material, however, was very responsive to treatment. The Caucasian East was unknown to Europe, which was easily captivated by its charm and novelty.

Fokine's choreography was good—at that time it was incapable of being anything else. But there was in it nothing new, no specially brilliant inspiration (as, for example, the "Bacchanal" in *Cléopâtre*).

[1] See footnote, p. 23.

Nevertheless, the ballet had a great success. As a spectacle it was splendid, dazzling, and colourful, and it had enough dramatic tension to hold the interest of the audience.

The fourth creation of the 1912 season was Nijinsky's first attempt at choreography. This was *L'Après-midi d'un Faune*, set to Debussy's music, with scenery and costumes by Bakst. This production is a very important one in the history of the *Ballets-Russes*. It marks a turning-point, the first step in quite a new direction, a second revolution.

It is difficult to determine how this ballet originated. Probably Bakst's continued enthusiasm for archaic Greek art played its part here. The visits to museums, to which Diaghileff was continually dragging Nijinsky, had also, of course, some influence. There is also in this ballet a strong stamp of Isadora Duncan, so belittled by Diaghileff and Nijinsky. But what is most apparent in this production is a craving for novelty, a striving to be "advanced," to be "the last word," Diaghileff's peculiar infatuation with "modernism" at all costs.

Against this tendency towards "modernism," this ambition to "shock the bourgeoisie," Diaghileff's collaborators, his artistic "parliament," fought continuously. For this reason the production of the *Faune* marks also Diaghileff's first divergence from his "parliament," the beginning of the parting of the ways with that group which, under his leadership, created the *Ballets-Russes*. It is true that some of them, more tolerant or more persistent than others, continued to collaborate for several years longer. It is true that there were many attempts to return to the "old guard" even in the post-War period. But, despite all this, the break was definite and inevitable. The first indication of this break, the forerunner of it, is *L'Après-midi d'un Faune.* This production was Diaghileff's first departure from the principles for which he strove, together with the friends, during his youth and early manhood. He abandoned the artistic principles which *Mir Iskustva* had fought to uphold. In addition, and this is extremely important, the production of this ballet brought with it the inevitable rupture with Fokine. What is important here is not so much the advancement of Nijinsky as a choreographer and the resulting resignation of Fokine, as the jettisoning of Fokine's main choreographic principles, the break with a tradition which Fokine had developed but had never sought to overthrow.

This break was not immediately evidenced in the years that followed. Bakst and Stravinsky continued to collaborate, Benois worked with Diaghileff in 1914 and again in 1923, and even Fokine staged ballets for him again, but there was a difference in all this. Instead of the joint friendly collaboration of a single group, there was a sporadic collaboration of its separate members; the "parliament" was dissolved. Derain became an alternative to Bakst, José Maria Sert to Benois, Nijinsky, Massine, or, say, Romanoff, alternatives to Fokine. All this, I repeat, was not immediately apparent, but if one looks for the first symptom, the genesis of the rupture, it is to be found in *L'Après-midi d'un Faune.*

This ballet was done in the style of a Greek bas-relief coming to life. The story is simple. Nymphs, frolicking and dancing together, are observed by a Faun, who begins to chase them, becomes inflamed, and tries to seize one of them. The Nymphs flee, and the Faun is left with one of their veils. Carrying this veil, the Faun climbs a cliff in the background of the stage, lies down on the veil, and becomes immobile. The curtains fall.

Diaghileff and Nijinsky based the choreography of this ballet on principles quite new to the ballet. The dancers were bare-foot, the movement was heel and toe, the plastic form was that of profile, like a Greek frieze, and the dancing consisted of a change from one "Greek" tableau to another. Classical dancing was entirely omitted; no points, no positions, no feet *en dehors* were permitted.

This was a novelty in the *Ballets-Russes*, but otherwise there was nothing original about it. In 1904 Isadora Duncan had already shown us much of what Nijinsky did here.

Bakst's scenery and costumes were again excellent. The Faun's piebald tights were decorated here and there by sewing on vine clusters, and a wig, like a low helmet with short horns, gave the Faun an appearance of youthful animality. The Nymphs' costumes were light and airy. All this was simple, beautiful, and at the same time original.

One of the unsuccessful features of this ballet was the music. Debussy's tone poem is splendid in itself, full of grace, taste, and subtlety. But it did not correspond to the action on the stage. This almost abstract music, the work of a refined musical aesthete, and the simple erotic story which Nijinsky constructed for it had nothing in common.

Was *L'Après-midi d'un Faune* successful? From the financial point of view it was a decided success. The box-office receipts were large. It was also in rather a questionable way an artistic success, a *succès de scandale* which created an uproar. This success all sprang from the Faun's final phallic movement, a theatrical indecency.

There are several versions of the origin of this phallic movement. Prince Argoutinsky has told me that one of the vine clusters, which were made of glass and which hung below Nijinsky's body, broke during the dance, and, when Nijinsky lay down on the veil, he could not immediately find a position in which the broken glass did not hurt. If this is the case, the movement originated by chance, and only later, when it was seen what an invaluable advertisement was provided by the uproar and controversy aroused, became a definite feature of the ballet. According to the recollection of the stage manager, Grigorieff, however, the scene was rehearsed quite deliberately just as it was given at the first performance.

Whatever may be the truth, the phallic movement played a decisive part in the success of the ballet. When the curtain came down there was an outburst of talk in the auditorium and protests and hisses were heard. Diaghileff gave the order to repeat the ballet. By this bold decision he scored a victory on the first evening of the performance. Whether the public's indignation changed to astonishment, or it was simply Diaghileff's obstinacy which prevailed, applause broke out when the curtain fell after the repetition of the ballet.

Nevertheless, the following day saw the scandal in the public eye. In the *Figaro* Calmette gave vent to indignation in a trenchant article, and before long he was answered in as biting a tone by the famous sculptor Rodin, a friend of Diaghileff's. The controversy in the Press continued, passions were aroused, and personalities indulged in. The whole of Paris was divided into two camps and in the newspaper war they stopped at nothing. The "success" of the *Faune* was assured. Crowds flocked to the theatre to see for themselves the indecency which could arouse such passions.

It is hard to say whether this phallic movement was consciously invented by Diaghileff (or Nijinsky) for the sake of publicity. Probably not. Diaghileff, especially at that time, did not like to let commercial considerations interfere with art. It may more probably be ascribed to Diaghileff's desire to "shock the bourgeoisie," to produce astonishment by his daring. But once the scandal had broken out, with its tremendous free advertisement, Diaghileff knew, of course, how to exploit it as a real master of his business. In 1916, after the first performance of *L'Après-midi d'un Faune* in the Metropolitan Opera House, New York, Diaghileff tried to revive a similar newspaper sensation. Notices appeared of the rumoured police ban on the ballet and a few short articles on the subject appeared, but the uproar created in Paris by the Calmette–Rodin controversy could not be equalled.

What do the results of this production, in brief, amount to?

First, it was in its own way a choreographic revolution. Not the same kind of revolution as was made a few years previously by Fokine, who evolved, added to, and freed from its routine and limitations the traditional art of ballet which he knew and loved. *L'Après-midi d'un Faune* was a revolution in the sense that it was a rupture with a long tradition, an attempt to create a choreography *in vacuo* without any relation to the past. Did this revolution

177

succeed? I think not. I cannot see in the choreography of to-day any influences of this innovation. Present-day ballet is related either to the "grotesque" of *Petrushka* or to the plastic form and architectural construction of post-War ballets.

Secondly, in this production there is clearly seen for the first time the ambition to be "advanced." This craving for "modernism" later played havoc with Diaghileff's work. When a work of art springs not from the compulsion to express something, but from a desire for novelty, a desire to "stun," it will seldom express anything of true value. It may very well be clever and amusing, but it will not be genuine artistic truth.

Thirdly, the *Faune* contains the germ of the disruption of the group which created the *Ballets-Russes*. This is the actual beginning of the cleavage with the "old guard," though its main importance, for the moment, was the clean break with Fokine and all his invaluable contribution to the collaboration.

Was there simultaneously a corresponding artistic gain? I think not. I think *L'Après-midi d'un Faune* is the beginning of decline. One may regret this, but, knowing Diaghileff, knowing the history of the development of the *Ballets-Russes*, one is forced to the conclusion that this stage of the process was inevitable.

\* \* \*

The *Ballets-Russes* tours of Europe started in 1912. During January, February, and March Diaghileff's company visited Berlin, Dresden, Vienna, and Budapest. The repertoire consisted of old ballets; no new productions were given, as they were not yet ready. In Germany the *Ballets-Russes* had no great success. The receipts were disappointing, and, although the Emperor William II himself attended the performance, there was no vital interest in ballet. The Germans as a whole are not very encouraging towards foreign art. There is no other country, I think, which has such a marked national outlook on art. The French and English, for example, began much earlier than the Germans to take an interest in Russian music. In Germany, the recognition of the importance of Russian music did not travel across the common frontier, but in repercussion from the West.[1] The art of ballet was non-existent in Germany. It was looked down upon and not considered a true art. It was not till 1929 that the *Ballets Serge de Diaghileff* had a notable success in Berlin, and this can be explained by the fact that at this time there appeared native ballet enterprises (*Jooss*) indicating a national interest in plastic art.

In Dresden the *Ballets-Russes* never met with any success. Here, too, the receipts were very small. Only three performances in all were given, but many members of the ballet company visited the famous picture gallery and were delighted with the Sistine Madonna and Holbein's paintings. *Carnaval*, however, left some trace on Dresden's art, perhaps just because Schumann's music and the Biedermeyer style were of German nationality. In any case, the famous Meissen porcelain factory executed, from the originals of Professor Paul Scheurich, six charming

---

[1] Liszt's enthusiasm in the seventies for contemporary Russian music was an exception. It left no mark on the musical life of Germany and in any case Liszt was a Hungarian.

statuettes of the characters in this ballet. The catalogue of these, however, contains no reference either to the *Ballets-Russes* or to *Carnaval*, describing the figures simply as "Tänzer."

In February the ballet was in Vienna. The atmosphere of the Opera House was very pleasant to work in. One could feel the fine old Court tradition. The politeness and orderliness, the tone of quiet assurance and tranquillity, resembled the Russian Imperial Theatres. The only difference was that here one had not to cope with the obstructionism of St. Petersburg theatre officialdom. The *Ballets-Russes* had a much better reception from the Austrian public than from the German. In Vienna, of course, they had ballet of their own and the remains of their own choreographic tradition, and, if the public was rather unkind towards the achievements of foreigners, nevertheless the interest and even understanding were there.

In the same month Diaghileff brought Benois to Vienna to discuss the production of a new ballet based on Debussy's music *Les Fêtes*.

The sight which greeted Benois' eyes was most unexpected. In perfect friendship and close collaboration with Diaghileff reigned—Kchessinskaya. She held, as it were, her own court, and her entourage included Nesterovskaya and Kandina. Matilda Kchessinskaya, whom the friends had for long considered almost the greatest enemy of the Diaghileff enterprise, from whom they continuously expected nothing but intrigues and unpleasantness, appeared to be on terms of hearty friendship with Diaghileff. In the Vienna Opera House they were preparing two acts of Tchaikovsky's ballet *Le Lac des Cygnes* (Petipa). In his

180

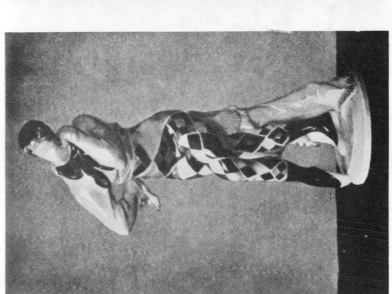

PLATE XVII

"TÄNZER" STATUETTES FROM ORIGINALS BY PROFESSOR PAUL SCHEURICH

*Executed at Meissen Factory*

PLATE XVIII

LEONIDE MASSINE, 1914

*Drawing by L. Bakst*

passion for altering and transposing things, Diaghileff made of this a muddled concoction, in which the meaning of the story was completely lost. Benois was displeased. He liked this ballet and remonstrated with Diaghileff about such "work."

"Listen, Serioja," he said, "nothing is left. One can't make head or tail of it."

"But even before I couldn't make anything of it," retorted Diaghileff.

As a general rule, Diaghileff disliked ballets with a theme. He did not care whether the story of a ballet made sense or not, whether it was understandable or not. In general, he liked in art the inconclusive and suggestive. Clear and definite meaning in anything did not satisfy him.

In painting his preference was for colour; he was, as it were, a gourmet of "colour-splash." In music he despised "form." He was quite willing to make in it unjustifiable cuts (*Sheherazade*) or to concoct in one whole quite unrelated compositions (*Cléopâtre*). He could not understand and considered it unreasonable for a composer to refuse to compose several additional bars for a completed work (*Les Fêtes*—Debussy). What mattered to him here, too, was the "splash" of sound, and not the general sense (form) of the whole work. He looked at the theme of a ballet in the same way. A succession even of disconnected things satisfied him. The theme, that is, the scenic form of a ballet, was of no importance to him.

Discussions began about the proposed ballet *Les Fêtes*. As usual, Diaghileff said to Benois:

"Now, you must discover what must be done with this music."

Benois suggested the construction of a ballet on the theme of a Doge's entry into Venice and an accompanying fête in the renaissance style of Paul Veronese. This suggestion was accepted, and the details worked out even down to the order of the dances and the allocation of the parts. The end of the ballet was to represent a night scene with lanterns. Benois returned to St. Petersburg to design the scenery and costumes. Unfortunately, this ballet was not produced. Debussy, who in his letters seemed amenable to anything, refused in Paris to add to his music some thirty bars which were needed for the action. Apparently his artistic conscience as a musician forbade it.

Benois's idea for a ballet in the Veronese style was carried out later in 1914 on another theme. This was *La Légende de Joseph*, with scenery by the Spanish painter José Maria Sert, costumes by Bakst, and music by Richard Strauss.

During the stay in Vienna they formed a circle of new friends, whom they saw continuously and who took a close interest in ballet. Diaghileff was especially intimate with the famous poet, Hugo von Hofmannsthal, and Count Harry Kessler. The latter was a close friend of the Empress of Russia's brother, the Duke of Hessen-Darmstadt. Sparely built, cultured, and a great lover of art, he was a grand seigneur of the old type.

If one remembers that it was just these two, Hofmannsthal and Kessler, who wrote the libretto for *La Légende de Joseph*, then one must involuntarily come to the conclusion that in Vienna Diaghileff was carrying on negotiations for the new ballet with them and with Benois simultaneously unknown to each other.

From Vienna the company moved to Budapest, where it met with striking success. The Hungarians enjoyed the colourful and "spectacular" qualities of the performances. The company retained the pleasantest memories of its stay. The tastes of the Hungarians and the Russians could scarcely have been more similar. There were continuous receptions, dinners, excursions, and even drinking parties. The Hungarian music closely resembled the Tzigane music familiar in Russia, the people of Budapest were affable, charming, and gay, and the visitors went away with the impression of having spent a lively holiday.

After the March and April season in Monte Carlo, the preparation there of new ballets for the year, and subsequently a six weeks' season in Paris, the *Ballets-Russes* arrived in London for a season at Covent Garden. Of the new ballets only *Thamar* was presented there. *Le Dieu Bleu*, judging by Paris, gave no promise of success, *Daphnis and Chloë* also seemed to arouse little interest, and they did not care to risk presenting *L'Après-midi d'un Faune* to the chaste English public. In 1913 Diaghileff was more daring, and the *Faune* was given on twelve occasions in the two London seasons.

Ballet always had a good reception in London. The English have no artistic chauvinism. The London public knows how to appreciate a spectacle, understands the artistic nature of ballet, likes dancing and the plastic form, and has the capacity of assimilating simply and directly an impression of beauty. There was already a specific ballet public in London, balletomanes, enthusiasts, and critics. The important thing is that it was not merely the artistic *élite* and drawing-room snobs who frequented the

183

ballet in London, but people drawn from various classes, of various occupations and tastes.

It seems to me that if the art of ballet is destined to survive anywhere, it is certainly in England. In Russia the survival of ballet was mainly due to the Tsarist régime, the Court atmosphere, the affluence and the conservatism which guarded all tradition, created the hot-house atmosphere in which ballet was preserved. There was no general interest in ballet. In England, on the other hand, there apparently exists precisely such a general interest. Ballet is appreciated not only by dignitaries and snobs, but by middle-class people, by shop assistants, typists, and postmen. It is this which guarantees the possibility of ballet flourishing in England. It answers a need of the public as a whole.

After a comparatively long London season (twenty-five performances) the *Ballets-Russes* again resumed their travels.

First they went to Deauville. This now famous watering resort was then just opening. Its founder, Cornuché, who once washed dishes in a Paris café and who later, with the support of Prince de Sagan, founded the world-famous "Maxim's," invited for the opening of Deauville the finest entertainment he could collect in the world. Tita Ruffo sang, Maria Barrientos, whose wonderful voice was then in its prime, also took part, and Enrico Caruso himself was expected. Without the *Ballets-Russes* this collection of celebrities would have been incomplete. The programme of five evening performances consisted of ballets which were beyond doubt or criticism: The "Polovetz" dances, *Les Sylphides*, *Carnaval*, and *Le Spectre de la Rose*.

*Petrushka* was not given owing to complications of scenery and properties.

Then the company moved to Germany, visiting Cologne, Frankfurt, Munich, and finally Berlin. This was the second 1912 season in the capital. The audiences were sparse and the receipts only moderate, but the contract was signed and had to be fulfilled. On these fifty-three performances given in Berlin in 1912 the manager who signed the contract with Diaghileff probably lost quite a considerable sum of money. At any rate the Berlin contract was not renewed for 1913, and in that year the *Ballets-Russes* made no appearance there.

After Berlin the company travelled to their beloved Budapest. They renewed their last year's acquaintances, who were already "old friends." Again there were receptions, dinners, and drinking-parties. This was in midwinter, in December, and here among the friendly and delightful Hungarians the rovers greeted the new year, 1913.

In 1912 Benois, as we have seen, did not actively participate in the work of the *Ballets-Russes*. He was occupied in Russia at the time. There was no definite quarrel between him and Diaghileff, but neither was there that intimate, friendly, almost daily collaboration which distinguished the previous years. This drifting apart happened naturally, almost by chance, but there was behind it in reality a deeper cause which those concerned perhaps did not realize. Diaghileff seems to have aimed at freeing himself from his "parliament." The victory had been won, and with it came greater self-confidence and a desire for greater independence. Bakst was more compliant. He could simply be

185

given a task and relied upon to execute it. Stravinsky, too, was not refractory. These two were mainly specialists, valuable collaborators each in his own sphere, but not "mentors."

Benois was different. From 1890 his influence had directed the whole of Diaghileff's artistic work. In matters of art he was the "teacher," the "guide." It is easy to understand that Diaghileff, aiming at independence, began instinctively to shun this influence, and with it also collaboration. As we shall see later, Benois did not definitely cut adrift from the *Ballets-Russes*. In 1914, and even in 1923, he again worked with Diaghileff, but his work then was temporary and sporadic, and did not produce the great results, the "creation of a new art," which was set in 1909, 1910, and 1911.

At the end of 1912 the *Ballets-Russes* suffered another important loss.

Michael Fokine left. The production of the *Faune* and Diaghileff's advancement of Nijinsky as a choreographer were the reasons. It was clear that Diaghileff was endeavouring to replace Fokine by his favourite and that, for this reason, Fokine's reign was drawing to a close. Even during the preparation of *Daphnis and Chloë*, when Fokine was not being given either enough time for rehearsals or the necessary new costumes, the coming break was evident.

Moreover, Fokine could in no way reconcile his artistic conscience to the new choreographic tendency which revealed itself in *L'Après-midi d'un Faune* and which was destined to be predominant in the Diaghileff enterprise.

For four years Fokine had been responsible for the

choreography of the *Ballets-Russes*, and he could not disclaim responsibility for what appeared on the Diaghileff stage. He had no wish to join the new movement, and even although the programme announced another choreographer, Fokine could not feel that it was outside his jurisdiction, so closely was his name connected with the *Ballets-Russes*. He did the only thing he could do—he left.

It is true that, like Benois, Fokine worked with Diaghileff again later. After Nijinsky's marriage in 1913 and Diaghileff's quarrel with him, Fokine again began to produce ballets for Diaghileff, but, in this case, the work was temporary and for one season only, and showed no great results.

# II

## 1913

FROM 1913 Diaghileff already begins to be the dictator, choosing his collaborators where he wishes, "creating" his own choreographers. He has already dispensed with his "parliament," and with his "fireside talks."

Owing to the impossibility of entrusting to Nijinsky all the choreographical work, Diaghileff, on Fokine's departure, invited the young Moscow *maître de ballet,* Boris Romanoff, to join him.

Two ballets were produced by him this season—*Salome* with music by Florent Schmitt, and scenery and costumes by Sudeikin, and the *Dance of the Persian Women* from Moussorgsky's opera, *Hovanschina.* Romanoff had a fair success with these, though they were not distinguished by any special daring or creative inspiration.

Romanoff did not join Diaghileff as a novice. In 1909 he had played one of the buffoons in *Le Pavillon d'Armide.* He was not only an excellent dancer but quite a talented choreographer. His comparative lack of success in this instance may be explained by the fact that all the care and attention were devoted to the two ballets produced by Nijinsky.

The first of these productions was *Les Jeux,* with music by Debussy and scenery and costumes by Bakst. The ballet is set in a garden adjoining a tennis court. A young man, dressed in a strange variation of tennis costume, runs

188

on the stage in pursuit of a tennis ball (which is unnaturally large). He is followed by two young girls. A
scene of light flirtation takes place, the girls become jealous
of each other, but finally agree to share the young man's
attentions, and the three form a sort of *ménage à trois*. A
second ball arrives on the stage; for some reason the
young people take fright and fly. All this is danced in a
manner vaguely suggestive of the movements of a game of
tennis.

In my opinion, this ballet is a striking example of the
consequences of the craving for novelty, the desire to
astonish and produce an effect even by trick methods. The
whole production was mere stupidity, completely devoid
either of common sense or of artistic value. Their search
for sensation had produced simply nonsense and absurdity.
As was to be expected, the ballet had no success.

If *L'Après-midi d'un Faune* was a negation of the choreographic traditions of the past, then *Les Jeux* is a renuncia-
tion of all tradition, all the past. *L'Après-midi d'un Faune*,
at least, is based on the past of ancient Greece, on a past
style. But *Les Jeux* is a departure from all style and all
epoch, it breaks away from all artistic lineage. During the
post-War period, Diaghileff gave us many similar productions; *La Chatte*, *Le Pas d'Acier*, *Le Renard* were
produced in exactly the same spirit.

It would be difficult to find a more false and erroneous
path in art. No art is ever born of itself. The Italian
Renaissance sprang from an enthusiasm for classicism,
Rodin would not be what he is but for Michelangelo,
and Rimsky-Korsakov is inconceivable without Bach. It
is only by feeding on the past that the creative genius

189

achieves originality. He does not need to try to be original, it is part of his nature to be so, it is the essence of his creative gift. Anyone who *strives* for originality is by that very fact confessing his lack of talent, his lack of precisely that gift for which he strives. To be afraid of the past is to be afraid of one's own talent, and to deny the past is to destroy the possibility of creating anything.

Diaghileff, in many respects a man of genius, was devoid of creative talent. Nijinsky, an instinctive creative artist, had little intellectual power. The collaboration of these two men had in this case no good results.

Nijinsky's second production this season was *Le Sacre du Printemps*. In my opinion this production cannot be condemned as much as *Les Jeux*. It is true that it produced an uproar, evoked protests and even a scandal, but, for one thing, the protests were directed more against the music than the actual production and, for another thing, the dislike arose, in my opinion, from a lack of understanding. In 1913 both the music and the choreography of this ballet were fifteen years ahead of their time.

The character of the tonality of Stravinsky's score, even to-day when our ears have been accustomed for many years to "modernism" in music, makes it difficult to accept, seems to many people "cacophony." It contains, however, a great deal of power, of "barbarism," of true primitiveness.

The theme of the ballet is a prehistoric sun-ritual of pagan Slav origin. Harmonious music is not suited to such a theme. What was required here was precisely "wild" sounds. Stravinsky is a great master of his craft and this "wild" score is a fine piece of work.

The scenery and costumes were designed by Rœrich.

190

*Le Sacre* in its theme is a return to a primitive prehistoric epoch, and Rœrich was a specialist in primitive cultures. He had already shown his mastery in this sphere in the "Polovetz" dances from *Prince Igor*. His scenery and costumes proved to be just right for this ballet.

Nijinsky's choreography could not help striking 1913 theatregoers by its strangeness and unusualness.

The movements were all distorted. There was no hint whatsoever of the ordinary ballet. Weird, almost convulsive movements closely followed the complicated rhythm of the music, and the dances produced a savage, almost terrifying, impression.

I can quite understand that a balletomane, visiting the theatre to delight in his beloved art, might fly into a fury at the unexpectedness of such a performance. Harsh dissonances confused his ears and his eyes beheld the convulsions of half-savage, half-animal beings.

Nevertheless, it seems to me that Nijinsky's sub-conscious instinct perceived an artistic truth. The *Sacre* is a prehistoric vision, confused, awe-inspiring, but true. To appreciate the choreography of this ballet at its true value it is necessary to have seen the negro dances of primitive African tribes. Of course, this production is not what is generally known as ballet, but if plastic form, even if distorted and combined with harsh, discordant music, can be called ballet—then this ballet was excellent. It was powerful, awe-inspiring, and impressive.

In recent years, twenty years after its first production, I have had no opportunity of seeing *Le Sacre du Printemps*, but I imagine that, after all the extravagances and experiments which have been made in the ballet form, it would appear neither strange nor even wild. The public can accept it calmly now, though in 1913 it produced an explosion.

During its first performance, the behaviour of the audience passed all the bounds of propriety. Almost from the first notes of the music, hissing and protests were heard and the noise, the shouting and vituperation did not cease for a single moment during the whole of the half-hour performance. Members of the audience jumped on their seats and yelled; there was almost a free fight. The lights had to be put up, and this produced some decrease in the noise, but immediately they were lowered again the uproar broke out with renewed vigour. Even the orchestra could not be heard above the noise. The performance was carried through and ended in a whirl of overwhelming scandal.

Theatre-goers are a strange and unpredictable crowd. At the second performance of *Le Sacre*, there was no repetition of similar scenes. There were isolated shouts and that was all. The third performance passed off without interruption. Finally, the public accepted the ballet and it has continued in the repertoire even until to-day.

The production of *Le Sacre* is the only illuminating example of Nijinsky's choreographic talent. In this production he showed more independence than in the two previous ones. In these, Diaghileff had not only "stuffed" him with ideas, explained the period, the meaning, and the style, but had also interfered continuously in the actual work of choreography. In *Le Sacre* Nijinsky alone was responsible for the dances. The strange, distorted movements were the products of his imagination, and Diaghileff only made a few minor alterations.

*  *  *

The *Ballets-Russes* travelled even more extensively in 1913 than they had done in the previous year. January found them in Vienna, where, in addition to their old repertoire, they gave two of the four new productions of 1912. *Daphnis and Chloë* and *Le Dieu Bleu* were not presented, as success could not be counted on. The great success of this Vienna season was *Thamar*, which was given four times in the five performances.

After Vienna, two performances were given in Prague, where the ballet had a great reception from the Czechs. In those days, anything Russian was well received by the Prague public. The Czechs made the appearance of Russian artistes an occasion for anti-Austrian demonstrations, speeches were delivered, processions organized, songs sung.

The aversion to the Austrians went to absurd excess in Prague. I remember being shaved by a barber, who cut my chin rather deeply. Involuntarily, I swore at him in Russian. The barber's despair was worth seeing. He begged my forgiveness, saying that he had mistaken me for an Austrian and, of course, would never have done such a thing to a Russian.

Visiting, *en route* from Prague, Leipzig and Dresden (where only three performances were given), the company arrived in London, where it was already clear that the *Ballets-Russes* enjoyed the greatest popularity. No new ballets were given; they were not yet fully prepared and, futhermore, new productions were generally reserved for

Paris, which absolutely demanded them. *Dernier cri* and sensation were indispensable conditions of success in Paris. The so-called *élite*, *le tout Paris*, in a word the social and intellectual snobs, were all-important there. On them success mainly depended, and they would have disliked forgoing their privilege as arbiters of taste in being denied the first sampling of a new, exotic dish. Of course, two seasons were being given in London. This had happened previously in 1911. In spring the old repertoire was given and in summer, immediately following the Paris season, the new productions were presented.

Eighteen performances were given in London and then the company returned by way of Lyons to Monte Carlo to prepare the new repertoire and to give performances in their favourite Casino Theatre. This small theatre, resembling in character some of the Imperial theatres of former times, is better suited than any other for the performance of ballet. The proscenium is immense and the ballet seems to take place in the auditorium itself. Every seat commands a view both of the stage and of the dancers' feet. The proportions of the theatre are such that they combine the advantages of a large stage with the intimacy of atmosphere of a small theatre. It was pleasant to rehearse and appear there. The beautiful climate of the Riviera, with its palms and flowers and blue sea, made every moment of repose a delight.

The season was a long one. Twenty performances were given, and in addition a great deal of preparation went on. Nijinsky always demanded many rehearsals for his productions. In the previous year *L'Après-midi d'un Faune* alone had required one hundred and twenty rehearsals.

194

In May the company left Monte Carlo for Paris, where its season was already a great annual event. They went to present their new productions for the judgment of the Paris "gourmets." The great scandal which was in store for them in connection with *Le Sacre* has been related at the beginning of this chapter.

After Paris, a second London season was given at Covent Garden. The new productions which had been already shown in Paris did not produce such a sensation here. They were received without demonstration. *Le Sacre* produced no scandal, but it aroused no enthusiasm and had to be replaced at a later performance by *Salome*.

After London the company was given a vacation and dispersed to various places. Diaghileff and Nijinsky went to Baden-Baden, whither Benois was summoned from Lugano in August to discuss the proposed production of a ballet to music by Bach.

These were the final days before Nijinsky's departure to South America. The contracts had been signed and the *Ballets-Russes* had to go. Diaghileff, who was obsessed by a fear of the sea, at the very last moment decided not to join the company. Nijinsky was left alone.

After Benois's arrival, the five or six days before Nijinsky's departure passed in Baden-Baden in gay and friendly fashion. Nijinsky was sprightly, youthfully gay, and in perfect health. There was a great deal of laughter and joking.

The Bach ballet was discussed. Benois had first had the idea of producing a ballet to seventeenth-century music. In 1909 he had thought of using some music by Montéclair which was discovered by the French brothers Casadesus.

Nothing came of the project then as the Casadesus were willing to allow the use of the manuscript of the score only on condition that the execution of it should be entrusted to them. The production of the Montéclair ballet did not take place till eleven years later, when Nijinska staged it in collaboration with the painter, Juan Gris. Its theme was the temptation of a shepherdess, and it was an unsuccessful variation of the pastoral from Tchaikovsky's opera, *Dame de Pique*.

In Baden-Baden, they discussed producing a ballet on the theme of Apollo and his triumph, with music by Bach. The music was selected and arranged. At this point Benois and Diaghileff parted. Benois went to Moscow, where he was engaged on a big task for the Moscow Art Theatre.

The production of this Bach ballet was not realized. After the war Benois revived the idea for Ida Rubinstein, using this time the theme of *Les Noces de Psyché*. The ballet was beautifully staged, but the unsuccessful performance of Ida Rubinstein herself was the cause of its failure.

Even to-day Benois says that he very much likes the idea of "dancing Bach," and regrets that the Baden-Baden project never matured. He considers that not only Bach's *bourrées, chaconnes,* and so on—in other words compositions named after dances—but even his preludes and fugues are quite suitable for ballet.

Professional musicians are generally horror-struck at the sacrilegious thought of "dancing" Bach. I, myself, do not agree with this attitude. I think that Bach could be danced, and that there is no sacrilege in this. To believe otherwise implies a denial that choreography is an art. The rhythm and energy of Bach often seem to me to demand interpretation in movement. But the task, of course, is exceedingly difficult. It demands a choreographer who is on the level of that immense, outstanding, solitary genius, Bach. Just as it would be stupid to stage a splendid plastic to cheap and trivial music, the choreography worthy of Bach would require to achieve a degree of fusion which has never yet been attained.

Also it seems to me fundamentally wrong to invent a theme to "dance" to Bach. Whether it is the triumph of Apollo or a sentimental pastoral that is chosen makes no difference; whatever the theme it will not be appropriate to Bach. Except for special large works of a religious nature, Bach's music has no programme. It is music for its own sake, a logic of sound, a rhythmic expression of musical beauty—and nothing more. It must be danced only in that way, interpreted by a logic of rhythmical movement alone, without story, without "sense"—by pure choreography.

It is in this direction that Massine has been making his first attempts in symphonic ballet. But however interesting these attempts are, however absorbing is this path with all its possibilities, only the first preliminary steps have been taken on this long and difficult road. It is still a long way from Bach.

The fusing of music with ballet without using the intermediary of a theme occurred accidentally quite early in the history of *Ballets-Russes*. Fokine introduced it. An example of it is to be seen in the charmingly poetical interpretation of Schumann in *Carnaval*. The impression derived from this musical choreographic progression is absolutely unified and strikingly poetical. It is nearly always received

197

with rounds of applause. Another instance of this method is provided by *Les Sylphides* in the version by Benois and Fokine. At the Imperial Theatre, under the title of *Chopiniana*, this ballet had a theme—even Chopin himself was represented on the stage. In the *Ballets-Russes* version the theme has disappeared. The elegiac style of the scenery, the Taglioni *tutu*, and the romantic, ethereal character of the choreography, coincide beautifully with Chopin's music. The spectator is not aware of any need for a story.

The choreographic construction of the two examples I have given above are based on the purely classical dance, and this differentiates them from Massine's recent attempts. But this is a matter not of choreographic style but of the absence of any other theme than the musical one. It is possible that in years to come the new plastic will evolve its own "scale" of pure movement, but, at present, it remains at the descriptive stage and if it is capable of interpreting to some degree dramatic music, as, for example, Tchaikovsky's Fifth Symphony (*Les Présages*), it is still far from the ability to express "pure" music. The new choreography cannot, in my opinion, express Bach. Massine's experiments fall short, perhaps, because, in interpreting symphonic music, he makes it to a certain extent thematic. "He employs a literary choreography." Of course, many symphonic works have a "literary" quality, but the true path, which is a difficult one but also a much more interesting one, lies, in my opinion, in abandoning all theme and even all expressive movement, in striving for the fusion of pure sound with pure movement.

\* \* \*

The South American season in the autumn of 1913 has no intrinsic importance in the history of the *Ballets-Russes*. The repertoire contained none of the new ballets of the year, except *Salome*, which was given only twice. The thirty-two performances given in Buenos Aires, Montevideo, and Rio de Janeiro were, of course, successful. The Diaghilevians were regarded there as unquestionable notabilities, and they were received with that foretaste of delight which is usual on such occasions.

This was the first trans-Atlantic journey of the *Ballets-Russes*. They had conquered Europe and were now embarking on a world-wide career. After 1913 their trans-Atlantic journeys were repeated at short intervals. Their success, especially in North America, became increasingly marked, and seasons there became regular. In the future, though it was a distant future (after Diaghileff's death), the influence of these journeys showed itself in the choreography of the ballets. Such productions as *Union Pacific* both in theme and style are influenced by America. When one sees this ballet, one involuntarily regrets that the Russians ever crossed the Atlantic.

As was mentioned previously, Diaghileff at the last moment failed to join the company. The ballet departed under the supervision of Baron Günsburg.

On the boat to South America there occurred something strange and inexplicable which caused the relations between Nijinsky and Diaghileff to be severed. Romola Pulsky, who pursued Nijinsky everywhere, contrived, with the help of Baron Günsburg, to get her prey and became the fiancée of Vazlav Nijinsky. The wedding was hastily arranged in Buenos Aires. Nijinsky's fate was sealed.

199

The marriage cannot be explained as due to any infatuation of Nijinsky for his bride. Romola Nijinska herself relates in her book how, on the night of the wedding, her husband went to his own room and locked himself in for the night. Neither was it due to a desire to emancipate himself from Diaghileff. In the first place, we have seen how gay and care-free the pair were only a few days before Nijinsky's departure (that is, about a fortnight before the wedding). In the second place, it is doubtful if it would have been worth while to have recourse to an absurd wedding in order to attain this emancipation.

From Nijinska's own book we know that Vazlav never paid her the slightest attention. Why then did he marry her?

The key to this enigma would seem to lie in Nijinsky's cloudy intellect, in his normal passive nature, in his complete impracticability. He usually went where he was told to go. Diaghileff led him to the stage and to art, Romola Pulsky and Günsburg to the altar. He just went. Probably he did not even ask where he was being led or for what reason. He was ordered and he simply obeyed. To people who knew Nijinsky this cannot seem either improbable or absurd. Outside the stage, this "god of the dance" had no actual existence.

The part of Baron Günsburg in these events is difficult to understand. He could not have been ignorant of what he was doing and of the consequences which threatened Nijinsky through this absurd marriage. Nevertheless, he helped in it. Why? Perhaps simply owing to his natural flippancy. Perhaps he had his own ideas and reasons. A person who knew intimately both the parties concerned and the circumstances of the case, has told me that his surmise is that Günsburg was not averse to occupying Diaghileff's place in the *Ballets-Russes*, and the break between Diaghileff and Nijinsky might have suited these plans. Perhaps there lies the explanation. . . . In any case, the marriage was not in the interests of the Russian ballet, but it did serve, in the opinion of many, to hasten Nijinsky's ruin.

# 12

## 1914

IN December of 1913 Diaghileff appeared in Moscow, where Benois was engaged in staging *La Locandiera* by Goldoni in Stanislavsky's Theatre. He brought with him the new three-act opera by Stravinsky, *Le Rossignol*. This opera was Stravinsky's "favourite offspring." As early as 1910 he had composed nearly the whole of the first act with the fishermen's aria and later he continuously returned to the work.

"All the same, I'll finish *Le Rossignol*," he would repeat.

In the course of three years Stravinsky's opera was gradually completed. It showed signs of the three years it had taken to compose. In that time Stravinsky had developed rapidly and his evolution was noticeable in the three acts of the opera.

In spite of his big task for Stanislavsky's Theatre, Benois immediately agreed to take the matter in hand. He designed all the costumes in Moscow in the rare intervals between his other work. Nevertheless, he worked on these designs with the greatest care. The costumes were executed in St. Petersburg by the costumier Carfi, an old man and a very fine costume artist. Bakst always worked with him and was his great friend. In St. Petersburg also the décor was being executed from Benois's designs.

Diaghileff signed a contract with Drury Lane in London for the production of *Le Rossignol*. This was a direct commission from the London Theatre which paid all expenses. However, the scenery was being constructed according to the proportions of the Paris Grand Opera, and Diaghileff whispered secretly to Benois:

"All the same, the *première* will be in Paris!"

How he succeeded in persuading "his" Englishmen to consent to this remains a mystery.

It was in Moscow, too, that they became engaged on the production of Rimsky-Korsakov's Opera, *Le Coq d'Or.* Benois stubbornly insisted on this production. He had a special admiration for this opera, the last and best work of the composer. Diaghileff opposed the suggestion, because he had no idea of how it was to be done. Having seen a performance of *Le Coq d'Or* in Zimin's private opera house, he was terrified by the poorness of the production and feared to undertake the opera.

For a long time Benois had had ideas of his own about the methods of producing opera. Opera as a "spectacle" had never satisfied him and he considered it impossible to attain a unified artistic impression by conventional methods. The appearance of the artistes, their lack of dramatic ability, the restrictions of conductor and prompter, all this was offensive in opera and yet seemed unavoidable. It seemed to Benois that a possible way out was to separate the functions of singing and acting, and have a different set of persons for each function. The unity of the work, he thought, could only gain by this. He proposed to Diaghileff to stage *Le Coq d'Or* in this way. The novelty of the idea probably appealed to Diaghileff and he gave his consent. The production was decided upon.

Benois at once went to the woman painter, Goncharova, to settle about the production of the opera. Natalia Goncharova was then a young painter at the beginning of her career. She was married to Michael Larionov, a painter who did a great deal of work for Diaghileff later. Goncharova and Larionov lived and worked together on the best of terms and in the closest collaboration.

Benois was especially enthusiastic about Goncharova's talent and his enthusiasm was not misplaced. Her staging of the opera proved brilliant.

The original suggestion was to station the vocal performers in the orchestra pit, thus giving over the stage completely to the dramatic and ballet performers. This idea had to be abandoned, however, owing to lack of space in the orchestra pit. The chorus and soloists had to appear on the stage, but they were neutralized as much as possible. They were placed in the shape of two pyramids on the right and left of the stage. Their high-necked costumes made them stand out magnificently against the general scenic background.

The opera singers were not persuaded without difficulty to accept such effacement. It is true that they were permitted, at the end of the performance, to come forward and take a bow, but this did not quite atone for their doll-like part in the eyes of singers accustomed to hold the centre of the stage.

Fokine also for quite a long time protested and did not want to have anything to do with such a production but they succeeded finally in winning him over.

In spite of the artistic success of Goncharova's staging, Benois was not completely satisfied with it. She had per-

PLATE XIX

DÉCOR FOR "LE ROSSIGNOL"

*By A. Benois*

PLATE XX

DÉCOR FOR "LES FEMMES DE BONNE HUMEUR"
*By L. Bakst*

formed her task splendidly from the point of view of an easel artist, but her work was perhaps not so fine from the purely theatrical point of view. This was particularly evident in the third act where she failed to emphasize the eerie mood.

*Le Coq d'Or* is often interpreted as a comic opera, almost an *opéra-bouffe*, and its inner meaning is lost. Like the fairy tale by Pushkin, the story constructed on it by Rimsky-Korsakov is imbued with a strange and terrifying unreality and prophecies of evil. The whole story of the Shemahansk Queen, who at the end of the tale "suddenly is not there, as if she had never been there," this ephemeral heartless instigator of fratricide, this instrument of death and destruction to simple-hearted, ignorant people, is not so simple as it seems on the surface. This subterranean terror, of course, is not easy to convey on the stage, but the essence and the inner meaning of the opera lie in that and without it it loses all importance.

In Paris, the dramatic performers were supremely good. Both Boulgakoff (King Dodon) and Cecchetti (Astrologer) were wonderful. Karsavina was particularly good in the rôle of the Shemahansk Queen. The performance was wonderful and had a great success.

All the same, it did not give the desired impression of an entity. The words, with their meaning and lack of connection with the action, constituted an interference. The result was a kind of distorted poetry recital with musical accompaniment. The combination of music, the spoken word, and the stage may or may not be considered successful, but it is the main convention on which the art of opera is based and to alter this convention in a work already constructed on that basis is difficult and perhaps impossible.

If one adopts a strictly purist attitude to the problem of the fusion of arts, one may question whether the union of sound and word is essentially organic. Of course, we have been accustomed to such a union for many centuries, but, all the same, I do not think that the song of the nightingale has any sort of meaning. It seems to me that it simply pours out its notes and creates music.

When a composer starts from the words and develops a musical meaning for them, as did Wagner, Moussorgsky, and even Schubert in *Doppelgänger*, then I, personally, am not offended by the combination of word and sound. Here the sound consists of the development of a musical content for the word. But, when the composer starts with the music, as is the case with Verdi, Glinka, Tchaikovsky frequently, and Schubert also (in *Serenade*, for example), and adds the words to the music, then this seems to me unnatural and the words seem superfluous and even a hindrance.[1]

What is music in its essence but the art of sound? Is it not with sound that the composer must commence? From the purist point of view is not "music arising from the word" harmful to the "music of sound"? To understand the charm and freshness of wordless singing, even in contemporary music, one has only to listen to Rachmaninoff's short but charming *Vocalise*.

The combination of plastic with music seems to me

[1] How many people remember the words of Schubert's *Serenade* or of Rimsky-Korsakov's "Song of the Indian Guest"? or of the "Hymn to the Sun" from *Le Coq d'Or*? Very few, probably. Yet these melodies persist in the memory. The words involuntarily fade from "the music of sound," which does not require them.

organic. The idea of plastic outside music, outside sound rhythm, appears absurd. The word is an independent element more foreign to music than life plastic. The fusion of these three artistic media in one can, in my opinion, scarcely hope to give the impression of a complete entity.

* * *

After Nijinsky's wedding it became clear to Diaghileff that further collaboration with him would be impossible. In the winter a telegram was dispatched to the dancer announcing that Diaghileff no longer required his collaboration. Another choreographer had to be found. It is quite natural that Diaghileff should decide immediately to try to attract Fokine again to his enterprise. This, however, was not so easy. After his successes abroad, Fokine at last began to be given work at the Maryinsky Theatre; moreover, after the disappointments of the previous year, he was not very willing to return to Diaghileff. An intermediary had to be found. After much persuasion, Fokine finally gave in. Not without reason he considered the *Ballets-Russes* as his choreographical child and he was probably involuntarily inclined to work there with those among whom he had created for himself a world name.

The 1914 productions, *Le Coq d'Or*, *La Légende de Joseph*, *Les Papillons*, and *Midas*, were all his work.

None of these ballets proved important and they did not remain long in the repertoire.

*Joseph* was the realization—on a different theme—of the Veronese-Renaissance Ballet, the idea of which Benois suggested to Diaghileff in Vienna. The scenery was entrusted to José Maria Sert and the costumes to Bakst.

In the part of Joseph in this ballet, a young man, scarcely more than a boy, who had just joined the company, made his first appearance. This was Massine. Diaghileff discovered him in December 1913 when he was finishing his training at the Moscow Ballet School. Massine had a strange, still almost childish, face. His almost unnaturally enormous eyes were intense and serious. Looking at him, they were all that one could see. It seemed that he consisted only of a pair of eyes and some additions. Perhaps Diaghileff alone understood at that time what an acquisition for his enterprise and for ballet art as a whole this young man represented. Diaghileff—with his flair for discovering talent—made no mistake on this occasion. Massine was not only a brilliant dancer but had keen artistic perceptions. For many years the Diaghileff enterprise was based on his gifts as a choreographer. He revealed himself not only as an artiste of culture but as a real creative genius, and if the art of ballet is alive and in a highly flourishing condition to-day, it is indebted for this in no small measure to the genius of Massine.

The rehearsals for *Joseph* went with a swing, but one of them was marred by a scandalous incident. The music of the ballet was composed by Richard Strauss who himself conducted at rehearsals. He expressed annoyance with members of the orchestra for unpunctuality (they often neglected to turn up). Strauss said something offensive to the French, something of the sort that "nothing else could be expected of a degenerate race." The newspapers seized on this and exaggerated it. The incident was settled only with difficulty.

Misia Sert, the wife of the scenic artist and an old friend

of *Ballets-Russes*, was present during the rehearsals, very much at home there. She could be seen sitting on one of the benches which were placed in various positions in lieu of scenery.

Fokine bustled about nervously. His relations with Diaghileff were still strained.

The preparation of *Les Papillons* progressed more easily. This ballet was conceived as a sequel to *Carnaval*. It represented the departure of the guests after a social evening. Generally, it was given as a curtain raiser. The music, as in *Carnaval*, was Schumann's and even the costumes were taken from *Carnaval*. The scenery, painted by a young and gifted Russian painter, Doboujinsky, portrayed two arbours and between them the representation of a fountain. This was very charming and poetical in its conception. This short ballet proved quite pleasant; it delighted the public but it was not an important success. It could not be compared with its predecessor *Carnaval* and did not remain long in the repertoire.

The fourth new ballet was *Midas*, with music by Rimsky-Korsakov's son-in-law, Steinberg, and scenery and costumes in the style of Mantegna by Doboujinsky. This ballet had no success and in later years was not revived.

As a whole, the creative work of the 1914 season cannot be considered successful. The only considerable attempt to present something original was *Le Coq d'Or*. Benois conceived a new method of producing opera, but even he himself was dissatisfied with the results. In staging the same opera at the Grand Opera in Paris (1927) he did not revive his previous ideas. *Le Coq d'Or* had some success

209

but it was followed by no further attempts in the same direction. The production remained an isolated experiment.

During the work in Paris, the friends made persistent attempts to make peace between Diaghileff and Nijinsky. Everybody joined in this, and talks and discussions on the subject were continually held. Nijinsky was known to desire reconciliation and renewed collaboration. He often visited Benois in his hotel and, with a loquacity unusual in him, expressed his confused plans and ideas about ballet. In spite of the constant pressure of friends, Diaghileff remained obdurate and replied with denunciations of Nijinsky. His vexation had not yet passed and he was not prepared to be reconciled. He wanted to demonstrate his power and to avenge himself on Nijinsky. At last, after much persuasion, he promised to give Nijinsky a part to dance in London. This, however, only made matters worse as Diaghileff did not keep his promise and thus put Nijinsky in a disagreeable and embarrassing position. This only prolonged the quarrel.

The spring season in Paris was a great triumph. Stravinsky's *Le Rossignol*, in particular, achieved great success. All the old friends, some of them now regarded as belonging to their "own," were present. Cocteau was already collaborating in the work, writing the programmes, bustling about and helping wherever he could. The silent and extremely delicate Marcel Proust was also of the company. Misia Sert and her husband were already like members of the family. They met in the evening and dined and supped together. At one of these dinners, in the now defunct Voisin, they reached agreement about the production of a new renaissance ballet. D'Annunzio wished to write the libretto, Reynaldo Hahn the music, Benois took upon himself the staging, and Rouché, who was present, promised to present it at the Grand Opera in the beginning of the 1915 season.

In 1914 there was a big Russian season in London. At Drury Lane they presented the Ballet and Opera. In addition to the old repertoire, this year's new productions were given. In the mute rôle of Potiphar's Wife in *Joseph* there appeared a young and very beautiful singer, Maria Kouznetzova.

Of the operas, Stravinsky's *Le Rossignol*, Borodin's *Prince Igor*, and *Hovanschina* and *Boris Godounov* by Moussorgsky, were given.

It was a brilliant season. The ballets had a huge success and produced great enthusiasm. The whole of London society went to Drury Lane. During the performances Diaghileff did nothing but move from box to box, receiving compliments and expressions of pleasure. In the same way, in seventeenth-century Spain, the author went round the theatre collecting bouquets and presents from the public and, loaded with these, looking like a Christmas-tree, retreated to the stage. As seemed unavoidable, Benois and Diaghileff had a quarrel here. In Paris Diaghileff had promised to make some changes in the production of *Le Rossignol* for London. Of course, he did nothing of the sort, and Benois and he quarrelled on the subject. This recurrent quarrel was terminated on the following evening by a gorgeous supper at the Savoy.

After the London season the company bade each other good-bye and in the spirit of peace and friendship went their separate ways. None of them foresaw how long, painful, and in some ways irreparable, this parting was to be. They intended to rest, to recuperate their strength, and to return in the winter to their beloved work.

Benois went to St.-Jean-de-Luz, Ravel's birthplace. The composer and he lived there in adjoining houses and went together continuously to see the dances of the local peasants, the Basques. Already they had ideas of a Spanish ballet. Ravel was planning the music which later took shape in his famous *Bolero*. They were preparing to plunge into work and new artistic endeavour . . . and the War descended like a thunderbolt.

# 13

## CONCLUSIONS

IF one surveys retrospectively these first six years of the creative development of the *Ballets-Russes*, one cannot help feeling the desire to sum up these years of endeavour, creativeness, and victory.

What were the results? What was achieved?

Firstly, of course, a new ballet art was created. The old classical Imperial Ballet was revolutionized. In place of the former Petipa fantasies, in the traditional rut, a vital dramatic content was instilled into the productions. In place of the formal and pompous ballets of the Maryinsky Theatre, there appeared ballets imbued with style, intimacy, and emotion. Instead of conventional prettiness and decorum, the performances were daringly and sometimes poignantly beautiful.

The revolution was accomplished in the very first years of the *Ballets-Russes*. *Les Sylphides*, imbued with the elegiac mood, with the ultra-worldly romanticism of the thirties, and the "Polovetz" dances with their wild beauty, were staged as early as 1909. In 1910, they were followed by *Sheherazade*, with its bright Eastern variety of colour, and by *Carnaval*, a dramatic ballet-miniature strictly in the style of Biedermeier. Finally, 1911 gave us *Petrushka*, a ballet-mime, a moving choreographical tragedy.

The revolution in choreography terminated simultaneously with the revolution in presentation. Fokine, adhering strictly to the basic principles of the classical Ballet School, even in his first ballets, developed, expanded, and infused with new life the choreographical "scale" on which that School was founded. The choreography, following the scenic action, became a plastic pattern, fluent and full of meaning. Expressiveness replaced the traditional smooth "prettiness," emotion was given free play in the ballet, and, finally, the production of *Petrushka* was the first experiment in the choreographical "grotesque."

On the heels of this first revolution in choreography, there follows another. In 1912, the public, who had not yet had time to assimilate Fokine's reforms, was offered by Diaghileff *L'Après-midi d'un Faune* and, in the following year, *Le Sacre du Printemps*. This second revolution is distinguished by a complete break with classicism and by a striving for novelty. This is the modernism which is to dominate in the post-War period.

Secondly, the *Ballets-Russes* of these early years made an important contribution to the artistic side of the European theatrical world. The participation of painters in theatrical production is the main evidence of this. In Russia this was not a new practice. At the end of last century, Sava Mamontov, the famous Moscow art patron, induced young Moscow painters to help him in his private opera enterprise. In its own day, this innovation caused a great deal of noise and argument, but, by the time of the first *Ballets-Russes*, it was such an established custom that Golovin and Korovin did continuous work for the Imperial Theatres. In Western Europe in 1909 it was unheard of for painters to take part in theatrical work. The scenery and costumes were entirely in the hands of theatrical professionals. After the overwhelming success of the *Ballets-Russes* in the early years, painters in Western Europe began to work for the theatre and, in course of time, this collaboration developed and extended.

Thirdly, the work of the Diaghilevians was splendid propaganda for Russian art in the West. The interest in Russian culture increased not only among the select few but among the general public. This is particularly evident in the field of music. In concert programmes and in opera repertoires, Russian composers began to feature more and more frequently. The names of Rimsky-Korsakov, Moussorgsky, Borodin, Rachmaninoff, Glazounov, Stravinsky, and even Prokofiev, became quite familiar. Without the huge publicity given by Diaghileff to Russian art, this popularity would have been much less easily achieved.

Fourthly, the *Ballets-Russes* revived the long-since-defunct interest in the art of ballet. They created, as it were, a ballet public. You can now meet, especially in England, persons who really value ballet, balletomanes in the best sense of the word. This love of ballet has penetrated to the mass of the public. If Covent Garden can maintain every year a three-month season of Russian ballet, then it is due to these first years of constructive effort when the resounding success of the *Ballets-Russes* laid the foundations of European balletomania.

* * *

How can the overwhelming success of the *Ballets-Russes* from their first inception be explained?

Mainly, it seems to me, by the enthusiasm and extra-ordinary creative inspiration of several very gifted young

215

men, by the bold, adventurous spirit and unconquerable energy of their leader, and by the absolute independence of spirit and unmercenary outlook of the whole group of friends.

From childhood, Benois had dreamed dreams of the ballet. Were these dreams realized? Yes, but the drama lies in the fact that the ballet of his dreams, as soon as it was realized, began immediately to be transformed into a mechanical thing, a hunt for "— isms," something quite foreign. The dream, when it began to flower, began at the same time to decay. Once upon a time these young hearts fell in love with the Sleeping Princess and brought her back to life; but she could not remain alive. "Progress" killed her.

# 14

## BUSINESS ASPECTS

ANY systematic description of the business side of *Ballets-Russes* is very difficult, perhaps impossible. This aspect of the enterprise is full of romantic adventure, flippant daring, recurrent catastrophes, and last-minute rescues.

If one remembers that Diaghileff began his enterprise without a penny, that, during the whole course of his career, he had no continuous dependable monetary support, that he did not even have a bank or any other establishment to advance him a systematic credit, that he, on the other hand, managed to build up a business which even in 1911 had a budget of over 2,000,000 gold francs, that, for twenty years without a break, he carried on this enormous ballet enterprise, and that, in addition, he died a pauper, one involuntarily throws up one's hands and cannot understand how all this came about.

The business side of *Ballets-Russes* can, nevertheless, be divided into certain periods. These periods are arbitrary, depend upon circumstances and not on Diaghileff, and have no definite limits. From the commencement of his activities up till 1910 may be called the Russian period. Then follow the years 1910–14, the time of highest artistic achievement and greatest commercial success; from the financial point of view this period, though by no means consistent, is self-supporting. Then came the War and the years immediately afterwards up to 1923, a period of depression and sometimes of collapse. Finally, from 1923 to 1929 follows a comparatively peaceful period at Monte Carlo.

The greater part of the first "Russian" period is pre-ballet. The activities covered by these years are continuously developing and changing and lead ultimately to the creation of *Ballets-Russes*. The foundations upon which the later creative work of Diaghileff and his friends will be built are already clear. From *Mir Iskustva* to the Châtelet performances of 1909 the line of creative activity is unwavering. The Diaghilevian personnel, his "staff," remains unchanged throughout this period, but, at first, there is no direct connection with ballet. This is the epoch of *Mir Iskustva*, of exhibitions, of concerts, and of opera.

The first patrons who lent financial support to Diaghileff's enterprises were Princess Tenischeva and Sava Mamontov. Without these two people *Mir Iskustva* would not have existed. Princess Tenischeva was a wealthy woman and a great lover of painting, and Sava Mamontov was a railway magnate and art patron who, quite apart from Diaghileff, played a considerable rôle in the history of Russian art and particularly in the theatre.[1]

The financial support given by these two people was regular and reliable only in the first year of the journal's life. Princess Tenischeva soon withdrew her support. She was probably influenced by the sneers and attacks of the press hostile to *Mir Iskustva*. A caricature was even published in which she was represented as a cow milked dry. It is probable also that she was displeased by Diaghileff's

[1] Among other things, he discovered Chaliapine and introduced him to the public in his private opera-house.

method of sparing no expense and no outlay which he considered necessary for artistic reasons.

Mamontov, unfortunately, lost his fortune soon after the inception of the journal. His crash was sudden and produced a sensation. He was an honest man but speculated rashly. He went, as it were, beyond the bounds, and it is sad to remember that this remarkable man had to go to prison.

After this Diaghileff had no private resource in Russia behind his enterprises. He no longer had a definite Maecenas. The financial aid which he nevertheless obtained privately had to be returned in one way or another—either by procuring a decoration or a patent of nobility or by some other service. This is already not a question of patronage but of "deals."

Diaghileff was a past master of such dealings; he almost always managed to procure the desired reward for his "patron." Although he was disliked in official circles in Russia and had powerful enemies at Court, he knew how to achieve his purpose. There were enemies and there were obstacles, but he also possessed staunch and loyal friends who were not without influence and numbering among them even members of the reigning family. When the widow of the Grand Duke Vladimir Alexandrovitch refused to sign the petition for a patent of nobility for the Riga manufacturer, Diaghileff found other means. The manufacturer became a nobleman and the *Ballets-Russes* received the £10,000.

These "deals" may seem to the reader repulsive, "in doubtful taste," but if one remembers that the money was employed solely for constructive artistic enterprises, for the

219

glory of Russian art abroad, that there was no shadow of personal financial interest attached to them, they appear in a more acceptable light. All the more so that such "deals" are by no means confined to Russia. Such arrangements have always taken place in every country and under every régime—and always will take place. Whether the "donations" are for charity, for the support of a political party, or for art, does not alter the nature of the case.

Diaghileff also knew how to obtain Crown subsidies—and this, despite the fact that from 1901, from the time of the *"Sylvia* scandal," he was looked at askance by the Court and not trusted by the Tsar. The attitude of the official authorities towards Diaghileff's enterprises had the same characteristics as their attitude towards everything else. It fluctuated with the wavering personality of the Tsar, Nicholas II. There was no consistent, firm line of policy. Sometimes subsidies were successfully extracted, sometimes not. Sometimes a promised subsidy would be withdrawn at the last moment. Sometimes—and quite often, too—Diaghileff's petitions were granted. The deficit on the Paris exhibition of 1906, which cost 300,000 roubles and brought in only 25,000 roubles, was covered out of Crown moneys. The 1907 concerts in the Grand Opera and the production there in 1908 of *Boris Godounov* were also subsidized by the Russian Crown. Subsidies were continually requested and often granted. Only, they could not be taken for granted or depended upon. As we saw earlier, the grant of £1,000 in 1909 was cancelled at the last moment. It is true that Diaghileff's requests were generally made through intermediaries and that these intermediaries were often grand dukes and the nearest relatives of the Tsar, but nevertheless the final authority rested with the Tsar himself. And, in spite of his bad relations with Diaghileff, his consent was often obtained. Apparently everything depended on whether the individual responsible for the final report on the matter to the Tsar was a friend or an enemy of Diaghileff.

About 1909, when Diaghileff and his ballets had their first great success, his treatment by official Russia becomes more definite, becomes definitely negligent. The probability of receiving support and subsidies decreases. Perhaps even a certain antagonism is noticeable. The Russian diplomatic missions abroad receive circulars informing them that it is undesirable to give any support to Diaghileff's enterprise.

The reason for such treatment is difficult to discover. Was it, as some thought at the time, the consequence of offending the all-powerful Matilda Kchessinskaya, who remained outside the Diaghileff enterprise? Or was it the work of influential ballet conservatives who deplored "these decadent ballets"? Or was an objection raised by the directorate of Imperial Theatres, which realized perfectly that the Diaghileff enterprise was in opposition to theirs? The truth of the matter is not known.

We have seen Kchessinskaya on terms of close friendship with Diaghileff in 1912; no official steps of the Imperial Theatres directorate are known to us and it is doubtful whether the old balletomanes went further than senile mumblings in their side-whiskers. The effect, however, is plain—Russia had turned her back on Diaghileff as early as 1909, many years before he himself turned his face away from the fatherland.

In 1909, Diaghileff's enterprise still showed a heavy

221

financial loss. The operas were very costly to produce and brought small returns. At the end of the season, Diaghileff's personal luggage was seized at the railway-station. Gabriel Astruc, Diaghileff's manager at the time, tells the story in his book. He only omits to add that the belongings were seized by his—Astruc's—order. This did not prevent Diaghileff from collaborating with him for many years to come.

This Astruc was a strange type of man. He was a professional theatrical manager but not at all a quiet, cool-headed business man. Excitable in temperament, enthusiastic, full of idealistic and artistic pretensions, he bustled about and took the credit for everything to himself. *Ballets-Russes*—they were his. He discovers them, he manages everything, he alone understands everything, knows everything, directs everything. Before long, he will produce himself such an *entrechat royal* as was never seen before. At the same time, he conducted the business side of the enterprise with intelligence and did not squander a penny. It is probable that, all things considered, Astruc lost a considerable amount of his own money in the *Ballets-Russes*, as Diaghileff was a hard bargainer. There were continuous frightful money squabbles between Diaghileff and him, and Diaghileff rarely emerged the loser.

In 1910 another strange and curious figure, Baron Günsburg, becomes attached to the ballet and begins to take a keen and financial interest in it. Baron Dimitri Günsburg came of a wealthy aristocratic family of Jewish bankers. He was fond of dress, rather a snob, and worshipped the *Ballets-Russes*. Everyone liked this apparently frivolous but excellent man. He was rich and often helped

Diaghileff financially. His advances never reached the figure of 400,000 roubles, as has been stated in print, but he often gave Diaghileff loans up to the limit of 100,000 roubles. This financing, however, was never either regular or business-like. It was in the nature of a "good turn" to a friend. If he had the money in his pocket, he gave it, but if, that morning, he had bought, let us say, a *bibelot* or antique and had no money handy, Diaghileff had to turn to someone else. He often bought, without consulting anyone, very expensive things for the ballet (for example, draperies of antique material which seemed to him suitable for a production and which were thrown away later). He jotted down his advances to the *Ballets-Russes* on his shirt-cuffs and fell into despair when a shirt with an account on it had gone to the laundry.

"I remember it was 18,000," he would shout. "Only the shirt has gone to the wash, and it was all noted down there."

Apparently Günsburg considered his shirt-cuff an unquestionable proof and Diaghileff himself never doubted the force of such a document.

The years 1910–14 were the most successful of the *Ballets-Russes*. From 1911 tickets for seats were all sold previous to the performances. The houses were packed and the receipts enormous. Nevertheless, even at that period there were continual money difficulties.

Incidents like the following were common. About ten minutes before the curtain was due to go up, Diaghileff would rush to the business manager, Svetlov, and say:

"I must have 5,000 francs immediately. X refuses to appear until he gets it. We can't ring up the curtain."

"Where are they to be found?"

"Go to Astruc at once. Perhaps he will lend it."

The agitated Svetlov would hurriedly call on Astruc, who sends him to the devil and refuses the money. Where next? . . . To Argoutinsky. He distrusts banks and always keeps his money at home. Finally, the 5,000 francs required are given by Argoutinsky. Svetlov rushes to the theatre with the money and the curtain rises, though somewhat belatedly.

Misia Sert relates that at one of the performances with *Sheherazade* in the programme, when the theatre was filled to capacity and the drawings were over 60,000 francs, Diaghileff rushed into her box. It appeared that the costumier was demanding 4,000 francs and refused to deliver the costumes before receiving the money. The curtain could not go up.[1] Misia Sert had to rush home and fetch the money.

This last-minute search for money was a general occurrence and the work was always carried on in an atmosphere of financial crisis. Diaghileff was a master at extricating himself from the most precarious situations. How, where, and from whom he got the necessary sums was often impossible to determine, but it is certain that in that heyday of the ballet he never failed to find them.

One may imagine that any man with the rudiments of business habits would find it very difficult to deal with Diaghileff in money matters. Astruc at one time thought of forming the *Ballets-Russes* into a company. The capital was found; everything was ready for a preliminary general

---

[1] The box-office receipts could not be touched until the tax had been levied.

meeting of the shareholders. The scheme collapsed, however, owing to the fact that no balance-sheet could be submitted. There were simply no balance-sheets. No books or ledgers even were kept. There were only small torn bits of paper with scribbles which nobody but Diaghileff could decipher. These slips of paper were usually thrust in various pockets of his wearing apparel, in his suits, overcoats, tail-coat, or anywhere. These bits of paper and Günsburg's shirt-cuffs constituted the whole book-keeping system of this 2,000,000-franc business.

This was absolutely typical of Diaghileff's attitude to money at that time. He despised it, using it as a slave to serve his god, beauty. To accuse Diaghileff of dishonesty would be ridiculous. He was the antithesis of a money-grabber; he had no respect for money, either his own or other people's, and for that reason business men probably found him difficult to deal with.

Not only was Diaghileff an honest man, but he was strictly unmercenary. Everything centred for him in the realization of his artistic purpose, in the active service of art and beauty. Money was only useful for this and, in itself, had no interest for him. He believed in his organizing powers, was confident that he would find the money as well as everything else indispensable to his work, and continuously undertook a venture, not only without having a penny in his pocket but without knowing where he was to raise the money.

Owing to this, collaboration with Diaghileff in these early years always had a spice of romantic adventure. Neither he nor his friends had any feeling of security in their positions. Everything was created in an atmosphere of risk, everything was under query, everything was capable of collapsing at the last moment. They were conquistadors in the realm of art, animated by a faith in their aims and by confidence in their leader's powers of overcoming obstacles.

In general, this confessed money-muddle, this business recklessness can be explained by the basic relationship of Diaghileff and his friends to the enterprise.

Diaghileff was neither a professional of the arts nor of the theatre. He was neither an impresario nor a theatrical speculator. He was a gentleman—a Maecenas. His whole attitude to his pre-War activities was that of a Maecenas and not of a business man. That he had no money of his own and had to find it from outside sources was unimportant. If he had had money of his own he would have used it. Expense was of no account. The artistic result was all-important. It never entered his head to think about the expense of a material or the cost of improving the stage machinery. The method of reasoning was generally as follows: (1) The cushions, let us say for *Sheherazade*, following Bakst's designs, require an absurdly expensive material. (2) For this purpose money must be found. (3) Where is the money to be found? The idea of using a cheaper material was absolutely excluded. The first essential was to create and to create according to plan, but how and when it was to be paid for was a secondary consideration.

For such a point of view one can, of course, accuse Diaghileff of being unbusiness-like. But it appears to me that any other attitude to money would probably have automatically prevented him from creating that great art which, under the name of *Ballets-Russes*, won for itself world-wide fame and remains the main influence on the art as it exists to-day.

Art flourishes in the hands of a Maecenas and withers in a purely commercial atmosphere. But for the lavish spending of Louis XIV, Versailles would not exist; but for Ludwig II of Bavaria it is doubtful if we should have Wagner's operas; the Moscow Art Theatre absorbed the whole fortune of the merchant Alexeiev-Stanislavsky. One must give money to art, and when it begins to show a profit that is usually the sign of the beginning of decline and decay.

The War years and the years immediately following are years of depression and sometimes of disaster for Diaghileff. He was alone. His friends and intimates were dispersed in various quarters of the disjointed Europe. There remained on his hands a complete organization, a whole ballet company; it, too, partly dispersed but only waiting a summons from him. The shells burst, the bullets whistled, and people were killed in their hundreds of thousands. Nobody was interested in *pirouettes*, *entrechats*, and *fouettés*. Offers of contracts became rare. Instead of being submerged in them, they had to be searched for.

In 1915 the ballet came almost to a standstill. There was one charity performance in Paris and several evenings in Italy and Switzerland. At last, towards autumn, the position looked like improving. Otto Kahn invited the *Ballets-Russes* to the Metropolitan Opera House, New York. Diaghileff collected his company with great difficulty, by persistence obtained Nijinsky's release from an Austrian internment camp, overcame his terror of the sea, and departed with his ballet for the U.S.A. For the moment,

227

the company was provided for, but Diaghileff himself could not earn in America the money which he required for his urgent personal needs.

Influenced probably by his wife, Nijinsky sued Diaghileff for 500,000 gold francs as "arrears of salary." If one remembers Diaghileff's system of book-keeping, it is evident that he was bound to lose the case. He could not have had any proofs of money paid to Nijinsky or any expenses on his behalf. Diaghileff's salary was arrested and he again remained penniless.

Beginning from these War years, Diaghileff's business attitude changes. Gradually he becomes the professional ballet-impresario. His constant assistant and stage-manager, Serge Grigorieff, begins to keep account books. It is true that Diaghileff strictly forbids him to show these books to anyone, but still they are being kept. The romantic adventure is over, and the business attempt has begun. Diaghileff begins to watch the expenses closely, to economize, and to cut from the estimates all those expenses which he does not consider absolutely essential. According to Grigorieff, Diaghileff showed exceptional capacity in this direction. Nobody knew better than he how to beat terms down to the lowest figure, nobody knew better how to reduce expenses without apparent detriment to the enterprise.

But such an existence and such type of work were strongly against Diaghileff's inclinations. The professional nature of his position weighed on him and wearied him. Besides, the pre-War success was not maintained. The new productions and experiments produced no great impression. The auditoriums were often far from full, and the receipts often failed to justify the expenses. Moreover, he was no longer a young man. He became tired, and the monotony of the work bored him. He himself had little faith in what he was doing.

"Something different must be done," he would say to Grigorieff.

"Well, what's to be done, Serge Pavlovitch? One must live," his assistant would answer.

"But something must be invented. Just wait. I'll invent something yet," Diaghileff would repeat.

Meeting old friends, he sighed, groaned, and complained.

"Do you think I'm not tired of it all? But I can't drop it. What would I do with the company?"

He began to be indifferent even to his own ballets. After the production of *La Chatte*, a ballet in which there is neither sense, beauty, nor even a cat, and which is one frenzied straining after *le dernier cri*, questioned by one of his friends as to what it all meant, Diaghileff answered:

"Oh, drop it! Don't I know myself! Simply two people persuaded me and a third produced it, and that's the result!"

After the War, Diaghileff's affairs went badly. From season to season, from performance to performance, the work dragged on anyhow. Contracts were few and money scarce. Towards 1923 the position became quite desperate. Even Diaghileff found difficulty in wriggling out of it.

At the very last moment came salvation in the shape of a steady contract with Monte Carlo. Diaghileff heaved a sigh of relief. At last, after many years of trouble and uncertainty, he felt firm ground beneath his feet. A definite income for the ballet was assured, and some sort of refuge which they could consider their own provided for the

229

homeless wanderers of the *Ballets-Russes*. The very atmosphere of Monte Carlo was pleasant to Diaghileff. At heart, he was a disappointed courtier. The Court of the Prince of Monaco resembled in some degree the atmosphere of the Russian Imperial Court, which had always attracted Diaghileff, and in which he had never been allowed to play a part. Now, he paid court to the ruling family. He was something in the nature of a Minister of Fine Arts at the Court of Monaco. But the chief thing, of course, was that the worry and threat of disaster no longer disturbed him.

The last six years of Diaghileff's life were more secure financially. He was no longer young, his fighting fervour was dying down. Doing the same thing, sinking into the rut of a ballet impresario, bored him. He was tired, too, of the "search" for sensation and of "modernism" and wished to rest from it all.

In short, Diaghileff's career was already virtually finished. He could go no farther. His death was timely.

# 15

## DIAGHILEFF

I DID not become properly acquainted with Diaghileff until 1916 in New York. I had known him by sight, of course, since before the War. He was a well-known figure in old St. Petersburg. In drawing-room and dress circle he was pointed out: "Look . . . do you see . . . over there . . . it is Diaghileff!" He caused the same excitement as a foreign celebrity.

He was a massive, rather flabby figure; his famous quiff of white hair stood out at the top of his high forehead in the middle of his silky chestnut hair. His mild face had no outstanding characteristics, his lips were thick and juicy, he had a dazzling row of teeth. You were impressed by his manner—quiet and lazy and in some way condescending— the manner of a very important and rather bored *grand seigneur*. He did not abandon this manner of nonchalant importance and apparent indifference even when speaking to the great people of this world or when he was in desperate need of something he was trying to attain. At the same time, and especially in his latter years, he was exquisitely polite, ever the man of breeding and culture; but he was a master in making felt through this politeness the weight of his own importance and his utter self-confidence. This was my impression of the man as he was pointed out to me in the centre of the theatrical crowds of St. Petersburg.

Diaghileff was not popular in the Russian capital; many people even hated him, but all paid tribute to his forceful personality. There were many reasons for his unpopularity. The chief was that he did not seek popularity, he did not care whether people liked him or not. Superficial and worldly success he could and did attain. Though he was not liked, he was invited everywhere: no door was closed to him, and the people who disliked him most were those who most eagerly sought his society.

The Diaghileff–Filosofov group was large, but it was not part of the social clique of St. Petersburg in which Diaghileff moved in later years with such ease. St. Petersburg did not encourage "outsiders," especially when they were not protégés of members of the fashionable circle, but on the contrary forced themselves on society.

Nor, on the background of St. Petersburg's absolute social simplicity, was Diaghileff's grand manner very convincing. His top-hat tilted at an angle, his monocle, his studied nonchalance reeked of pose, and of a pose which was not typically Russian. It will be seen later that Diaghileff was indeed always acting . . . and for Paris he acted brilliantly. In St. Petersburg one could not act the *grand seigneur*, one must be one.

In Diaghileff pretension and pose were obvious. Among Robert de Montesquiou and Boni de Castellanes—the flower of the Parisian *précieux*—his manner passed as a slightly florid lordliness; in St. Petersburg it did not convince.

Furthermore, Diaghileff had achieved his success and made a name for himself outside Russia, almost as if in opposition to Russia and her traditions, in the teeth of

PLATE XXI

[*Sasha*

SERGE DE DIAGHILEFF

PLATE XXII

DIAGHILEFF'S OLD NURSE
*Drawing by L. Bakst*

official Russia. In the eyes of the Imperial Theatre he was a rebel, a defiler of the classical ballet in Western Europe. Finally, he was not in favour at Court. It is possible that his somewhat dubious reputation was responsible for this. His homosexuality was no secret, and his continuous financial difficulties were common knowledge. Long before any ballets were produced unfriendly tongues were asking: "Where does he get the money on which he lives?" and the gossip did not stop at this. Altogether he was a prominent and much-discussed figure.

This attitude was revealed in the fact that he never received a Court appointment, despite the intervention of very important people, including a Grand Duke. The position of Gentleman of the Chamber, which he greatly coveted and which to him would have been the crowning glory of his St. Petersburg success and would have helped his work abroad, was denied him. He had no ambition to be a professional in the world of art, or a theatrical impresario; he sought always to be the *grand seigneur* type of patron of arts. A Court distinction would have helped him in this rôle, a rôle which he sought, not only because it was more to his taste, but because it was better suited to his business and was the atmosphere in which his possibilities could grow and develop most widely.

But official recognition was denied him. In this respect St. Petersburg was very strict. There were cases where for years very prominent people were refused admission to Court. As an example may be cited the case of the wife of a very well-known politician, a Cabinet Minister of many years' standing. In Diaghileff's case he was recognized *de facto*, but *de jure* recognition was not for him because it would have constituted official "consecration."

I remember the feeling of excited curiosity and awe, mingled with a sense of daring and wrongdoing, with which I always looked at Diaghileff.

I was introduced to this awe-inspiring man in New York. We were fellow-guests at the same hospitable table in the Ritz Hotel. A soft, fleshy hand lay in mine. Diaghileff looked tired and displeased, as though everything—his work, the people, and even this dinner—bored him. There was nothing "awe-inspiring" about him. His conversation was extremely clever and pleasant. I remember that he tried to prove to me that such Russians as achieved success in creative art were often stupid. In a few words, quoting Tchekov and Stanislavsky as examples, he showed how mistaken it was to confuse creative power with intelligence and how a stupid creator could at the same time be great. He did not mention the ballet, and it seemed tactless to broach the subject. The usual small talk at that time *de rigueur* in America was something quite foreign to him. Diaghileff was a genuine and brilliant conversationalist, interesting, intelligent, and agreeable—one could not help but pay attention to what he had to say. At the same time he did not monopolize the conversation; he himself knew how to listen. His conversation generally did not arouse controversy; despite the mildness of his words, there was something of unquestionable authority in what he said, to which no one could take exception.

On every occasion when I met him in America Diaghileff filled me with a sense of fatigue and sadness. This seemed real, and not the assumed languor which was part of his old make-up. He did not like America, and was not at home in the midst of the hectic prosperity of the New York life of that period. He had gone to New York in search of funds, and had encountered nothing but worry and trouble. The friends of his early victories were dispersed about Europe, thousands of miles away. A war had separated him from them.

Among his old friends Diaghileff was quite a different being. Drawn into their intimate circle when quite a boy, during the nineteen years from 1895 to 1914 he had shared all his work, all his hopes, all his life with them. During that period of his work he was bound spiritually to this artistic circle. Benois still keeps a letter from him dealing with his early work of the last century. In it Diaghileff reproaches Benois for a lack of warmth and enthusiasm in the creation of the *Mir Iskustva*, which was then being formed. In this letter he draws an exact and picturesque description of his own part in the mutual work of collaboration. Here is an extract from the letter, which is dated June 14, 1898:

When you are building a house you are surrounded by God knows how many masons, carpenters, joiners and painters. You don't know how many worries you will have to encounter in the building or in other directions. It may be the bricks, the rafters, the mortar, the wallpaper or some other trivial matter. The one thing that does not worry you is the façade—believing in the friendship and artistic capacities of the architect you know that the outside appearance will be beautiful. But just the opposite transpires. Covered with dust and perspiration you clamber out of the scaffolding and planks and your friend the builder tells you that he cannot build the house and, in any case, *why* build it? Is it really necessary? Then, and only then do you appreciate the loathsomeness of bricks, of the smell of the glue and paint, and the stupidity of the workmen.

This extract gives a clear picture of what Diaghileff considered to be his part in their joint work. He took on himself the technical side of the business, building a practical interior to an artistic façade, and this façade he left entirely to his artist friends. Another characteristic feature of this letter is the stress which is laid on the façade, and not on the building itself. His whole life was spent in building façades; he was not a constructor of a solid building. In the words of Benois, he was not an architect but a pyrotechnist, and the magnificent palaces which he created crumbled in the dust the moment after they were erected.

To all this must be added that their joint work was made to appear as if it were his own. At about that time Diaghileff published an elaborate monograph on the eighteenth-century Russian portrait painter, Levitsky. This publication was an example of Diaghileff's attitude towards "work." The whole of the documentary portion which had been compiled after considerable technical research bore his signature, and he made the edition his own by putting his name on the binding, but the critical article on Levitsky, written in proper literary style, was neither made nor signed by him.

Diaghileff, as has already been stated, was not a personal creator of art. He was an organizer, not a man of ideas. For not a single ballet or even part of a ballet was he responsible. He was a first-rate "lightning conductor," a marvellous "battery" which could be charged with electricity. His whole career is marked by the influence of someone or other. First it was Filosofov and Benois, the one in ethical matters and the other in the artistic sense: later, at the time of the ballets, it was the whole group of friends who gathered at the "tea table." Later, after the war, there were the sporadic figures of the Parisian artistic vanguard.

Until things began to take definite shape in the creative laboratory he was liable to give way before the critical onslaught of his collaborators. They would shout: "That's enough about your national Russian ballets . . . cheap trash," and he would give way and subside.

Even in the realm of music, of which he was passionately fond and in which he had had some technical training, he did not attempt to create anything, although it was in this sphere that he came nearest to doing so. He had a passion for correcting and "cutting," and undertook nearly all the cutting and rearrangement of the ballets. The music of *Cléopâtre,* a miscellaneous assortment from the works of Russian composers, was put together by Diaghileff. He was able to do this with a certain masterly skill, and liked the job. Even in the days of *Mir Iskustva* he always attended to the cutting out of the photographs for the blocks. To what extent this can be counted as creative work is another question.

Collaboration between the friends in the days of the early ballets was of an extremely close and intimate character. During the St. Petersburg period they usually forgathered at Diaghileff's almost every evening. Diaghileff insisted that they should see each other every day, and like a spoiled and capricious beauty would demand:

"Why can't you come to-day? . . . You must. . . . Very well, we won't start at all . . . we'll drop the ballet."

These evening teas at Diaghileff's were the inner laboratory where all the friends joined together in the preparation of their undertakings. He had a ground floor flat in Zamiatin Street, neither large nor luxurious. In the first room you entered stood a large Bechstein grand piano, which he had brought from his home in Perm. The rest of the furniture consisted of seventeenth- and eighteenth-century pieces which he had collected during his journeys abroad. Many were the ballets which were created in this room. Valechka Nouvel usually played the piano—he was good at reading music. When the theme of the ballet had been decided upon and it was time to start "stuffing," Fokine, a professional pianist, was invited. Fokine was not of the intimate Diaghilevian circle, and, being looked upon as one of the "ballet," he was not invited to the preliminary gatherings. The next room was used by Diaghileff as the reception room. Here he received business callers and officials. Next came the dining-room, then the bedroom. The evening meeting usually took place in the dining-room. There stood the samovar, the cakes, the buns, and the jam. At first Diaghileff's old nurse presided over these gatherings. He ill-treated her, roared at her, yet at the same time tenderly cared for her. To the friends she was a member of the family. They all shook hands with her, and Benois kissed her. When she died her place was taken by Vasili Zouikoff, Diaghileff's devoted slave. These teas were long affairs, starting usually at 9 p.m. and lasting until three in the morning. Nine-tenths of the conversation had nothing to do with their work; they would chatter and gossip until suddenly, perhaps at one o'clock, they remembered why they were there and began to discuss the work in hand.

238

In this atmosphere there was no pose about Diaghileff—none of the Serge de Diaghileff, *grand seigneur*. He was just himself. Hot-tempered, unbalanced, and sometimes rude, he was not easy to get on with. In the days of *Mir Iskustva* he once got terribly angry with Bakst, who, it appeared, had let slip to his brother, a journalist, an editorial secret. The brother promptly made use of it. With the help of his cousin Dima, the infuriated Diaghileff threw Bakst out of the flat and his overcoat and goloshes after him. Such violent physical measures were not regarded with favour by the friends, and there was a storm of protest. C. A. Somov even wrote him a letter saying that so far as he was concerned everything was finished. Two months later he had to be formally introduced, like a complete stranger, to Diaghileff, though within a fortnight of the incident the good-tempered Bakst was once again sitting at the same hospitable table, his overcoat and goloshes lying peacefully in the entrance hall, ready for the next outburst!

Diaghileff was difficult also on account of his whims and fancies. He had an almost ridiculous fear of infection. The following is a typical conversation:

"Well, everyone quite well at home?"

"Yes, but my son has a cold."

"What! A cold! Are you sure it isn't tonsillitis?"

"Of course not; just a slight cold in the head."

"All the same, I think you had better sit over there, a little further away from me."

The same fear of infection caused Diaghileff never to ride in an open carriage. He was afraid of catching glanders, a disease peculiar to horses. In summer, no matter how intense the heat, one had to travel with him in a closed carriage; he would not allow one window to be opened.

"No, leave it alone," he would snap. "Can't you see there is a cab passing—the horse will sneeze, and we shall catch glanders."

During 1907, the cholera year in St. Petersburg, he paused before every looking-glass to look long and intently at his tongue, fearing to see that it was turning black. Some idea of the stupid limits to which the fear of infection carried him can be gathered from the fact that when Benois on one occasion telephoned to say that he could not join them as scarlet fever had broken out in the building where he was, Diaghileff in all seriousness sought assurance that he would not catch the disease over the telephone.

He was also a prey to superstition: the spilling of salt, the number thirteen, passing under a ladder, were to him certain omens of misfortune. Heaven help you if you put your hat on a bed in his presence. He would shriek hysterically: "Take it off, take it off immediately!" and would not be pacified until it was removed.

He probably had an equally superstitious regard for religion. He had icons hanging in his rooms, and always made the sign of the cross before them. But it is doubtful whether he was imbued with any real religious feeling; at any rate he never displayed any interest in religion. The friends at one period developed an enthusiasm for such matters, but Diaghileff was merely sceptical, saying that such occupations were a waste of time.

Behind all these whims there was of course the constant fear of death, a fear which, combined with that of old age, possessed Diaghileff all his life. Towards the end of his career it was easy to influence him by saying that he was old, and that was why he didn't understand the matter in hand. At such a remark he would at once give way and agree to things with which he was not really in favour. His terror of travelling, and in particular of sea journeys, was founded on this fear of death. He was haunted by the premonition of death by drowning, and it was probably owing to this that he had not the courage to go with the company to South America on the fateful occasion when he allowed Nijinsky out of his control, and lost him for ever. Only the hopelessness of the position in Europe forced him to the decision to go to New York in 1916.

This constant fear of death might give the impression that Diaghileff was an arrant coward. This, however, would be a mistake. He was afraid of no man, nor of material difficulties and business catastrophes. He was a born fighter, and was at his best when in the thick of the everyday struggle. It often seemed that he created difficulties for himself in order to overcome them. Whether this was so or not, the fact remains that he did not run away from trouble, and the many catastrophical situations in which he found himself were a direct consequence of his seeming lack of desire to prevent them.

In 1910, for instance, Diaghileff was in search of capital for the launching of his London season. George Edwardes, a relative of Benois and a prominent figure in theatrical London, received him with the utmost cordiality. Edwardes took upon himself the whole organization, and everything pointed to the season being an outstanding success. On his return to Paris, Diaghileff received a series of letters from London containing all manner of inquiries in connection with the production. He did not reply to a single one of them. At last Edwardes lost patience, and wrote saying that it was impossible to carry on with a man who was so unbusinesslike. The result was that the probability of a London production was thrown once more in the melting-pot, and the whole procedure of raising capital had to be gone over again.

It is possible that another reason for this was Diaghileff's negligence and laziness. No greater contrast in a man could be found than this combination in Diaghileff of extreme laziness and frenzied energy. He scarcely ever answered letters: books he never read. When in St. Petersburg or on the Lido he took his coffee and read his newspapers in bed, and never rose before eleven. At the country estate in Russia where he spent his holidays he did absolutely nothing except indulge occasionally in a little mushroom gathering, a recreation which he greatly enjoyed. Apart from such expeditions he never walked (he loathed walking), and on his trips to town he used a closed carriage. To persuade him into any business was not an easy matter, but when he took something in hand he attacked it with an energy and capacity for work which seemed unlimited. During the ballet seasons in Paris he no longer stayed in bed until eleven—he was up at eight. There were days when, according to programme, he made no less than thirty-six calls. He liked any kind of technical work, and spent many hours with the carpenters, joiners, and other workmen. These people were absolutely devoted to him; he knew how to deal with them, talking in a language which they all understood, always exquisitely polite and never abusive or "superior." Rudeness he reserved for his equals or social superiors. For skilled workmen he had great respect, and they knew it. With such people as Skamoni, who was in charge of the *Mir Iskustva* printing office, or with Valz, the manager of theatrical machinery, Diaghileff could do just what he liked. He achieved wonders with them and trusted them implicitly.

There was no limit to the passionate enthusiasm with which Diaghileff threw himself into his work once it was undertaken. He was never a calm, systematic, and consequent worker, but rather a sporadic and explosive fighter. At the same time his explosive outbursts at work were enormous and lasting. Because of this characteristic, work with him was never dull or monotonous.

Great master as he was in finding it, money as such did not count with Diaghileff. He never saved. It was just the means to an end, something which was necessary if his undertakings were to reach a successful conclusion. His whole life was a series of financial disasters. So early as 1909, after the first ballet season in Paris, his luggage was seized for debt on the railway station. After the War the complete scenery of various productions was often taken and sold by auction, and when in 1923 the Russian Ballet found a home and sanctuary at the Court of the Prince of Monaco in Monte Carlo, it was a salvation at the eleventh hour, as Diaghileff was in another financial corner.

Diaghileff's success, nevertheless, must not be attributed merely to his sporadic fighting qualities. In twelve short years after his start in the 'nineties, having gone through his inheritance and without the help of any influential connections, the man had become the head of a huge international undertaking and a world-famous celebrity.

The fighting spirit was not enough; other qualities were needed in order to go so far. Diaghileff had them.

Personality was the most essential. Diaghileff had an inborn and spontaneous power of bending people to his will; even his most intimate friends succumbed to his dominating influence. They fought against it, but in the end they did what he wanted. The periodical quarrels between him and his collaborators—as a rule they occurred at least once every three months—were very much in the nature of an explosion of their subconscious revolt against this domination. In his presence one not only found it difficult to resist him but even sought to please him. He involuntarily inspired a desire to create, a desire that he should approve and be wildly enthusiastic. It is possible that had it not been for his presence as the central, though not the creative figure, many of the ideas which formed the basis of the Russian ballets would never have been created.

The same influence manifested itself not only with everyone with whom he had business dealings but with people he met casually. He was an inborn leader, ever capable of subduing others. At the same time he was not a stupid "dictator"—in the creation of the ballets he allowed his collaborators every freedom in the purely artistic sphere. This, incidentally, might explain his lifelong friendship with Bakst. Bakst in business, as in everyday life, was the most easygoing of men. He was Diaghileff's right-hand man, his trusted "aide" for years. He would give way in everything except his artistic convictions—this Diaghileff did not expect of him. It was only in later years, long after the war, when the artistic direction of the productions, under various influences, took a course with which Bakst's artistic conscience could not become reconciled, that he became indignant against this breach of tradition and finally developed a hatred of Diaghileff as the betrayer of their common ideals. He wrote him an extremely rude letter which was handed to Diaghileff in a restaurant during lunch. It began with the words "You useless old slipper," and was unprintably rude. Diaghileff read it and handed it across the table to Benois, saying "Read that. He is completely mad." The break was final. They never met again.

Another characteristic of Diaghileff was his extreme capability. Despite his dislike of study, he passed out of the St. Petersburg University with honours. The whole of his career as a student was marked by his enthusiasm for music, painting, travelling—everything, in fact, that was not in the university curriculum. Yet he passed out with honours, owing mainly to his wonderful memory which recorded the smallest and often most unnecessary details.

He also had quite an exceptional way with people. By some deep infallible instinct he understood them and knew how to treat them in order to get what he needed out of them. In Paris the following is the type of incident which frequently occurred. Vasili Zouikoff would enter the room and announce to Diaghileff that Mr. X had called. Mr. X was some disagreeable creditor. Diaghileff would wink at his friends: "Now you will see how I will manage it—it will be done in no time." Outside the door would be heard voices raised to an enthusiastic pitch, and the creditor would depart, all smiles, and not a penny the better off!

Diaghileff's lightning changes from the Russian sitting

at ease at his tea table into the snobbish dandy were extraordinary. A comb through his hair, monocle thrust into his eye, and he would sail into the next room—Serge de Diaghileff, the Russian *grand seigneur*, a little weary and important—to see the caller. His friends did not wholly approve of such transformations. The catchword invented by Serov—"It's good for business"—was used, with a shrug of the shoulders, in such circumstances. Diaghileff sometimes achieved miraculous results. For instance, no one ever understood how he succeeded in persuading Beecham, who had financed the production of Stravinsky's *Le Rossignol*, to allow the *première* of this opera in Paris.

His intuition was uncanny. On one occasion he drew Benois's attention to their mutual friend, M. A. Vroubel, a brilliant and seemingly quite normal painter.

"Vroubel, you know, is qualifying for the madhouse . . . you will see . . . and Bakst will follow him."

Vroubel went insane within two years, and the strange end of Bakst which even mystified the doctors was not unconnected with an unfounded conviction of imaginary ailments—which in some way proved the correctness of Diaghileff's prediction.

Another proof of Diaghileff's uncanny tuition was his flair for discovering new talent, particularly in the musical sphere in which he was better able to use his own discrimination. Such finds as that of the practically unknown Stravinsky were remarkable. Vladimir Dukelsky and Igor Markevitch were later discoveries. In the *Mir Iskustva* days he helped quite a number of painters—Sapounoff, Sudeikin, Paul Kouznetzoff, Krymoff, and many others—to come into their own. In the realm of ballet one can point

246

to Massine and Lifar as two of his finds. At the same time it is true to say that Diaghileff considered that he had created rather than discovered these last two. When one of his lucky finds was remarked upon he would say:

"What are you talking about? I could make this plate dance if I wanted to!"

Both in his handling of people and in his personal relationship with them Diaghileff was unblushingly practical. He was a master in the art of putting them in an embarrassing position and turning it to his own advantage. Other people's time he never bothered about. An appointment for four o'clock would be kept at six, and in two minutes the whole business would be effected. He used his personal charm and snobbish skill quite consciously as a weapon to achieve his purpose. In the one or the other rôle he was quite irresistible and always got what he wanted.

His cynicism did not show itself at once but developed gradually. In his youth he was rather a prude, a modest and naïve young man, but with the passing of years and in the light of his experience he developed a contemptuous and cynical attitude towards mankind and life in general. He was no longer shocked by indecent jokes—he began to make them himself. No man was faithful, he would say, and no woman pure; everyone had his price, and vice reigned everywhere. Selfish theories became a hobby, and in his dealings with mankind he became unfriendly and morose. Such of his sayings as "The weak must perish, they must not be helped" and "One must be above the petty squabbles and cares of mankind" were strongly flavoured with Nietzschism. He was indignant when he saw anyone give alms to a beggar and was contemptuous of charities and social work. He only approved of the service of art as this was the service of beauty—an abstract thing, the cult of which was so strongly developed in himself. For beauty everything could be justified—it was finite, the highest purpose of his life's work. In this theory of a superman and in the worship of beauty are to be seen the remains of German influence.

Despite this general unfriendly attitude towards mankind, Diaghileff was deeply and genuinely attached to a small group of people. Family feeling ran strongly in him. Dima Filosofov, his cousin, was the close companion and faithful friend of his youth. Their ways inevitably parted in later years, but the attachment remained. He was devoted, almost with fatherly tenderness, to his two young stepbrothers. They lived with him for many years, and he treated them as though they were his own children. The sister of Dima Filosofov, Zina, and her husband, Ratkoff-Rognoff, were equally dear to him, and it was at their house that the friends often gathered in St. Petersburg. Another cousin, Kolia Diaghileff (a rather mediocre 'cellist, but of good principle) also spent much of his time with him.

Yet another who followed in Diaghileff's train in the old days was another relative. His name—Wissenka Proteikinsky—like everything else about him, was strange. He was one of the types portrayed by Dostoevsky, a mystic and Christian, and a fervent admirer of religious philosophy and its prophet—the author, Vladimir Solovieff. Proteikinsky was incredibly dirty; he never washed or changed his linen. He adored funerals, and if ever by chance he met one in the street he would certainly join it and piously accompany the cortège to the cemetery. That it was the funeral of an absolute stranger had no consequence! At meetings of religious and philosophical societies in which the friends at one time took part he was a tireless orator, and often confounded bishops and priests by his particular gift of argumentation.

One day Wissenka did not make his usual appearance. After some time had passed Diaghileff began to worry and went in search of him. He found that poor Proteikinsky was ill and had not left his room for a month. The smell of the room was enough to make anyone ill. Diaghileff literally dragged him out of bed and took him to hospital. In the bath Wissenka revived: the novelty, the delight of splashing about in the water affected him like a child. After he was washed and put to bed he was given some sweets. . . . Wissenka ate them . . . and promptly died!

The list is not yet exhausted. Another who was very dear to Diaghileff up to the date of his death was his cousin Pavel Georgevitch Koribout-Kubitovitch. Of ancient Slav extraction (he was the descendant of the Lithuanian king, Gedemin), in all his bearing Koribout-Kubitovitch resembled a Russian boyard of the pre-Peter the Great days. He was of affectionate disposition with a yearning for self-expression, but none the less a good diplomat and a far from stupid man. He was continuously attached to Diaghileff, and sometimes relieved Vasili Zouikoff as Nijinsky's protector against the outside world. In general he was a very agreeable and harmless man. Diaghileff was very fond of him and trusted him implicitly.

Vasili Zouikoff, of course, is still another who must be counted among the intimates of Diaghileff. He was nearer to the type of Russian Leporello than to the classical idea of the well-trained servant of Western Europe. A confidant, intimately acquainted with all the details of the life of his sometimes difficult though adored master, he served him with an almost dog-like devotion. Zouikoff was often consulted by others of the group who sought his opinion and relied on his elemental peasant good sense. We can be certain that if Zouikoff was ill—but not of a contagious sickness—Diaghileff would be the one who would apply the compresses, take his temperature, and so on. Zouikoff's wife often took up his duties when he was engaged in the guardianship of Nijinsky. Diaghileff was extremely kind and attentive to her, and her boy, who at that time studied at the ballet school, was equally well looked after and cared for.

Of other close friends of Diaghileff much has already been said in this book. The relationships between Diaghileff and Benois, so full of intermittent quarrels and reconciliations, are already known to the reader. In spite of all the ups and downs their friendship endured for forty years, and, warmed by the fire of mutual regard, although they followed different paths in their quest for truth and beauty, it only came to an end at Diaghileff's death.

Nouvel, too, maintained friendly contact with Diaghileff until the latter's death. Their quarrels were more frequent than those between Diaghileff and Benois—but everyone quarrelled with Nouvel, indispensable though he was. After the War, when owing to circumstances Nouvel lost his position as a Government official and "entered the service" of Diaghileff, he had much to bear. His master was not without leanings towards psychological sadism and was very fault-finding and disagreeable towards him.

For years Bakst and Diaghileff were bound by the ties of a close friendship. Easy-going as he was, Bakst never failed to give back as much as he got—shriek for shriek, abuse for abuse. These shrieks and abusings, however, were the favourite pastime of the old days of the "Pickwickians," when the epithets of "rotter" and "beast" were almost terms of endearment.

Diaghileff had an especially soft spot in his heart for the painter Serov, who, however, was everybody's darling and the incontrovertible moral authority among the friends. Unfortunately, this remarkable painter and delightful man died at an early age, succumbing in 1911 to the first attack of angina pectoris.

Another name is linked to this galaxy of talent, that of Prince Argoutinsky-Dolgoroukoff. He joined the group in 1907 at the time of the production of *Le Pavillon d'Armide* in the Maryinsky Theatre. Argoutinsky was a St. Petersburgian by birth, and by his relationships he belonged to what is usually called "high society." Nevertheless, he was far from the type of a man-about-town. He was an original, silent, and reserved man, possessed by an almost maniacal passion for collecting art treasures. His rare and almost infallible judgment in art was something on which the friends relied. He had an established reputation in St. Petersburg as an expert in paintings, and was often invited to the Imperial Museum to give his opinion of proposed purchases. One became accustomed to his monosyllabic replies. He would gaze thoughtfully at a picture. and murmur "Yes . . . yes . . . yes" or "No . . . no . . . no." He gave no explanation of such Pythian pronouncements, but everyone knew that that "Yes" or "No" was right and well-founded. In spite of his taciturnity Argoutinsky was capable of strong feeling on all vital subjects. Deeply religious, he often made great sacrifices for those who were dear to him. At the same time there was a strangeness in his dealings with people; he was prone to take sudden and unexpected dislikes.

"X is a disgusting creature," he would suddenly say.

"But why? What is wrong with him? He is quite a pleasant fellow."

"No. . . . Didn't you notice what hands he has!"

Argoutinsky had to be understood from half a word, sometimes without words. Diaghileff, master of intuition, found in him a friend from whom he was only parted by death.

Diaghileff was closely attached to this band of friends and relatives, and showed his affection in every conceivable way. He worried about them when they were ill even to the point of sentimentality, and when possible looked after them. Reconciliations after a quarrel were usually made up of embraces and, on Diaghileff's part, of tears. This warmth and sentimentality was practically unknown outside the confines of the intimate group. The world at large saw only the exterior—the creator-organizer, adroit, efficient, and exacting.

At work he was implacable, even cruel, but he also had the knack of awakening the most dormant conscience, of demanding and obtaining sacrifices, of making people work for love and not for money. He himself was the first to make sacrifices, and by force of example he made others do likewise. A half-joking reminder that he was a descendant of Peter the Great often fell from his lips. There is actually a legend that Field-Marshal Count Roumiantzoff was Peter's natural son. The Count's daughter was Diaghileff's great-grandmother. This descent is of course doubtful, but Diaghileff, when on the subject, stressed it with almost schoolboyish enthusiasm. Benois, however, told me that he had a clearer understanding of Peter's nature and character since he had studied them through the prism of Diaghileff's personality.

Although Diaghileff was not a creator of art, and even though his friends were far from enthusiastic over his taste, his artistic realizations often bore traces of his personality. One exceptional trait marks the whole of his activity from his early youth, ever since the days of his first exhibition. It was the desire to impress and astound, to astonish the bourgeois—an impish delight in "hair-raising." One of his first exhibitions was devoted to the so-called "Glasgow Boys"—Lavery, Guthrie, Patterson—about whose painting he was enthusiastic. In addition it delighted him to puzzle St. Petersburg society with an art which they at that time could not understand. This trait was not at first noticeable in his ballets. For a long time the "parliament" of his friends restrained him with their veto.

"I want to leave them open-mouthed," Diaghileff would say to explain a sensational effect. His friends would resist, arguing and demanding that the work should be kept within the limits of a strictly artistic creation. Thus did the friends spend their most productive years, in the days of *Mir Iskustva* as well as in the ballet period, in a constant fight with Diaghileff's attempts at "hair-raising." The creators did not seek to astonish and perplex people, they simply created on the lines they found possible; but in spite of their opposition the "hair-raising" crept in, both in the days of *Mir Iskustva* and of the ballet. Not only the bourgeois but also the *élite* were startled. Even if only in the way in which he served his dish, in the decoration of the theatre, in the snobbish insistence on a worldly and social atmosphere, in the unexpectedness even of such trifles as the programmes, from which every vestige of advertisement was suppressed, Diaghileff managed to get what he wanted. Probably even without all this Diaghileff would have succeeded in his "hair-raising" because the art which the Diaghilevians brought was in itself too new, but this collaboration combined with the continuous struggle between the clear creativeness of the friends and the Diaghileff "hair-raising" brought into existence the success of the masterpieces.

From 1912 the first signs of the victory of his "hair-raising" direction, which was to reign after the War, began to show themselves. They were to be seen in *L'Après-midi d'un Faune* and *Les Jeux*. Although, to continue the culinary metaphor, the dish is served in the same unexpected way, with all the old brilliance and wonderment, the essence of the dish itself somehow does not seem to taste so good.

This love of creating astonishment is one of Diaghileff's special characteristics. It was not due to commercial considerations, nor was it instinctive advertisement, but rather some inward desire to astound. Like everything else with Diaghileff, it was not actuated by mercenary motives, though, of course, once it proved successful Diaghileff was not against reaping the fruits of his work, and generally managed to do so very successfully. This characteristic of Diaghileff supports Benois's observation that he was not a builder but a pyrotechnist. It is very true to say that Diaghileff had no taste for lasting things, he rebelled against routine and had no desire for a quiet, humdrum existence. He was a nomad, and therein truly Russian, with every external and inward indication of his "wanderlust." This roving instinct was so strong that in post-War days he never lived in either of the two small flats which he had in Monte Carlo and Paris. His secretary stayed there, his belongings were there, but Diaghileff himself stayed at an hotel.

In the last years of his life his established position as a theatrical impresario weighed heavily on him. He groaned and sighed and even complained, but he knew that he could not give it up.

"It is all very well," he would say, "but what shall I do with the company?"

As a distraction he took up the collection of Russian books and found a thrill in the acquisition of first editions and rare books. He talked about his treasures with the same verve that he had used in the past for an eighteenth-century painting.

In such talks the old friends recognized in the aged and weary Diaghileff their old Serioja. As far as he himself is concerned, death took him at the right moment. He could go no further, and to retrace his steps would not have been his desire. His work was done, and all that lay before him was an artistic cul-de-sac.

It is impossible to write about Diaghileff without referring to another of his characteristics—his homosexuality. People usually allude to this subject either with disgust and jeers, treating it as something degenerate and immoral; or, as do some of its adherents, in terms which are partly apologetic, partly in praise. Neither the one nor the other seems to me to be entirely right. In my opinion, unisexuality is neither a virtue nor a vice: it is inherent. In any case it is not something which is acquired, like vice or amorality, nor is it a sign of degeneracy. Homosexuality has always existed; it can be encountered in the pages of ancient history, in the times of Ancient Greece, in the Middle Ages, and in the turbulent days of the Renaissance. It still exists, and it does not seem to have become any more widespread. The only difference is that in our days, when everything is done so openly it seems to be flaunted before our eyes, and it is in this publicity that we see signs of degeneracy. But the trouble in this case is not so much a question of unisexuality as of sex in general. The tendency of a certain type of English literature is a regrettable sign in this direction. Such books as the *Well of Loneliness* and *Lady Chatterley's Lover*, which treat intimate sexual matters in a pictorial way, are, to my mind, a sign of moral decay. Their authors try in vain to justify such works on the grounds of their social and psychological importance. In vain do they dedicate such books to their wives and even daughters as serious and much-needed enlightenment. These problems have always existed, and people have known how to handle them in the days when this shameless-ness and publicity did not exist. That it does exist is something for which such authors have to be thanked. In the decline of the ancient Phœnician state people un-blushingly performed the sexual act in public places—such sexual shamelessness is a sure sign of moral decay, and therefore of degeneracy.

There is, of course, something abnormal in homosexuality. Procreation, the natural purpose of sex, is lacking. But if this is to be the criterion, are there many normal people in the world? Abnormality among heterosexualists or so-called normal people is unlimited; it is difficult to meet people who have a natural sex understanding.

The rather widespread idea that genius and unisexuality are in some way related is equally fallacious. It would perhaps be more true to say that talent, being in itself abnormal, often carries in its wake some other abnormality, which may quite conceivably be expressed in sex wrongness. This, however, does not necessarily reveal itself in tendencies towards homosexualism. Count Leo Tolstoi, for example, was undoubtedly abnormal, and in the sense of sex, but this abnormality found expression in hypertrophy, in an unusual power of normally directed sex instincts. This is abundantly clear from the reminiscences of his wife and after reading such of his works as *Kreutzer Sonata* and *Father Sergius*. It would be a still graver error to regard unisexuality as a sign of genius. Although it is perhaps true to say that many gifted people have been homosexual or bisexual, it is quite wrong to put it the other way and say that all homosexualists are geniuses. Among them you can find as many dull and untalented people as you wish. Though talent may be conditional upon abnormality, the reverse, that abnormality is conditional upon talent, is absurd: if this was the case, all lunatics would be geniuses.

The position, so far as Diaghileff's circle is concerned, is clearly defined. Among the creators of modern ballet Benois is an absolutely normal man; Bakst, although a great admirer of women, was erratic and extremely depraved; Diaghileff himself was a non-depraved homosexualist.

The Bakst and Diaghileff types are interesting as a study of sex analysis. In their later years they were both quite open on the subject and discussed it frequently. Diaghileff was a theoretical apologist of homosexualism. He maintained that to be a creator of art it was essential to have the instincts and understandings of both sexes in order to be able to understand and interpret life from both points of view. He disliked women and treated them with contempt. Marriage he regarded as simply dangerous. Whenever he heard of the death of some married man he would say: "There you are, I always told you so! I am not a bit surprised, it is the most harmful thing in the world. . . . You can expect just the same . . ."

He maintained that all great men were homosexual, and quoted Frederick the Great, Julius Caesar, Wagner and Tchaikovsky, and others as examples. At the same time he was in no sense depraved, but rather monogamistic, true to his attachments and holding his friends in genuine regard. In contrast to Bakst, he liked to talk about his inclination for quiet "family" life and the lack of any desire for amorous adventure.

Bakst was quite the opposite. He was a passionate lover of women and was always in the throes of some hysterical and mysterious romance. His depravity, it seems, dated from the time of a liaison many years before with a French actress in St. Petersburg. There is no need to enter into details of his depravity, it would not be worth while; but if I was asked which of the two I considered the more normal and more healthy in his relations to sex, I should say Diaghileff. Just as he was an apologist of homosexuality, so was Bakst of his love of women. Each tried to prove that theoretically and aesthetically he was right, but it was a hopeless task. They had their own opinions, and nothing would shake them.

There is a general but mistaken point of view that all homosexualists are effeminate, it being supposed that in their psychological make-up some feminine traits have displaced the male. This may be explained by the fact that the onlooker is often struck by the womanly touch which is undoubtedly there and which is dubbed "effeminate." This is far from being always the case. Homosexualists, who both in their manners and outward appearance produce this impression of "womanliness," are generally far from lacking in masculine characteristics. It is not so much a case of psychological "inversion" as of a psycho-sexual broadening—they are men and women at the same time. Among them are often to be met people with strongly developed masculine characteristics; people, for example, who are absolutely devoid of fear. There are unisexualists among American gangsters, they are to be found among aviators and boxers. In them is also to be found that partial moral blindness which is an attribute of great men, even supermen. The amorality of Julius Caesar and Peter the Great were characteristic. We must agree, it is true, that neither were pure types of homosexualists, but it is sufficient to read Suetonius's description of the young Caesar, scratching his elaborately curled head with a no less elaborately manicured nail, to see in him what we regard as effeminacy.

The psychical emotions of such people have a tremendous

range; it reaches from tearful sentimentality to sadistic cruelty, amorality and a total contempt for human life. Their ranks are filled with great men and great criminals. The creator of the infamous Russian Tcheka, Felix Djerdzhinsky, may be taken as an example of the latter. He doted on children, and when they were in his surroundings he would shed tears of pure tenderness, yet at the same time he could send thousands of innocent people to the scaffold.

This wide psychological range gives them sometimes attributes which are unattainable by others. Diaghileff's instinctive understanding of mankind, his almost feline deftness in dealing with people is undoubtedly a characteristic of the feminine side of his make-up, whilst his knowledge of how to use this power, how to dominate men and achieve what he set out to do betrays his strong or masculine side. He was in fact a combination of man and woman, a blending of adroitness and strength. Without both it is doubtful whether he would have achieved his success.

Diaghileff had many feminine traits of character. He was capricious, jealous, and easily offended. Jealousy had a great influence on his work, an influence which had by no means a negative effect. He was extremely jealous of any manifestation of rivalry or competition in his work; it was the cause of many of his quarrels with his friends, especially with Benois and Bakst. If Bakst collaborated with Rubinstein, or perhaps Benois with someone else, Diaghileff would always be moved to recrimination and abuse. "Unfaithfulness" was something which he could not forgive.

The elementary idea of unisexuality is that it can be divided into two distinct classes—the masculine or active, and the feminine or passive. This, like most other theories on the subject, is erroneous. The purely masculine or purely feminine types are seldom met. As a rule they are people of mixed psychology, and the constituents of the mixture are so varied that it is quite impossible to say what quantity goes to the making of one or the other. It would be quite wrong, for instance, to regard Diaghileff and Nijinsky respectively as masculine and feminine homosexualists. There is no doubt that Diaghileff possessed the stronger and dominating character, but Nijinsky was far from being effeminate; there was actually far more of the woman in Diaghileff than in him.

Another mistaken though less widespread opinion is that the inclination towards homosexuality is a sort of outcome of depravity. This idea is caused by a decided leaning among homosexualists towards bisexualism, or sexual relationship with both sexes. It is often thought that if a man can have sexual connections with a woman, then his indulgence in similar relationships with a man must be a form of depravity. Inborn bisexualism, however, is by no means uncommon. The whole East can be taken as an example. Furthermore, if depravity is to be recognized in such cases, then the relationship of a homosexualist with a woman—that is, with the sex towards which he has not an instinctive leaning—must in this case be depravity.

That homosexualism is inborn cannot be doubted. Plato made reference to it in his *Symposium*, and it has been proved scientifically. From this it does not follow that it is a normal manifestation—in just the same way one can be born left-handed or colour blind. Diaghileff was such a born homosexualist, but of a more pronounced type. It is probable that throughout his life he never had sexual intercourse with a woman.

At the end of the last century, when he tried to keep his inclinations secret from his friends, there were occasions when he made allusions to his imaginary orgies with women. These stories were most unconvincing, and were probably invented as a screen to hide the truth.

As far as I know, from 1895 until his death Diaghileff had only seven liaisons. They were all of long duration and enduring, and in nearly all in addition to mere sensuality there was genuine attachment. At the present time all these people are alive, and for reasons which can well be understood it is better not to refer to them. The one exception is the liaison with Nijinsky. In the first place this was in its time almost public, and secondly Nijinsky's wife admitted it in her book.

It is difficult to give the exact date of their meeting, but it appears that they were introduced in 1907 by the Prince X of whom Romola Nijinska speaks in her book. In any case there was no liaison or other unusual relationship between them at that time.

Diaghileff had a secretary, and Nijinsky did not count as an important factor in his life. As we have already seen, the beginning of the romance dates from the first Paris season of 1909. From that moment they became inseparable. They lived in the same hotels, travelled together, spent their holidays in Karlsbad and the Lido.

Diaghileff thereafter began to act differently in the question of his unisexuality. He ceased to hide it—his open cohabitation with Nijinsky made this impossible. He had the choice either to hide it and not to live with Nijinsky, or to live with him and thereby admit his inclinations before the public eye. He chose the second course.

If one remembers the general attitude of the public towards homosexuality in pre-War days, one must assume that such a decision was not easy to take. The scandals of Oscar Wilde and Count Eulenburg were still fresh in the memory. Unisexual people carefully and fearfully made secret of their inclinations; to be considered a homosexualist was a disgrace. Nowadays, when such people no longer hide themselves, when it has become almost fashionable to be considered unisexual and normal people are looked at almost with disdain as some survival of the past, it is difficult to appreciate the courage with which Diaghileff reached his decision. It is probable that his affection for Nijinsky was so strong that he had no option but to take this course. Diaghileff's attitude during this liaison might be termed neutral. He did not proclaim his unisexuality or preach about it to everyone, but at the same time he made no attempt to hide it. Their lives were completely united, and on the rare occasions when they were separated Nijinsky was guarded by Vasili Zouikoff and others from every external contact and worry. It would be a mistake to regard this guardianship as a sign of a desire on Diaghileff's part to be the sole "possessor" of Nijinsky. The main reason was the latter's complete helplessness in everyday matters. Everything had to be done for him: railway tickets taken, rooms booked at the hotels, bills paid. He was as helpless as a child, and the position was still more complicated by his breathless rise to fame and the need to protect him from his too zealous admirers. He was also the ballet's main attraction, and it was important from the point of view of his work that his peace of mind and normal life off the stage should be maintained. Having in view his childish temperament, his overwhelming success, and his importance in the Russian ballet it cannot be doubted that any manager would have taken the same steps to guard Nijinsky under similar circumstances. He was certainly the *grande passion* of Diaghileff's life, and genuine affection and attachment were the guiding powers in their relationships.

Diaghileff spared no effort in his attempts to advance Nijinsky and make him world-famous. He tried to develop and uplift his understanding of art by taking him to museums and discussing with him creative art. He introduced him to prominent artistes of the day, and in fact did everything possible to raise him to his own cultural level. As we have already seen, he was not successful. There was too great a difference between the professional dancer and the artistically developed Diaghileff.

To raise Nijinsky to the level of an averagely developed person, let alone to the cultural development of Diaghileff, was a hopeless task. The amount of labour, effort, and attention which was given to this is hard to estimate. For this reason it is more easy to understand the weight of the blow which Diaghileff received in the news of Nijinsky's marriage. It was not only a *dépit amoureux* but a feeling of resentment against what was felt to be rank treason, a betrayal of affection and even of art.

Diaghileff managed to live down his own personal loss, and about two months after he received the telegram from Nijinsky from South America informing him of his marriage he had established another liaison which was to prove long-standing and reliable. But it was a long time before he forgave his "betrayal" by Nijinsky. He was filled with bitterness, and even nursed thoughts of revenge.

In 1914, when another man had replaced Nijinsky in Diaghileff's affections, the latter refused to become reconciled with his erstwhile friend, and even went out of his way to hurt him and publicly humiliate him during his stay in London. The hints at attempts on Nijinsky's life in New York during 1916 are certainly baseless. Diaghileff was not so primitive as to resort to such lengths, nor were they necessary, but the wound had still not healed and his feeling of resentment remained.

# 16

## ALEXANDRE BENOIS

ONE can speak of the great influence of Bakst on the Diaghileff ballets, one can point to the important part which Fokine played in their creation, one can write of the considerable contribution of Stravinsky to the work, and of Nijinsky's genius on the stage, but one has to say something quite different about Alexandre Benois.

A study of the history of the *Ballets-Russes* leads to the irrefutable conclusion that if it had not been for him they would never have existed, if Diaghileff in his early years had not had that chance meeting with Benois there would have been no *Ballets-Russes*. At the same time there is no doubt that Diaghileff would have made a great name for himself and would inevitably have left his mark on life, but it is doubtful whether this would have been in the realm of ballet.

Diaghileff was never a lover of ballet in the sense of being a "balletomane"—he had even no real leaning towards the theatre in general. In his early days he was merely a young man of good family with a liking for music and instinctively inclined towards ordinary social life without any definite purpose or aim. After his introduction, in 1890, as the cousin of Dima Filosofov into the circle of the "Pickwickians" he was drawn little by little into the sphere of their interests and yielded to their influence. The artistic tendencies of this circle were clear and well-defined. There Benois reigned and his influence was dominant. Not only in the very earliest days but in the later work of *Mir Iskustva* and in the creation of the ballets until 1912 his work is apparent. The impressions of childhood, the atavistic leanings, the preferences of Benois are to be found in the whole of the Diaghilevian productions during that period. From 1892 to 1912, or in other words, until the time when the *Ballets-Russes* had already taken shape, Benois's influence was decisive.

We can see that the achievements of Diaghileff during those years were directed according to the taste of Benois. First of all, in the painting, with all its retrospective leanings, the branch of art which was dearest to Benois and quite foreign to Diaghileff's nature; then in the ballets, another passion which had possessed Benois from his early childhood and made him a real lover of ballet long before he met Diaghileff.

The seeds of this love of painting and of the ballet were deeply implanted in the heart of Benois, the roots are to be found in his very nature and in the atavism of his first childlike impressions.

His grandfather Louis Jules Benois was born of a family of French farmers in the Brie province of France two years before the death of Louis XV, in 1772. To escape the French revolution he emigrated to Russia and after various ups and downs he settled at the court of Paul I and Maria Feodorovna, serving as *maître d'hôtel* in a similar capacity to the famous Vatel during the reign of Louis XIV. He was a cultured man and a poet. Of his nineteen children, eleven lived to a mature age. He died of smallpox in 1824. Benois's father was born in 1813 and lived to a great age.

He was a decorative architect, a lover of the arts, and a talented designer. Alexandre Benois himself was born in 1870. His fate also was to emigrate, but this time it was back to France to escape the Russian revolution. His mother was born a Cavos. Her grandfather, Catarino Cavos, an *emigré* from Venice, was in his time a famous conductor and composer, and by his patronage of its creator, Michael Glinka, he had a considerable influence on the history of Russian music. Benois's maternal grandfather, Albert Cavos, was a court architect and a specialist in the construction of theatres. Nearly all the Imperial Theatres were either built or rebuilt by him. So, from both sides, Benois was endowed with an inheritance of artistic-cum-theatrical atavism.

On his father's side this inheritance had one other definite peculiarity. Owing to the extraordinary longevity of its various members the historical past had for Benois a special significance. His grandfather was born and reached manhood in the eighteenth century. Benois's father remembered both him and his stories, with the result that what is to us merely history was to Benois something which was alive and related to a not far distant past; he had a consciousness that the French eighteenth century was quite near, whilst his father talked of the romanticism of the 1830's as if it were of yesterday. In this way an intimate sensation of a *living* past was created. Benois loved this living proximity of bygone days, throughout his life he has been a warm, almost passionate, devotee of the past.

Let us hear what he himself has to say on the subject:

"If through me new things have been created it has

certainly not been of my choosing. I would deny the usefulness of innovation, of the special preparation of anything new. I cannot deny the fact that as novelty ripens the old decays, but I am sorry for the "old." I should like to preserve everything in it that is precious and beautiful. My whole outlook on life is to an extreme degree sentimentally reminiscent, I find it hard to destroy even an old slip of paper. After all, the past is the only real thing in life, the future does not exist and the present is merely fiction."

Actually this cult of the past proved to be something new. This love of things historical, so deeply imbued, was the motive power of Benois's innovations.

"I am not a conservative in the exclusive sense of the word"—he would say. "I do not attempt to preserve the past, at any rate, in the form in which it existed, but I always deeply regret the loss of anything good, of anything belonging to the past which had value, which had every right to enjoy existence and never ceased to prove a joy and consolation. My psychology is perhaps that of an English conservative, a believer in progress on the foundation of the value of the past. It is possible, however, that in addition I had a premonition of the approaching upheaval in Russia. All my life I have taken photographs, made notes, and collected, and I have now a great accumulation of such things. I have spent a fortune on it—works of art, curios, engravings, statuettes, toys, examples of peasant work—some of these things may seem strange and unusual, but each is a definite reminder, in its characteristics and strangeness, of the period."

His love of the past and for the collection of its beauties

and its rarities was endowed on Russia by Benois even in pre-War days. In a whole series of brilliant volumes and numerous monographs and articles he shared his work with the Russian public. A few examples which serve as a sufficient reminder are his historical volumes *The Art Treasures of Russia*, his monograph on "Tsarskoe-Selo," and the articles in *Mir Iskustva* on "Bygone Days," in which much of the historical material may be attributed to Alexandre Benois. All these works were completed at the end of the nineteenth or the beginning of the twentieth centuries, or in other words, just at the time when, under Benois's influence, Diaghileff was becoming enthusiastic about Russian art and was the driving power behind *Mir Iskustva*; just at the time when he edited his monograph on the eighteenth-century portrait painter, Levitsky, and arranged his historical exhibitions of paintings in St. Petersburg and Paris.

If one recalls the direction which the development of the *Ballets-Russes* took in the sense of theme one can see clearly the touch of Benois's leaning to the past. *Sylvia* is the re-creation of the ancient mythology combined with some transposition of later romanticism; *Le Pavillon d'Armide*—the epoch of ostentatious baroque intermingled (in the dance of the lame faunes, the bacchantes, and the terrifying figure of the Marquis) with Hoffmannism; *Les Sylphides*—an elegy of the 'thirties; *Cléopâtre*—the ancient world; *Carnaval*—typical Biedermeier; *Sheherazade*—the Arabian East; *Petrushka*, in the decorative sense and locale—Old St. Petersburg, and in its psychological emphasis—again Hoffmannism. Even *Le Sacre du Printemps* is a vision of the distant past.

Thus in all the pre-War productions there is an element of the revival of the past. One can only see in the opera *Le Coq d'Or*, by Rimsky-Korsakov, any fairylike abstract production, and even in that there is the Hoffmann touch of terrifying unreality. The only ballet of pre-War days which broke the link with the past was *Les Jeux*. This was modernism, quite up-to-date and devoid of any historical tradition. Such productions were more numerous after the War, as, for example, *Le Pas d'Acier*, which was ultra modern and without a trace of the past. But this already was beyond the influence of Benois.

"Nowadays," says Benois, "innovation has become a profession. Meyerhold is an example of this, it is a sort of Ersatz creativeness of which anyone is capable. Diaghileff was inclined towards such things and we often had to restrain him. If we did anything revolutionary it was done involuntarily, we issued no 'challenge.' We hated 'isms' as being the most repulsive manifestations of vulgarity. Things which are new, in my opinion, must come naturally, when they are *in* their creator. Such, I think, was the case when we were creating our ballets. Despite all my worship of the past I realize that what we did could not be reckoned pure reproduction. The creation, let us say, of *Les Sylphides* or *Carnaval* would have scandalized the generation of the 'thirties. But in this lies the essence of the mysticism of creativeness, that which is involuntary and often intangible. And in this lies the difference between the imitator and the creator. Our 'originality' was due rather to the fact that our relations towards art were different from those of all our contemporaries. We felt this most strongly in Paris, where nobody in the theatrical world gave himself wholly

271

to art. Our delight and faith in what we did, our absolute independence, the absence of any mercenary motive, may have seemed strange and new. Independence is rooted very deeply in the very basis of my nature; I could never have become an efficient employee or government official. I am incapable of submitting to outside pressure. It gave me, for example, special pleasure to produce in Soviet Russia the *Dame de Pique*, by Tchaikovsky, with its glorious triumph of Catherine II. It was not without its dangers, but at no cost would I have denied myself the ideas which attracted me. I am quite able to restrain myself without outside pressure. I had often to do so during my collaboration with Diaghileff, but when people begin to insist (and it is the rule with irreverent government officials), I cannot work, I become tired and, in a word, am useless. I cannot allow myself to be tied in any way and can submit to no shackles except those of religion. Yet this inborn objection to discipline has not prevented me from working during my whole lifetime, even with method and tenacity of purpose.

"Our dissatisfaction with the Russian Imperial Theatres dates from the trouble over the production of *Sylvia* in the Maryinsky Theatre. The whole company of *Mir Iskustva* painters responded enthusiastically to the invitation of the Director, Prince Wolkonsky, the more so because the idea of producing *Sylvia* was ours (and particularly mine). We put all the best that was in us into the work—to find that the officials still held the view that painters were people who had to be kept at a distance. They gave their orders but would not allow us scope for our ideas—we were like jilted lovers. The same thing happened two years later with the production of Wagner's *Götter-dämmerung*, the full control of which was entrusted to me by the new Director of the Imperial Theatre, Teliakovsky. My efforts were successful, but I was still made to feel that the 'distance' remained the same. The next invitation, to produce *Le Pavillon d'Armide*, came from the Assistant Director, Kroupensky. (At the time I had contributed several articles to the newspapers and in them I had not spared Teliakovsky.) Once again I gave myself enthusiastically and wholeheartedly to the work, but once again the venture ended in a row. Later we produced our own works. Diaghileff began his productions in Paris. We entered into it with a spirit of defiance—'Now we will show you! You wouldn't have us! You didn't want us! Then we will do it ourselves!!' "

Traits of his temperament, of his enthusiasm and his boisterous quick temper are not obvious to the casual acquaintance of Alexandre Benois, particularly now when the years have done their work. Short in stature, thick set, with a slight stoop, he gives an impression of unvarying affability and of one who despite a brusque but good-natured humour would be warm at heart. There is no trace of the explosive disposition; he is always pleasant and it is easy to talk to him, he never overwhelms one, however ignorant one may be, with his really boundless knowledge.

One day as I was leaving Benois's apartment with Prince Argoutinsky I told him that I could never imagine Benois breaking windows, shrieking curses on the whole theatre, throwing cases about, and so on.

"But why can't you?"—answered the Prince. "Can't

273

you see that under a surface of culture there dwells in him an absolute savage?"

The pronouncements of Argoutinsky always need commentaries. He spoke, of course, not of any physical likeness to a savage, but of the fact that there is in Benois a certain primitiveness and natural freshness as opposed to decrepitude. With the normal continuity of generations he should have been born in the twenties of last century, it is possible that he really belongs to that epoch, an epoch incomparably more fresh and untouched by decrepitude.

Even in the artistic sense, in his make-up he depicts the St. Petersburg of that period, a period of enlightened dilettantism and encyclopedism. The father of Russian music, Glinka, considered himself a dilettante, and in later years the group of the so-called "Big Five" did not consist of professionals: Rimsky-Korsakov was a naval officer; Moussorgsky, an officer of the guards; César Cui, a military engineer; and Borodin, a professor of chemistry. Analogous examples can easily be found in the realms of painting, sculpture, and literature. Of course the word "dilettante" in the sense in which it is now used would have been entirely inappropriate, either to the Russian creators of the beginning of the nineteenth century or to Alexandre Benois. They all attained the highest level of professionalism in their work, but in speaking of their inner personality and of their psychological outlook they cannot be referred to as professionals. Despite the fact that their achievements were often works of genius, they were not specialists and they did not concentrate either in their lives or in their work on one thing alone.

Once when talking to Benois I asked him to what artistic profession he would say he belonged.

"I myself do not know"—he answered. "Perhaps the propagation of art if this can be called a profession. But to what I am most inclined I do not know even now, after a lifetime. If I am occupied with the theatre, then at the same time I must be writing on the history of art or painting a picture which has nothing to do with the theatre. I am always working simultaneously at some side-line which is of equal importance. Thank goodness I did not become a musician in addition to all this. I have probably no less a gift for music than I have for painting, but there is one organic defect—I have no idea of metre. I have a perfect sense of rhythm, I can easily remember not only the outline of a melody but also the harmonic runs. . . . I can improvise . . . but to write down the score is beyond me. . . I cannot do it because the music and counting to me seem to cancel each other out. I can improvise both musically and choreo- graphically. The pastime which I enjoyed most in my childhood and in my early youth was the dancing which I performed to the remarkable improvisations of my elder brother Albert.[1] Unmusical dancers who have no sense of rhythm always irritate me: I could never understand how any ballet performers could dance and at the same time count to themselves—when they ought to be carried away by their rhythmical instincts. For the rehearsals before the staging of a dance it is necessary and even indispensable to count the beats, but in the actual performance this should

[1] The opinion of the Russian composer Glazounov on this subject is of interest. He told me that: "Albert Benois improvised brilliantly, very few of us professional musicians could do it as well as he did."

give way to the instinctive sense of rhythm. It is strange that although I am the son of an architect I have never been able to do anything higher in mathematics than simple arithmetic. I am a musical cripple, but I do not regret this—the theatre, painting, the study and criticism of art have sufficiently dispersed the activities of my life."[1]

Benois's musical gifts and peculiarities played an enormous part both in his life and in the creation of the *Ballets-Russes*. The choreographic improvisations of his childhood to the music of his brother formed the basis of one of the greatest ballet innovations of the Diaghilevian enterprises —a choreography which expressed the meaning of the music instead of merely a dancing to musical accompaniment.

It is true that in the eyes of the wide public of Western Europe the palm for this historical innovation belongs to Isadora Duncan, but in so far as it relates to the *Ballets-Russes*, Duncan was only a coincidence, the realization of a want which had long been felt and known. From his early childhood Benois had no other conception of a dance and when, in 1904, Duncan made her first appearance in St. Petersburg he went into raptures on seeing the spectacle of the realization of his long-cherished dream. In addition, Benois was the only one of the circle of friends who had the combined gifts of painter and musician. He was capable of being entranced by sound which captivated him. At the same time he responded to music plastically, with pictures,

---

[1] It is curious to note that the musical defect of Benois, a descendant of Franco-Italian emigrants, is specifically inherent to Russian folk music. Real Russian folklore knows no metre; ancient songs and traditional church singing cannot be forced into bars for scoring.

and with action. The whole of *Le Pavillon d'Armide*, of *Sheheraȝade* and *Petrushka*, and much also in *Cléopâtre* were created by the music-inspired visions of Benois.

In addition to the purely artistic ideas, leanings, and inventions of Benois, this capacity for musical-plastic creativeness lies at the root of many other things in the *Ballets-Russes*. In the inner laboratory where these ballets took shape—at the meetings of the friends at Diaghileff's St. Petersburg apartments—there was a constant stream of what might be termed Pythian oracular pronouncements from Benois whilst under the influence of music.

If, as he says, the encyclopedism of Benois did disperse the activities of his life it in no way detracted from the thoroughness of his attainments in each of the branches of art which fascinated him. Benois is perhaps not encyclopedic in the usual sense of the word, but rather, a combination in one man of several first-class specialists. As a painter he ranked amongst the foremost in Russia. As a professor of art he is undoubtedly one of the highest authorities and an expert. His works as an art critic are classics, and by his work in the theatre he is known throughout the world.

His enormous reserve of culture and erudition made Benois an artist of a special type. He is one of those creators who cannot be imitated, his creations, whether they be in painting proper, or in the theatre, are the result of this reserve. They are buildings which have grown on a foundation peculiar to him. His work was made possible, and can only be understood, through this foundation. Benois can be copied—but to do as he does is impossible.

The artistic importance of Benois in the history of the

art of the early twentieth century is still far from being appreciated. Those who came in touch with him mainly in the theatre in some way narrowed down his rôle—they overlooked Benois the historian. In Paris there are many who to the present day take him for a theatrical scenic painter. On the other hand, those who came in touch with him as a scientist forgot him as the theatrical creator. In actual fact his influence on his contemporaries is much wider and deeper and was mainly the result of his encyclopedism.

One day after the War Bakst, who was sitting with Prince Argoutinsky (they saw each other almost every day), said to him:

"I am probably one of the foremost painters of the day, but what will remain when I am gone? . . . Drawings . . . sketches. . . . But Benois . . . he will live in history."

And it is true. No one could write the history of Russian art without giving due regard to the enormous influence which Benois had on it. His personal artistic ideas directed the course of the revived Russian art into quite a new channel. He was the "motive power" of the revival created by *Mir Iskustva,* which changed the whole artistic atmosphere of Russia.

The revival of interest in Russian antiquity, in the paintings of the eighteenth and nineteenth centuries, in Russian artistic literature was due to his influence, to his personal leanings. As a development of this his influence is apparent in the museums and in collections. Interest in provincial monuments, in old palaces, furniture, and country mansions began to reveal itself in a wide public. It was apparent even in the printing and editing business.

278

The type which was used assumed a more ornate appearance, the paper was of better quality, rich and beautifully bound volumes were published in abundance. New and more searching cultural and artistic investigations were undertaken, taste became more refined and became the demand even of the public at large.

The great influence of Benois on world art is less well known though none the less real. So, if the *Ballets-Russes* had an importance in the realm of Western European creativeness, and this is difficult to deny, then this importance must be attributed to the man who, at the time of its creation, by his personal influence defined its artistic individuality and method of presentation. This man was Alexandre Benois. From *Le Pavillon d'Armide* to *Petrushka* he was the inspirer of the ballets. His thoughts and his leanings are the foundation of the character of the *Ballets-Russes* of that period, the purely decorative work is only a secondary part of his activity.

The art of Benois is of the type peculiar to the Russian nobleman's culture, which is little understood in the West. For some reason it is not regarded as "Russian." In Germany and France the music of Tchaikovsky is not looked upon as Russian. "What Russian music is this?"—they say. "It is the same as Mozart and Schumann." For some reason they expect something quite different when the art is classified as Russian, something of a folk-lore type, something even exotic, otherwise it is not acknowledged as being "national." The work of Rimsky-Korsakov with its folk-lore characteristics is regarded as Russian but that of Glinka and Tchaikovsky is not. Both the latter composers are typical examples of the Russian nobleman's culture. To understand this does not appear difficult. There is not one foreign reader who will get it into his head to demand folk-lore from such representatives of this nobleman's art as Tolstoi or Turgeniev, yet it is from their work, uncoloured by any exoticism, that they should be able to appreciate what is meant by this same nobleman's art. It is understood better in England. To the English a symphony by Tchaikovsky is Russian music; for some reason they are able to recognize in spite of its technical method and manner of execution the psychological complex of the work and the national physiognomy of the author.

Benois's art shows these same traits carried to the extreme. This art is St. Petersburgian, reared on the culture of St. Petersburg, it has even less specific popular shade than the music of Tchaikovsky. The folk-lore which is to be found in it (*Petrushka*, for example) is real St. Petersburg and not provincial. But this does not mean that it is not Russian. During its two hundred years as the capital of Russia St. Petersburg has developed a quite original culture. Westernism, transplanted to the Neva, produced quite a different bloom on its new soil. In this sense Benois must be considered a Russian national painter; his Franco-Italian descent is of no material importance. His family lived for 130 years in Russia, and during that time played an active part in the upliftment of the culture of St. Petersburg. Would anyone think of questioning the nationality of an American whose family were immigrants during the eighteenth century? One only needs to have a little understanding of the old Russia in order to see the nationalism of the St. Petersburg culture. To us Russians the Sixth

Symphony of Tchaikovsky is much nearer in spirit than the folk-lore style of Rimsky-Korsakov.[1]

When one remembers the old St. Petersburg as sung by Pushkin, the product of two hundred years of cultural creativeness, then in spite of one's self one thinks of Alexandre Benois, the brilliant, talented, and typical exponent of this special culture, which we all loved and which we now only recall as something long laid to rest.

The whole childhood of Alexandre Benois was imbued with the spirit of this old, patriarchal St. Petersburg with its wide, hospitable, and ample culture, and its cosiness of family life.

The old family house of his parents was very large, the circle of close relations numerous. Cousins, nieces, children, aunts, and uncles—all were often gathered there at family dinners or in the evenings when they talked and played

[1] To musicians, who may be outraged by such a statement, I must explain the foundation for this remark. Genuine Russian folk-lore can be distinguished from the fake by several main characteristics: (1) unrhymed verse; (2) rhythm, which is based on the number of syllables and cannot be confined with any strict metrical form; (3) the dance songs, in strongly accentuated rhythm (two- and four-beat metre) are exceptions to this rule; (4) the three-beat metre is unknown in Russian folk-lore; (5) in songs written in the minor key the dominant chord is also minor (the augmented seventh in the minor scale is absolutely unknown); (6) modulations are made only to the key of the dominant (major to major, minor to minor); (7) the foundation of choral singing is not harmonic but linear—the whole construction of the score should be horizontal and not vertical.

Glinka and, following him, other Russian national composers also, including Rimsky-Korsakov, infringed the above observances. They handled Russian folk-lore material as a Western European composer might have done. The great Russian music was created in that way, but, from the standpoint of genuine folk-lore, these composers were far removed from the authentic material.

together. His father was so fond of being surrounded by his family that the evening gatherings were held in his study which, on such occasions, was like a fairground. Neither the chattering nor playing which went on around him interfered with his work. He sat quietly at his large and imposing writing desk, glancing from time to time at the members of his family who surrounded him, joining in from time to time in the general conversation. On the table stood a lamp, a large, complicated object which was a survival of the days before the petrol lamp was invented. The oil which it burned was, in Benois's childhood days, not always easy to obtain. The use of matches was also not allowed by Benois's father. On the same table there was always a bundle of long wooden splints, called "fidibus," which, when needed, were lit from the fire which burned continuously in the fireplace. In a drawer of the table there was always a tinder in reserve. This tinder glowed beautifully and gave off a delightful aroma.

The older members of the family seated themselves in the same study around tables on which petrol lamps burned and the children played in the adjoining ballroom, rushing about in the endless corridor which had so many mysterious corners which were ideal for games of hide and seek. Like all children, one or the other from time to time caught some contagious sickness, then the rest of the family was removed to their grandfather's house. Playtime then was continuous. Being some years younger than Shura Benois, the children of his grown-up cousins played the part of "supers" on the stage in his enterprises.

When Benois was ten years old he was given his own room. This "red room," the floor of which had been

painted by the direction of his father with a complicated
design, was the cradle of all Benois's future artistic activity.
Here were held the magic-lantern shows; here, too, were
given the performances of his marionette theatre. One of
the first productions was *Harlequinade*, performed with
dolls which his grandmother Cavos had brought from
Venice. His later enthusiasm for the ballet *Pharaoh's
Daughter*, in which Zucchi acted with such incomparable
art, showed itself in an extremely complicated production
on the same subject. For the performances a high stage
made of boards was erected and on this the closest friends
of Benois and his future wife and her brothers were permitted to stand and operate the dolls. The lighting effects
were achieved by means of the raising and lowering of the
wicks of petrol lamps placed under the legs of the assistants.
The smell and the smoke were terrible, but providence saved
them from any outbreak of fire. In the same "red room"
Benois began the accumulation of his artistic library. He
very soon collected a mass of journals and foreign art
editions. And finally in this same room the meetings of the
"Pickwickians," the future creators of *Mir Iskustva* and
the ballets, were held.

Benois's tender years were marked by the great happenings
of Carnival (it was this Carnival, nearly forty years later,
that was re-incarnated in *Petrushka*). A sort of saturnalia
was held where crowds of people gathered together, stalls
and merry-go-rounds were erected, bearded old men vied
with each other in their shrieking to attract the people.
There were marionettes, noisy bands, conjurers, organ
grinders, harmoniums, Russian (or as they were then
called, American) scenic mountains, drunken or merely

merry loungers, peasant women and boys. All these mingled in one colourful whole, one extraordinarily amusing crowd. Smartly dressed children of the gentry, in their fur coats and accompanied by their governesses, mingled with the shabby street urchins. Society ladies and peasant women mixed together in one good-humoured crowd. Only the girls of the strict and exclusive Smolny High School were not allowed to mix with this gay crowd. They were driven in carriages round the stalls but were not allowed where the people revelled. Theirs was a handsome and pompous procession—it consisted of about twenty large and ornate carriages with coachmen and footmen in red liveries, two pairs of horses to each carriage, in which were seated eight girls with their class mistresses. As the procession moved slowly round the stalls one could see avid eyes peering through the windows.

There were several large wooden theatres in the centre of the fairground and in some of these the traditional *Harlequinade* was performed. This tradition was kept up until 1880. In the theatre at Egarev the performance remained mute, a real pantomime, but at Berg the fairy-like poesy of the action was marred by dialogue.

It was at Egarev that Benois, at the age of four, received his first theatrical baptism. This spectacle left a deep mark in his psychology, he remembered it in all its details and it was the deciding factor in many of his future leanings.

The story is well known. Pierrot and Harlequin, two lackeys in the house of the rich Cassandre, are both in love with their master's daughter, Columbine. Pierrot, who has lost his previous position as an unsuccessful poet, is the type of under-lackey. He is envious of Harlequin and engineers various plots against him. In the first act, while he is asleep, Pierrot kills him, cuts him up and goes away, after heaping the pieces up near the door. The fairy appears and with her magic wand assembles the pieces and Harlequin comes to life again, and not only that, but he receives a magic baton (Benois dreamed of this magic baton and prayed that it might be given to him). Then Harlequin begins to avenge himself on Pierrot. The next five or six tableaux are full of the adventurous pursuit of Harlequin and his kidnapping of Columbine. Before the eyes of the audience he disappears through trap doors, jumps into a mirror and into the large clock which hangs on the wall, appears in a burning fire, out of a steaming cauldron, and so on. Finally, both he and his pursuers find themselves in a very terrible hell in which enormous demons try to catch them. The performance ends with an apotheosis in which pink Cupids with flowery garlands descend from the skies to witness the marriage of Harlequin and Columbine, and the pursuers are transformed into wild beasts. The whole is accompanied by flashes of Bengal flares and a number of scenic tricks.

It seems that from these pantomimes Benois retained a love of spectacle, as such, and a tendency to regard the theatre not so much for the portrayal of philosophy, thought, music, or morality as for pure spectacle. This attitude later developed in Benois into balletomania, a love of the most spectacular of theatrical arts—the ballet.

In Benois's family the love of the theatre was traditional. His grandfather, assisted by his father, was a builder of theatres. In the Grand Theatre,[1] that huge classical temple, which was only a few steps from Benois's home and in the same street, his grandfather had a box in the second circle, near the Imperial box, specially furnished with antique Venetian furniture in rococo style. Tuesdays were set apart there for subscribers to the Italian opera. Louis Benois (later the Rector of the Academy of Fine Arts), who was fourteen years older than Alexandre, was a lover of Italian opera, and after Shura was ten years old he often took him to see the performance from the family box. But Shura was much fonder of the ballet performances and he used every pretext to persuade his doting parents to take a box for every performance. It was one form of celebration of his birthday on April 21st. Later, when his cousins grew up, two boxes had to be taken and the outings began to take the shape of a family picnic. They took chocolates, sandwiches, and bonbons with them, and during the interval held a real children's party in the small ante-room, in which tea was served from the theatre buffet.

But it must not be thought, as has already been mentioned, that in those days the glorious Russian ballet was very popular. During that period there was a prejudice against the ballet, with its bare legs, as being something immoral, suitable only for children who did not understand things and for depraved old men. The front rows of the stalls, which were occupied by the real lovers of the ballet, were usually well filled, but otherwise the auditorium

---

[1] The Grand Theatre was demolished in 1891 and on its site grew the ugly, banal building of the Conservatoire. Just opposite the Grand Theatre stood (and still stands) the Maryinsky Theatre, which was later so regrettably disfigured with "embellishments."

was deserted. Interest in the ballet was not revived until the appearance of Virginia Zucchi. There was no dearth of wonderful Russian performers even then. Outstanding were the ballerina, Evgenia Sokolova, and the plain but especially charming Gorshenkova. Madame Vazem was beautiful and Maria Mariusovna Petipa, daughter of the famous ballet master, entranced everyone with her piquant charm. Among the men, the juvenile lead Gert, the wonderful character dancer, Kchessinsky (father of the future ballerina), Stukolkin, and Lukianov must be mentioned. Litavkin was inimitable in the *genre gracieux*, whilst the Hungarian Bekeffi, one of the first foreigners to obtain a continuous engagement in the Imperial Ballet, electrified the public with his fiery performances of national dances. Later, in 1884, the slender and very pretty Alice Nikitina greatly helped towards the success of Delibes's ballet *Coppelia*.

Conscious love of the ballet began to develop in Alexandre Benois at about the time when he became enthusiastic about *Coppelia*. The appearance of Zucchi in the following year opened his eyes and converted him for a time into a real "balletomane," in which he was supported by his future fiancée and her family. Out of their own savings the young people took a box in the third circle and from there in a very boisterous way showed their appreciation. At the end of the performance they would rush to the stage door and once again pay honour to the objects of their adoration as they entered their carriages. This acute form of balletomania lasted for the whole of the three years that Zucchi spent in St. Petersburg and was revived with new force when Tchaikovsky's *The Sleeping*

*Princess* was produced in 1889. At the same time *The Sleeping Princess* was not so much the triumph of any one artiste as of the whole ensemble. Its actual creators, in addition to the great composer, were the then Director of Imperial Theatres, Vsevolozhsky, who is responsible for the idea of the ballet and the invitation to Tchaikovsky, and the ballet master, Marius Petipa.

During the next year Diaghileff arrived in St. Petersburg and through his cousin Dima Filosofov was introduced into the circle of Benois. This chance meeting was to be the starting-point of the departure which in later years became famous under the name of the *Ballets-Russes*.

It is difficult to imagine two people who in their creative qualifications were more suited to collaborate with each other, yet at the same time one could seldom meet two characters who could make such collaboration more difficult.

The artistic gifts of Benois, his enormous reserve of culture, his precise and fine taste, and his great artistic inventiveness—all these provided something which was lacking in Diaghileff. On the other hand, his impatience, explosiveness, helplessness in practical matters, his tendency to drop anything owing to a temporary distaste for it because of some unpleasant obstacle, were counterbalanced by the great fighting power of Diaghileff, by his unchecked pressure towards the attainment of a purpose, by all his genius for achievement. During the first seventeen years the whole of the direction of their activity turned on the artistic influence of Benois, but without the collaboration of Diaghileff these ideas of Benois would have remained just dreams.

Nevertheless, this mutual and indispensable collaboration did not pass without collisions, and even very frequent ones. Diaghileff was a born dictator of the Russian, somewhat obdurate type. Benois was in essence an anarchist, reacting towards any pressure with revolts and explosions. There were several long and lasting quarrels and many minor ones between them. They were everlastingly being reconciled, which, however, was perhaps not very difficult, as there was undoubtedly a very sincere bond of mutual sympathy between them and they both had the sentimental turn of mind which so strengthens friendship. Their quarrels caused both of them pain, but at the moment of the outbursts they would curse and swear at each other with all their natural fire. Benois would usually jump up, shrieking, throwing things about, and rush out of the flat. Prince Argoutinsky often filled the rôle of peacemaker. With some difficulty he would run after the departing Benois and with his usual monosyllabic insistence would bring him back and make the peace.

After the War the artistic paths of Diaghileff and Benois went apart. Their collaboration became rare and sporadic, each went his own way. But the friendship between them remained and until the day of his death Diaghileff loved Benois tenderly, looked upon him as one of his nearest and dearest friends, and referred to him as his "teacher." Even now Benois recalls Diaghileff with that sadness which one feels only in the loss of those who are nearest and dearest to one.

If one sums up the creativeness of the first ballet one can distinguish in it three main powers: Diaghileff, the man of achievement; Benois, the artistic driving power, and Fokine, the choreographer. While these three powers worked in collaboration and were consumed with the same fire the *Ballets-Russes* were created and stood on a high artistic level. When they fell apart there began, though perhaps not at once, a noticeable and slow disintegration which drove the Diaghileff enterprise later on into an artistic *cul-de-sac*.

Alexandre Benois is now sixty-five years old. He lives in a small flat on the Quai d'Auteuil in Paris. From his windows he has a similar view of the trees and the Seine to that which his grandfather, the *émigré*, had before him. At his tea table in the evenings his numerous relations and friends gather round him. Here you can meet Nouvel, Somov, and Prince Argoutinsky. Children, nephews, near and distant relations all gather together round this table covered with biscuits and fruit. Tea is served by his wife and true friend, Anna Karlovna, his guardian angel from childhood days. It is fifty-five years since she helped her husband to control the dolls in his marionette theatre. No one could resist the charm of Anna Karlovna; there is no limit to her kindness and good nature. You sometimes see in her slightly astonished appearance a look of wonderment, as if she is surprised by the cleverness and charm which she finds in you and the others. Her very presence in the room makes it more pleasant and cosy and puts you in a calm and contented mood.

Alexandre Benois has not changed much during the last ten years. As of old, he takes an almost passionate interest in everything that he meets in life, in every article and in every person. A woman's dress, the way to prepare a dish, a new edition, everything interests and absorbs him.

PLATE XXIII

ALEXANDRE BENOIS, 1935

PLATE XXIV

LEON BAKST

His colossal, almost elemental kindness shows itself particularly in his love of children and animals. A cat is more certain to jump on to his knee than to that of another person, dogs follow him in the street, and children have to be literally dragged away from him.

If one calls upon him during the daytime one will often see such a picture: in an armchair, slightly bent forward, with his spectacles on the end of his nose, sits Benois. On his knee is one of his grandchildren. On the table in front of him is a large album with drawings by Busch. Benois is showing it to his grandchild and explaining:

"Now look here! Here is a school teacher! Look at his big pipe!... His spectacles are falling off.... Oh, look ... the bridge is cracking.... Splash!... he is falling into the water. Let us turn over.... Now look at this picture...." So the story continues until they reach the end of the book. The grandchild listens, immersed in the story, and only when the last picture is reached does he say in a serious, childlike voice: "Some more." Then he will think for a moment, remember, and add "Please."

# 17

## BAKST

BAKST is one of the most significant figures in the history of the *Ballets-Russes*, which was greatly influenced by his art as a painter. Nine of his twelve productions covered the period 1909 to 1914, that is, the period when that novel and original art came into being.

Bakst's personal imprint on the face of Diaghileff's masterpieces is deep and varied. *Cléopâtre, Sheherazade, Carnaval, Narcisse, Le Spectre de la Rose, L'Après-midi d'un Faune, Daphnis and Chloë, Le Dieu Bleu, Les Jeux,* costumes for *Joseph*—one and all are tinted with the vivid colours of his handiwork.

Egypt, the Arabia of the East, Biedermeier, classical antiquity, French romanticism of the thirties, India, and contemporary sport—all these, seen through the prism of his artistic phantasy, were reproduced by him on the stage. Bakst was first and foremost a genius in the costumier's and designer's art. The elements of the true art of painting, such as we find in the work of Titian and Delacroix, he did not possess. His efforts in that direction were—for him—a failure: there always seemed to be some shadowy attempt at reproduction. Even as a decorator and creator of stage effects he did not reach the highest level; his creative powers in this were not instinctive, he had to "invent." But when Bakst came to the human form and the problem of how to drape and adorn it, then his artistry

292

carried everything before it; in this he was the perfect master and innovator. He did not merely concentrate on colouring, but supervised every detail in shape and cut.

Bakst "found himself" fairly early in life. Several of his youthful efforts in pure painting were strongly flavoured with Teutonic "problems" in the style of the so-called Anecdotists. A sad-looking woman standing forlornly near a railway line, representing "Suicide"; an old man and a young girl sitting side by side on the seashore and looking in opposite directions meant "An Ill-assorted Couple," and so on.

Then Bakst made the acquaintance of the "Pick-wickians," and, together with Benois and Somov, began to try his hand at water-colours. In a surprisingly short time he developed a marvellous technique and began to reveal his inborn gift of colour. At this time he was noticed and taken up by Benckendorff, a wealthy man and noted in St. Petersburg as a lover of painting. Benckendorff, who was familiarly known as "Mitá," started to take lessons with Bakst and gave him the benefit of his patronage in every possible way. The lessons resulted, in the most part, in the young master of twenty-five summers altering and finishing the water-colour sketches of his fifty-five-year-old pupil. But the influence of this patron was material to Bakst's career. Bakst at that time was nothing more than a poor and unimportant young Jew who had a large family dependent on him. He rose steadily, thanks to Bencken-dorff's influence, and soon was giving lessons in painting to the children of the Grand Duke Vladimir Alexandro-vitch. He even stayed during the summer at the grand duke's palace at Tsarskoe Selo. Then, through the efforts of this same Benckendorff, he was commissioned to paint a picture immortalizing the celebrations in honour of Admiral Avelan in the Place de la République in Paris. Though strongly influenced by Menzel, the picture was good. Thanks to this offer, Bakst journeyed to Paris. He was twenty-six at the time. It is strange to think that this man, who was to lead so depraved a life, began his erotic career so late. After this first rather trivial experience of Paris, Bakst was for ever floundering, to the end of his life, from one complicated love affair to another. He was for ever quarrelling and making it up, and had to be constantly rescued, reconciled, reasoned with, or consoled.

On his return to St. Petersburg Bakst became one of the most active members of *Mir Iskustva*. He collaborated in designing vignettes and even touched up photographs. In whatever he undertook he revealed unusual knowledge and skill.

It was during this period that he began his stormy amours with a French actress living at that time in Russia. This liaison left its mark quite clearly on his future life. Bakst at that time was still young and inexperienced, and, falling into the hands of this knowing and wanton woman, he lost his head completely. He even threw up his work in order to follow her to Paris.

Benckendorff was in despair. He haunted his protégé's friends and implored them to do something: "Ce pauvre Bakst! Il est en train de se perdre! Il se perd!"

This affair, like all Bakst's love entanglements, was stormy and complicated. He kept quarrelling and making it up, and eventually he returned to St. Petersburg. He returned rather a different person, no longer the modest, retiring young Jew, but an experienced man who had tasted the bitter fruit of a *grande passion*.

Bakst was given his first theatrical work in 1900, the year when the Diaghileff group was first drawn into the circle of the Imperial Theatres. He staged a short French play, *Le Cœur de la Marquise*, in the Hermitage Theatre. Here his gift for theatrical costumes was at once apparent. The production was brilliant, the costumes entrancing. Unfortunately, the play was given only once, for a Court gala performance.

Two years later, in 1902, Bakst was asked to produce at the same theatre a small Viennese ballet called *Puppenfee*. He carried out the work brilliantly, with true inspiration. The production was so successful, the ballerinas' costumes so surprising and lovely, that the ballet was included in the repertoire of the Maryinsky Theatre and enjoyed a long and successful career. Bakst gave this old-fashioned Viennese ballet the flavour of St. Petersburg of the 1850's. He loved this production and longed in later years to revive it.

Whilst at work on *Puppenfee* Bakst made the acquaintance of Lioubov Pavlovna Gritzenko, *née* Tretiakoff. She was one of the three daughters of a well-known merchant prince. Of the other two sisters, one married Dr. Serge Botkine, the Court physician and a member of the Diaghileff circle, and the other the famous pianist and conductor Zilotti. Material and social considerations were never taken into account by the madly amorous Bakst. A romance sprang up and the young couple decided to get married. But this was not so easy. By the old Russian law marriage between a Jew and a Christian was forbidden. Madly in love, Bakst found that he would have to be

baptized. It was not easy for him to agree to this; all his
life he had been a good and orthodox son of Israel. He
was proud of his Jewish blood and of the religion of his
forefathers. In his youth one of his favourite subjects for
discussion had been the theory that Christianity was
nothing more than a feeble offshoot of that great and
ancient old tree, Judaism. He had even wished at one time
to paint a picture in which Judas would be Christ's favourite
disciple and the only opponent worthy of being pitted
against Him.

Conversion to Christianity proved a difficult matter for
Bakst. He pondered long and shrewdly over how he could
do this in the simplest and most practical way. At length
he sought out in Warsaw an Anglican minister who most
nearly fulfilled his requirements. "He is very nice," said
Bakst. "It will be quite simple and quick."

Returning from Warsaw, whither he had made the
journey for the sole purpose of being baptized, Bakst
began to make arrangements for the wedding. Another
hitch occurred. The authorities demanded proof of his
conversion—that he had gone to confession and received
Holy Communion. Bakst appealed to the Anglican minister
in St. Petersburg to give him the Sacrament.

"You must be confirmed first," said the priest.

"Well, confirm me, then!"

"I cannot do that. . . . Only a bishop can confirm."

"Well, where is the bishop?"

"In England. He only comes over once in three years
for confirmations."

"Will he be over soon?"

"No, he has just been."

So all that he had accomplished was to no purpose. Bakst had to abandon Protestantism and embrace Greek orthodoxy.

Bakst did not hesitate to emphasize to his friends that this change of religion was compulsory; he wanted them all to know that he was still a Jew at heart and that baptism was merely an unavoidable formality. He was annoyed, therefore, by the congratulatory letters which some of them sent him.

In spite of all this trouble, Bakst's domestic happiness was not of long duration. Troubled, apparently, by a tiresome conscience, he took to his bed during 1904, the victim, for the first time, of that strange malady which twenty years later, in a third and deadly attack, ended his life. There were all the absurd signs of an imaginary illness. Neither his friends nor his doctor saw anything alarming in it. There was not a symptom of real illness, not one organic defect. Baskt simply lay in bed and declared that he was dying. It was even comical, though, of course, Bakst always distinguished himself in this respect; he was comical in spite of his gravity, he was highly esteemed, respected, and loved, but he was always rather funny. He was teased and laughed at—as one of them said, he was a "continual operetta." Bakst was used to this; it had been the custom since his early childhood, and all his life he responded to his friends' waggishness and mockery with his usual good humour.

After their marriage the Baksts took a luxurious flat, where they often entertained their friends. One day they found Mrs. Bakst was there alone to greet them.

"Where is Levoushka?"

"I don't know what is the matter with him, he is ill."

"What? . . . Ill?"

"I don't really know what is wrong with him. . . . He is in bed and won't let anyone go near him. . . . He says he is ill."

In spite of this injunction the friends burst into Bakst's room. There he lay on an immense and elaborate bed, his pointed nose, his short-sighted eyes, and the shock of carroty hair protruding from under the bedclothes. The whisper of a weak, dying voice was heard:

"No . . . it's no use. . . . I can't carry on any longer . . . you don't understand, Shoura, but I am dying . . . woe is me . . . I feel that it is the wrath of Jehovah!" No argument to the contrary could shake his belief. Despite the doctor's assurances he kept insisting that he was dying. He would listen to no arguments or persuasion, and when his friends quoted the doctor's assurance he would answer: "As though he would tell me. . . . He is so kind, he loves me too much . . . and you . . . you wouldn't tell me either."

This illness of Bakst was not taken seriously by his friends or even by his doctor; they looked upon it as one of his extravagances and treated it as a joke.

Soon there were misunderstandings with his wife, mutual quarrels and recriminations. Bakst, it appeared, could not forgive her because he had on her account been baptized and had thereby angered Jehovah.

In 1905, at the time of the first Russian revolution, Benois took his family to live at Versailles. The Baksts followed him there. By that time they were quarelling almost every day; they could not be reasoned with or reconciled. Bakst was furious and abusive, and reconciliation was impossible. They parted for good then and there.

At the time, as a result of the rising tide of revolution which was sweeping Russia, a new law was passed granting freedom of religion. Bakst lost no time in seizing this opportunity of returning to Judaism and making his peace with his Jehovah. This return to Judaism had, nevertheless, legal consequences, because, although freedom of religion was allowed, the marriage of a Jew to a Christian still remained illegal, so that his return to his old faith meant the annulment of his marriage. He found himself not merely separated but divorced from his wife.

During the Russian Exhibition in Paris in 1906 the friends tried several times to talk to Bakst of his former wife. They always received the same curt reply: "Don't talk to me about that woman, I don't wish to know her."

One day one of his friends called at Bakst's hotel and knocked at the door of his room. He heard a commotion within, but the door was not opened. Surmising that there was a woman inside, the friend discreetly went away. Next day, to everybody's surprise, Bakst appeared at the Exhibition with his former wife. The mysterious lady in Bakst's room had been Mrs. Bakst! They lived together again and seemed to be the best of friends.

The complexities of Bakst's character were only noticeable in his matrimonial and love affairs; in his other everyday relations, in business and with his friends, he was an equable, pleasant, and even shy creature. With him one always felt happy and amused and at perfect ease, knowing that if Bakst was there everything would be pleasant and merry.

This combination of good nature with his involuntary drollness was the secret of Bakst's particular charm. It was fun to tease him, he reacted in an amusing and good-humoured way. Once Benois drew Bakst in a new Parisian coat with one button missing. He must have done it on purpose, because Bakst was always meticulous and fussy about his clothes. Bakst looked at the drawing and became quite excited. "Draw a button here at once!" he shouted. "I tell you, Shoura, you must put a button there, immediately!" His outburst was greeted with roars of laughter, and Benois, needless to say, refused to insert the button, and so the drawing remained.

The friends always treated his illnesses on account of Jehovah's wrath as a huge joke, and Bakst was not at all offended. Often he was too meek, and the friends had to take his part against Diaghileff. So, at the first performance of *Cléopâtre*, which was Bakst's first work for the *Ballets-Russes*, Diaghileff, annoyed for some reason, refused to send for him to come to Paris. Bakst was penniless in St. Petersburg and was unable to undertake the journey at his own expense. To the arguments of his friends all that Diaghileff would say was: "Well, what about it? He has done the *mise en scène*; isn't that enough for him?" They had to insist, almost force Diaghileff to send the money. Bakst arrived, not in the least degree offended or hurt. But although modest and gentle, Bakst, deep down in his heart, knew his own worth; he had enormous inner pride and self-assurance. When, as a lad, he was asked the usual question, "What would you like to be?" he always answered, "The greatest painter in the world." Later in life he considered that he had attained his ambition: "I am

PLATE XXV

LEON BAKST

*Sketch by A. Benois*

PLATE XXVI

MICHAEL FOKINE

certainly the greatest painter in the world; I am the Russian Veronese."

In religion he was equally unshakable; he considered ancient Judaism the highest and most significant of all religious doctrines.

In one respect Bakst differed completely from the other members of the Diaghileff group. He was a cosmopolitan. Neither in his taste nor in his art is there anything national, anything Russian. Benois, in spite of his origin, had absorbed the spirit of St. Petersburg; Diaghileff was a typical Russian; Stravinsky was St. Petersburgian to the minutest fibres of his being; but Bakst was an internationalist. Nor was he Western European in his art; his work was in some way not specifically but generally cultured. The whole diapason of his achievements proves this. In his work for the *Ballets-Russes* he encroached on an unusual number of styles and periods of different nations. He was as equally at home in ancient Greece, in a Persian harem, as on a tennis court. At the same time one feels that he, in spite of his genius, had no real "home." He could not have created *Petrushka*, a work that was St. Petersburg in every line and thought. Bakst did not seem Russian either in his manner or in his personality; he was very pleasant, very cultured, and cosmopolitan.

At the time of the first productions of the *Ballets-Russes* he was Diaghileff's faithful shadow. In painting he was a "Jack of all trades," and apart from his own work he gave a hand to everyone around him. Diaghileff and he were constantly bickering and abusing one another, but they had no real quarrels. They seemed to have been born to collaborate. Bakst's pliability in everyday matters and his

inborn good nature helped him to bear Diaghileff's way-
ward and rather tyrannical rule, and in the artistic sense
the freedom and scope that Diaghileff gave his craftsmen
was essential to Bakst's creative work. When on holiday
they usually separated, Diaghileff going, generally with
Nijinsky, to Karlsbad and the Lido, and Bakst to St.
Petersburg. The law passed in 1905 relieved him of any
vexations on acount of religion, at any rate until 1913,
when on returning to the Hotel Astoria, where he usually
stayed, he was unpleasantly surprised to receive a visit
from the police with an order that he must leave St.
Petersburg within twenty-four hours and settle inside the
zone reserved by law for Jews.[1]

There was a tremendous hullabaloo. Everyone stormed
and protested, attempts at string-pulling were made, even
a grand duchess intervened. It was all to no avail. It
appeared that the Freedom of Religion Law had been
qualified and that no evasion could on any account be
permitted. Bakst was obliged to leave the country in haste.
He found himself in opposition to the entire Russian
Government and its laws. He never returned to Russia, but
settled down in Paris, where he remained until his death.

During the War his collaboration with Diaghileff continued, and he was given the production of *Les Femmes
de Bonne Humeur*, to music by Scarlatti.

Bakst was once again parted from his wife, though this
time on friendly terms. She remained in Russia, and during
the Revolution, and particularly during the most acute

[1] This was the extent of country in which it was lawful for Jews to
reside. It included western and south-western Russia. They were not
permitted to live in the capitals.

years of Bolshevism, she suffered great moral and physical hardships. The conditions in which she lived can be judged from the story of the death of her faithful old servant Christopher. He was devoted to her and would not leave her. He used to go out each morning to get the few things needed for their modest existence. When he returned in the evenings he would go straight to his room. One day Christopher did not make his appearance. Mrs. Bakst waited two days, and then went upstairs to investigate. She found him dead in his room. It was in the worst days of Bolshevism, there was no telephone, and no means of getting help. The poor woman had to do everything herself—get the coffin, put his body in it, drag it down six flights of stairs into the street. There she put the coffin on a sledge and dragged it through the snow to the church-yard, and there with her own hands buried her poor Christopher.

There were no means of communication with Western Europe and Bakst knew nothing of his wife's plight. In 1920 Prince Argoutinsky managed to escape from Russia. Having crossed the frozen Finnish Gulf on a sledge, taking with him a large sack in which a precious collection of miniatures was hidden among potatoes, he reached Finland, and from there journeyed to Paris. He was not able to get in touch with Bakst at once, as the latter was just recovering from the second attack of his mysterious malady. Argou-tinsky had to write and explain as best he could. Bakst at last consented to receive him at Le Pecq, where he was living with a sister and niece who had managed to escape from Russia. Bakst gave the impression of being half crazy. "You know, I am nearly blind; I cannot look at the light," was his greeting. Upon hearing the story of his wife's sufferings he became very agitated, walking up and down the room and repeating: "No, no . . . don't tell me . . . it is so awful . . . we will talk about it later." After a while he calmed down, and eventually saw Argoutinsky to the station.

Bakst that day must have presented a strange sight to the people of Le Pecq, as he walked through the streets, collarless, with the Legion of Honour in his buttonhole, and blue spectacles shading his tired eyes. He seemed pleased, however, to see Argoutinsky, and insisted that he should come again. Argoutinsky succeeded eventually in making his wife's position clear to him, and even explained how he could send her some money. At the time Bakst was at the height of his fame and earning large sums of money. He began to send his wife a thousand francs a month. Benois, who was in Russia at that time, says that thanks to this money Mrs. Bakst was transformed in a day from a pauper into a rich woman. A thousand francs was a lot of money in those days; with so much the owner could have given dinner parties and entertained on quite a large scale.

The doctor who was treating Bakst at the time asked Argoutinsky to do his utmost to get Bakst out of the dismal atmosphere in which he was living. Argoutinsky asked him to go to Mentone, a suggestion to which Bakst not only agreed but almost jumped. They left the next day. Some time elapsed before Bakst returned in his normal frame of mind. Except to walk in the garden he seldom left the hotel, he slept badly, and was worried. At night he often called Argoutinsky. "My heart is beating like a hammer; I am alone . . . I am afraid," he would say in great distress.

Argoutinsky could rarely leave him. One day, after lunching out with some friends, on returning to the hotel he was met on the steps by a frightened proprietor, who told him that during his absence Bakst had been pacing from room to room; he was unable to settle anywhere, and was fearfully excited.

Bakst's condition gradually improved. He was able to take walks with Argoutinsky, and they even went by car from Mentone to Italy. At last Argoutinsky was able to leave him and return to Paris. Bakst followed him a fortnight later.

By this time his relations with Diaghileff were already very strained. The trouble was that some time previously Bakst had accepted the stage management of a revue at the Théâtre Marigny, and Diaghileff, with his natural jealousy, was angry that Bakst should collaborate with anyone else. The revue was not a success; not only was the production weak, but the whole enterprise broke up, and Bakst was not even paid for his work. His relations with Diaghileff were spoiled; they parted in anger. Diaghileff asked Argoutinsky to act as peacemaker. At the time Diaghileff had been entrusted by Stoll with the production of Tchaikovsky's *The Sleeping Princess*. It was expected that Benois, who was still in Russia, would produce it; but his escape did not materialize, and, through Argoutinsky, Bakst was asked to undertake the work. He set about it with zest. The production was very successful; it ran for three consecutive months and was performed ninety times. Unfortunately, it could not be revived, as the scenery, the costumes, and the effects were all seized for debts and sold by auction. Later, when Diaghileff wanted to put it on again in Paris, he had to content himself with one act and use the décor of *Le Pavillon d'Armide*.

All through this period Bakst was in communication with his wife. He wrote her warm and affectionate letters. Separated by thousands of miles, they were the best and closest of friends. Eventually he decided to get his wife and son out of Russia. Their reunion in Paris was very touching, but for Bakst somehow it was a disillusionment. He did not want to live with them; they separated, and he granted them a meagre allowance.

All this happened in 1923, the year of Bakst's final break with Diaghileff. It was brought about by Diaghileff's entrusting a French artist with the scenery and costumes for Stravinsky's opera *Mavra*. It was thought at first that Bakst would undertake this; he had even signed a contract to this effect. The root of the trouble may have been that in 1919 Diaghileff had entrusted the production of *La Boutique Fantasque* to Derain instead of to Bakst. This ballet was a new version of the same *Puppenfee* which, so far back as 1902, had been Bakst's first theatrical success and which he had always longed to produce again. Now he brought an action against Diaghileff and would not come to terms. Diaghileff once again asked Argoutinsky to act as mediator, but Bakst obstinately refused, saying: "You forget that I am a Jew, and my God is a God of vengeance." The affair went so far that under Bakst's instructions bailiffs were sent to the stage of the Grand Opera in Paris to hold up Diaghileff's production. All efforts were in vain; he stood his ground and refused to become reconciled. The fact that Bakst did not agree with the artistic tendencies of Diaghileff's new work must have played a part in this. He felt that Diaghileff had betrayed the artistic principles which they had previously had in common. So the entrusting of *Mavra* to another producer was the last drop in an overflowing cup. Bakst, so tractable in everyday life, was immovable where his artistic conscience was concerned. He would not give in.

There were no signs of another attack of his illness. He was gay, healthy, and on good terms with his other friends. He had just returned, in very good spirits, from a successful business trip to America.

In the summer of 1924 he undertook the production of *Antar* for Ida Rubinstein. During a rehearsal something happened which was to be followed by his last illness. He suddenly lashed himself into a state of great excitement, without any justification, and, bursting into wild and abusive shrieks, ran out of the theatre. It was all so unlike Bakst. From that day none of his friends saw him again. At first he kept to his bed in his flat, then he was transferred to Malmaison, where no one was allowed to see him. What was the matter with him and what he died of remains a mystery. To the usual signs of imaginary illness were added symptoms of a real disease. There was talk of arteriosclerosis and kidney and heart trouble, but nothing was definite or clear. It seemed as though his organism had suddenly heard him and, obeying his sick soul, refused to work any longer.

So died this strange man, so modest and at the same time so firmly convinced that he was the greatest painter in the world, so easy-going and yet, in the depths of his soul, possessing such a great store of energy and pugnacity; ridiculous and absurd . . . and yet a genius.

307

# 18

## MICHAEL FOKINE

MICHAEL FOKINE was never a member of the inner group of friends and creators of the ballet. He did not come into contact with it until the members of *Mir Iskustva* were approaching the age of forty. Only occasionally was he called into that workshop where they conceived and worked on the ideas which took shape in their ballet productions. Their plans, when they reached him, were usually more or less worked out and needed only the finishing master touch.

Fokine's career as a producer of ballets began quite independently of the *Mir Iskustva* group with the small ballet *Evnika*, in which he revealed his creative ability.

At that time and afterwards he was regarded by the encyclopedists of *Mir Iskustva* as an authority on one thing only. It must also be admitted that the cultural level of the Russian ballet was not high; ballerinas and male dancers were not educated people, their interests were limited, and they were not interested in art outside the narrow sphere of their immediate concern—the ballet. One could not discuss any other subject with them; they simply would not have understood the Diaghilevian topics of conversation. They knew how to dance and to act, and that was all.

In this milieu, of course, Michael Fokine stood apart. The co-ordination of the ballet with other arts meant something to him. He had an appreciation of music and the plastic arts, he could draw and painted in his spare time, and was one of the few men of the ballet who visited museums. He was an eagle among his likeable but simple and somewhat dull ballet colleagues.

Benois's first appreciation of Fokine was a very pleasing one. It was in the summer of 1907. On the recommendation of Nicolas Tcherepnin, and after the success of *Evnika*, Fokine had been asked by the theatre directors to stage *Le Pavillon d'Armide*. He went to Benois, who at the time was working on the décor of his ballet. Young and strong, with a pleasant face, an easy manner, and burning eyes, Fokine seemed to overflow with health and energy and the will to work. Even in that his first experience of joint creative labour he showed qualities which not only the ordinary ballet workers but even the best choreographers in St. Petersburg lacked. He *understood*. After one or two discussions this youthful "barbarian" began to know something of the style of the period. He had never heard of Hoffmann, but he soon realized how much was Hoffmannesque in the subject and in the dramatic part of the production. Intuitively he saw the required light and shade of the dance and the scene and knew how to bring it out. With great poetic feeling he made the goblin come to life, and in the same way he brought out the comic element of one of the *divertissements*, "Abduction from the Seraglio."

It at once became obvious that in Fokine there were creative possibilities quite unlike those of the old St. Petersburg masters of the ballet. Leaving Marius Petipa, a veteran who had been working on the Maryinsky stage for the last sixty years, out of it, even the young *maîtres de ballet* such as Legat were not capable of such subtleties. Petipa, who had rendered such invaluable services to the Russian ballet of the nineteenth century, was still devoted to the fairy-tale style (the style of *The Sleeping Princess* production). He, of course, could not have satisfied the requirements of men who came, as it were, from outside, in no way under the domination of the time-honoured theories and principles of the ballet world. Their experience of collaboration with Legat, as early as 1901, in the production of *Sylvia*, had shown the *Mir Iskustva* group that he also could not be made to understand.

The difference between Fokine and the other ballet masters was not in the tendency of his art or in some singular originality. It was a difference of quality. He was more talented and more alive than they were, he saw more clearly and more deeply, he was in fact more *kulturfähig* and more daring. Moreover, he was young and burning with the desire to create. Fokine did not aim at destroying existing things; he had, on the contrary, a very real respect for the old school, the school to which he owed his own mastery. In his art he was a "tolerant liberal," correcting and improving on the past, but in no way casting it aside. There was no affectation about him, he created with simplicity and never pandered to any of the new "isms." In this respect he was quite the opposite to Nijinsky and Diaghileff, who, in *L'Après-midi d'un Faune, Les Jeux*, and *Le Sacre du Printemps*, aimed chiefly at new forms and the upsetting of tradition. In this he differs also from the whole post-War work of the *Ballets Serge de Diaghileff*, in which innovation was always the deciding factor.

In our time there is a tendency to return to the methods

of the old days. The work of that highly gifted choreographer Massine is a return to the classics, to the "absolute" and the "ratified." It goes without saying that Massine, like Fokine in his day, must keep in mind the requirements of the age, but the foundation at the root of their work is the same.

Fokine was distinguished from his contemporaries of the ballet world chiefly by the warmth of his temperament and by the fact that his imagination was quicker and more vivid.

In private life he was a simple and pleasant companion who liked to entertain guests in his snug flat at the "five corner," and later by the Ekaterinsky Canal. He liked to joke and enjoy himself. At work he was a different man: the spirit of the dance took possession of him and he burned with an inward fire.

This is how Benois described Fokine at work:

"One must see Fokine at rehearsals to realize his significance. He becomes cruel, spiteful, and unbearable. He is obviously the *bête noire* of the officials of the Russian theatre, and naturally even among his comrades he has many enemies—dancers whom he has offended by his unrelenting exactness and his merciless criticism. But it is in this very cruelty and obduracy in his demands that Fokine proved himself the truly great artiste, so carried away by his subject, so eager to realize what his inspiration dictates, that to achieve this realization he is prepared to crush and break up all obstacles."

This fanatical cruelty in work is a common characteristic of the inspired creator. One of the most fanatical artistic workers that I have ever seen, C. S. Stanislavsky, behaved like a grand inquisitor at rehearsals. I remember one occasion where a young actor playing the part of a messenger had to repeat his entry sixty-four times. The part of this unfortunate youth consisted of five words—"From Ouglich to Boyarin Boris." It was not at all unusual for the actresses to burst into tears.

Fokine was a similar inspired fanatic. It was thanks to this that he adapted himself so easily to the Diaghileff group. They were all afire with the zeal and urge to create; Fokine suited the group as no other could have done.

Fokine's method when he was at work on the production of ballets was peculiar to himself. Before the rehearsals he would sometimes draw graphs of the mass movements on the stage. He might draw plans on paper, or with a piece of chalk he would mark out on the floor the big entries and groups. He was interested in the vertical as well as the horizontal scenic effects, which meant that sometimes he would ask Benois to go to the top of the house to see how it appeared from that angle. He seemed to visualize the groupings so dear to the hearts of cinema ballet masters and their all-seeing cameras.

He would compose the dances on the stage to the music as it was being played. He did not produce any passage to begin with in its entirety, but split it up, working at each part in detail, always adding and altering, and often not knowing how it would look when completed.

At times he would leave this mosaic work and in one stroke complete entire scenes or even the whole ballet. It was here that he produced some of his best work—the "Bacchanal" in *Cléopâtre*, the "Dance of the Jesters" in *Le Pavillon d'Armide*, the "Polovetz" dances, the Russian dance in *Petrushka* and *Le Spectre de la Rose*. All these he worked in their entirety.

312

No one can deny that Fokine had true and inspired creative powers. He was, moreover, daring, and not afraid to depart from the established aesthetic canons or to give play to his temperament. Many of his productions gripped and held the spectator.

It was in his time that an important secret of the art—the school of gesture—was lost. This traditional school, established probably in the days of Vestris and Noverre, lasted throughout the nineteenth century on the Russian Imperial stage. It was still upheld by the aged Gert at the beginning of the twentieth century. They were rare restrained gestures, very exact, and because they were so controlled they were very expressive.

In the *Ballets-Russes* there was only one such master of gesture—Nijinsky. He possessed it intuitively, and not because of any training. In the choreography of Fokine these plastic controlled gestures had been replaced by freer and more personal expressions of the mood.

Dramatic expression in production figured least in Fokine's artistic make-up; he even felt some revulsion for pantomimic art. This might have been because mime, in the State Theatre schools, was instilled as something very lifeless and stale. He was too young to have seen Zucchi, who had demonstrated what mime on the stage could mean. "What is the use of waving one's hands about?" Fokine used to say. He had to be told and almost shown how to "drag out bar after bar." On such occasions he seemed helpless and almost afraid. "Won't it be dull?" he would ask. It took some persuasion to convince him that anything which was truly expressive could not be dull. It is certainly true that *Le Pavillon d'Armide, Sheherazade,* and *Petrushka* all owe their success to that very significant truth brought out in each case by dramatic mime.

Owing to this fear of proving dull, Fokine was inclined to fill his stage to overflowing with performers.

In spite of the fact that he cannot be regarded as one of Diaghileff's intimate circle, Fokine must be looked upon as one of the most significant creative forces in the *Ballets-Russes*, no less significant than Bakst or Stravinsky. Two of the most brilliant ballets of the early days, *Cléopâtre* and *Carnaval*, came into the Diaghileff repertoire only through his medium. Fokine arranged them for some charity performances in St. Petersburg. It was thanks to his initiative and thought that they came into being.

The most significant fact is that without Fokine and his choreographic achievements the *Ballets-Russes* would have assumed quite a different appearance. To appreciate his particular merit and achievement one must perhaps be a Russian and remember the Imperial Ballet. Fokine astounded us Russians by his daring and originality. In the place of the highly respectable "prettiness" which we so well knew, instead of the well-drilled fairies, we saw the unbridled passions of the harem, scenes full of lyricism and poesy, and lively, colourful ensembles. Freedom, daring, and unity took the place of the former severe and absolute ballet routine with its *pas seul, pas de deux,* and so on. Fokine was an innovator, and his originality directed the whole current of ballet art into a different channel, where it will continue to flow for some time yet. He achieved this, of course, only in collaboration with the members of the group, but the part he played is lasting and invaluable.

314

# 19

# NIJINSKY

TO understand and appreciate Nijinsky to the full it must be known that he came of a family connected with the circus. I foresee much indignation and protests at such a statement: "What! Nijinsky! The God of the Dance! The highest, the greatest genius that the ballet art has produced . . . and you dare to mention circuses!"

But it is the truth, and, to my mind a necessary truth. Both his father and his mother were connected with the circus and to this day his uncle works as a clown in some show or other.

Without this circus lineage, these generations of acrobats behind him, it would be difficult to explain his extraordinary physical gifts. His lightness which was beyond all technique, his renowned *élévation* would be quite inexplicable. It would, of course, be absurd to credit the circus with all that this man accomplished, his genius was developed in quite another sphere—that of the ballet. Yet his natural and inherent physical gifts were due to and sprang from the circus.

There is, moreover, nothing degrading in the art of the circus; it attains the same heights as any other art. Did it not produce that wonder of wonders, Little Tich? Is not clowning the art of one of our most gifted contemporaries —Charlie Chaplin? The circus, nowadays, has become a forgotten art, it has been submerged and its possibilities are underrated by us. It is in approximately the same plight as the ballet art was in Western Europe prior to the advent of Diaghileff. Yet in the circus we find that which is most essential to art, namely, art-tradition. True classical clowning has not yet died out, its root must be sought as far back as the Italian Harlequinade and the Commedia dell'Arte. A good circus has traditions and therefore, style, in the true sense of the word. It is the branch of art which is on the brink of a renaissance, all it needs is a leader, and creators, who will raise it back to its true level as a great and noble art.

I think that Romola Nijinska was ill-advised when she carefully withheld in her book any precise information as to the "theatres" in which her husband's people worked. There is nothing shameful in the fact that these were, for the most part, circuses. Nijinsky's art ranks so high in the history of human achievement that the slightest detail is both important and essential, provided it throws some light on his unusual gifts.

Of all the people I have met in the course of more years than I like to remember, I can apply the term "genius" only to Chaliapine in his youth, and Nijinsky. In the latter there was something rare which was not to be found in other people. He danced as birds sing, with that joy and simplicity natural only to one who found dancing the one way in which to pour out his soul. He seemed to have been born for dancing and for nothing else. His every movement was natural, light, and unique. No other dancer used his hands, inclined his head or moved his body as he did. His movements were so plastic and yet so surprisingly simple and convincing: there was nothing artificial, strained, or faked about him. He seemed to speak to you from the stage in his own particular and natural language of movement, and you seemed to grasp the meaning of his message although you could never translate it into words.

His *élévation*, by which I mean the way he had of rising in the air, remaining motionless and slowly descending, has always remained a mystery to me; it seemed obvious that the law of gravity did not exist for him. He remained in the air as long as he pleased and returned to earth just when he felt like it, not when he was compelled. I have often pondered over this strange "illusion," longing to get to the bottom of it and to discover the "trick." I timed his leaps and tried them myself at home. My time was the same—I was young then and could jump. But whereas Nijinsky floated in the air, I saw myself through the looking glass falling heavily like a sandbag. The secret of this illusion might have been in the extraordinary plastic quality of his jump: it was so free and beautiful. Whether he rose or whether he fell, he swept into the air without the slightest effort and the lightness and beauty of this dive into space was beyond words. It might have been that the secret was in the impression he conveyed of all that he still had in reserve to give. In just the same way, certain Italian tenors, reaching the topmost and most dramatic note of their arias give the impression that they could go much higher. Having reached the top "C" they could, it seems, go up through the whole scale. Nijinsky gave the same impression of un-exploited and infinite possibilities. When he did his famous *entrechat* ten you were firmly convinced that he could do a twenty.

Nijinsky accomplished every variety of movement

with marvellous ease. In *Le Spectre de la Rose* there is a scene where, jumping from foot to foot, like children do, he would make the whole round of the stage. I can remember the audience of the Metropolitan Opera in New York—one of the most stolid and immovable audiences in the world—letting out, at the sight of him, something which was between a sigh and a groan. There was no applause—just that strangled cry. Nijinsky travelled through the air, just above, but never seeming to touch the ground. Like an autumn leaf he came lightly down.

*Carnaval* was another of his ballets. Nijinsky as Harlequin was something quite different. Like a bouncing rubber ball he rose and fell from the floor as if there was something there that refused to keep him but sent him on again into the next jump.

In another ballet, the classical *Les Sylphides,* he seemed to be caught up like a feather, his hands and feet just flashed in the happiness of an airy dance and his soul lived in it.

In *Petrushka* his movements were again quite different. His first dance on emerging from the fair booth, a Russian dance, was very *terre à terre*, rhythmical, and full of energy. It was the weird, mechanical dance of a clockwork doll, angular and full of kinetic temperament.

I pity from the depths of my heart all those who did not see him. No words can describe the lasting impression that he produced. It was a peculiar impression, he was so unlike anyone else, his manner was so clearly individual and personal. You could not say: "Woizikovski and Massine are different from Nijinsky because . . ." It would not have explained anything. In technique it is easier to explain

318

PLATE XXVII

VAZLAV NIJINSKY (IN SIAMESE COSTUME, 1911)
*By J. E. Blanche*

PLATE XXVIII

COSTUMES DESIGNED FOR NIJINSKY IN "PAVILLON D'ARMIDE"

*By A. Benois*

—one can say, for instance, that his technique was so perfect that it was no longer noticeable, looking at his dance you found it so simple that you felt that you yourself could have done it. But artistically, Nijinsky cannot be described or explained. When his career came to an end his art died, like the art of many histrionic geniuses. It has not been preserved by any mechanical means and those who did not see it will never feel it or understand.

In addition to this unique gift of the dance, Nijinsky had a great dramatic gift. He could be expressive—amazingly so. Petrushka's last gesture, when he appears above the fair booth and looks down on the terrified magician, doll in hand, was shattering. The outstretched hands and crooked fingers, the broken, puppet-like bend of the body, and the face grimacing tragically as in the throes of some macabre passion he seemed to be reproaching the magician: "What have you done to me? Why have you ruined my poor immortal soul?" The curtain fell on this arresting movement whilst the orchestra shrieked this tragic, unfinished and questioning phrase.

Nijinsky's influence on the art of the ballet was great. There had always been male dancers on the Russian Imperial stages. So long ago as the seventies, Gert the magnificent, was already renowned. The brothers Legat were brilliant dancers in a later period, and they were followed by others. Every year the Imperial schools sent out batches of highly accomplished pupils. Without this tradition of the St. Petersburg schools there would have been no Nijinsky. But the significance of male choreography changed with Nijinsky. Previously the rôle of the male dancer had been auxiliary, he had merely been the supporter of the prima ballerina. There had been male *pas seuls*, but they were short ones to which no one attached great importance. They merely gave the ballerina a rest. Dramatic talent, mimicry, and character dancing were more important in male dancing. It was only after Nijinsky that a man could take the principal part in a classical ballet. He made the male dancer the equal of the ballerina and established equality between the male and female elements of the ballet. In this way he influenced the moulding of the ballet art and of the librettos. Such productions as *Le Spectre de la Rose*, *Narcisse*, and *Petrushka*, where the male dancer takes the centre of the stage, did not make their appearance in the repertoire of the *Ballets-Russes* until its third season, late in 1911. This was the immediate result of Nijinsky's genius and his two years of overwhelming success.

Was the man a creator as well as a gifted dancer? It is a hard question to answer and any answer could only be surmise. According to the reminiscences of his wife Nijinsky was a great choreographic innovator. Unfortunately one cannot rely on her book as one which provides solid material on which to build. It is, actually, difficult to define Nijinsky's part in productions, hard to tell where he begins and where Diaghileff leaves off. It would have been easier if Nijinsky, after the break with Diaghileff, had proved his creative powers in some way. Unfortunately he did not do so. His attempt in 1914 to run his own ballet company in London was a sudden and complete failure. Whether Nijinsky had in him the makings of a gifted choreographer may be questionable, but there is no doubt that he was quite unsuited to the job of theatrical manager. Moreover, his enterprise in London was tacitly taboo—to go to the *Ballets-Russes* and to applaud and get enthusiastic about its productions was not only permissible, but was "the thing" in the snobbish social sense, but to patronize the Nijinsky productions was decidedly a social *faux pas*.

According to the account that Benois gives, Nijinsky's plans and ballet theories at that time (he was then seeking a reconciliation with Diaghileff) were hazy, naïve, and even childish. Benois was frankly sceptical about his ability for independent artistic creation. I believe the only attempt of Nijinsky in that direction apart from the 1914 London production was the ballet *Tyl Eulenspiegel* to Richard Strauss's music, which he did in America in 1916. It was only given three times and left no impression on the ballet art.

Nijinsky, during his friendship with Diaghileff, is supposed to have produced three ballets—*L'Après-midi d'un Faune*, *Les Jeux*, and *Sacre du Printemps*. It is hard to say who was the real author of these ballets. *L'Après-midi d'un Faune* certainly bears traces of Bakst's passion for archaic Greece. Bakst and Serov had just returned, delirious with rapture, from a tour of Crete and Greece. They did more than give verbal expression to their enthusiasm, the tour inspired from Serov the painting *The Rape of Europa*, and from Bakst *Terror Antiquus*. The ballet *Narcisse* must also be put down to Bakst's enthusiasm. We find the same idea in *L'Après-midi d'un Faune*.

Diaghileff always liked to push his fellow workers into the limelight; like the good owner of a large stable he loved his racehorses, he showed them off and was proud of them. This sentiment, naturally, was very strongly expressed in Nijinsky's career—the urge to make a choreographer of him was one of the few mistakes in Diaghileff's life. Nijinsky was his *grande passion* and Diaghileff found it difficult to view him impartially. His unmistakable genius and his overwhelming success as a dancer were not enough for Diaghileff, who did not love lightly. He believed that with his help and with the artistic milieu that he had built around him, Nijinsky would become an independent constructor. He was mistaken.

Just as the impression left by Nijinsky the artiste was so great and unforgettable, so the impression created by the man was slight and disappointing. I have never come across such a striking contrast. As a rule the talented artiste can be distinguished in private life. Sir Beerbohm Tree was a cultured and delightful conversationalist; Gordon Craig, when he chose, could be brilliant.[1] Diaghileff was one of the most brilliant conversationalists I have ever met. But Nijinsky was a nonentity, an absolute and thorough nonentity. After five minutes in any society his existence was completely forgotten.

I made Nijinsky's acquaintance as late as 1916 behind the scenes of the Metropolitan Opera House, New York. He produced a strange impression, he was silent, but not as people are wont to be silent. It was not the ordinary silence of an untalkative man, not that the dancer was averse to speech, but rather that he was not there at all. His manner of greeting you was characteristic—it was exaggeratedly and unexpectedly cordial. I have noticed the same thing

---

[1] I remember Tree's answer when I asked him what he thought of Craig. "Oh, he is very good to steal from." It would be difficult to describe Craig's quality more aptly.

in blind people. Whether he was intelligent or whether he was stupid I cannot say. I think he belongs to a class of people who cannot be described by either term. At any rate, if I called him stupid it would convey nothing. I think the neatest and at the same time the truest estimate of Nijinsky's intellect was given me by Misia Sert, one of Diaghileff's best friends. She called him an "idiot of genius." This is no paradox. In our enthusiasm over the "entity of an image" our admiration goes to the dancer's creative instincts and not to the conception of his brain, as for example, his rôle in *Petrushka*.

I am bound to say that he did not strike one as an ordinary man. Was he always pre-occupied with his art? I do not think so. I think rather that outside his work and off the stage he simply did not exist. There was something vague, childish, and even absurd about him; it seemed that if you took him by the hand and led him somewhere he would follow without asking where and why he was being taken. The story of his marriage proves this.

As a worker Nijinsky was untiring. Every day, for hours at a stretch, no matter where he was, even in the theatre, he could be found practising.

His physical build was most unusual. The top half of his body seemed to belong to one person and the lower half to another. You had to see him training to appreciate this to the full. From the waist up his body was that of a normally developed, strong, and healthy youth. Below that were thighs and calves with extraordinarily developed muscles. All that part of his body struck one as being abnormally developed and massive compared with the top half. On the stage, thanks to the costume and lighting this was not noticeable. There Nijinsky seemed to possess the figure of an Apollo. Off the stage his appearance, of course, was disappointing. With his pale face, his small and slightly Mongol eyes, and his thin hair, nondescript blonde in colour, he was not beautiful. Seeing him you could hardly believe your eyes. "What! This is the same Nijinsky who was just now so perfect in *Le Spectre de la Rose?*" It was simply unbelievable. That same colourless figure seemed queer and unhuman in his ballet working garb; he repeated the same steps, leaps, and *entrechats* a hundred times.

Let us hear what Alexandre Benois has to say about him.

"He was a modest, quiet, and silent youth. I cannot remember any of his conversation—he had none. If he had not been the famous Nijinsky he would have passed quite unnoticed. I remember when they came to see me in Montagnola—Diaghileff, Stravinsky, and Nijinsky—it was a week of reconciliation. I can remember all the details and all the conversation. There was Diaghileff and Stravinsky, but no Nijinsky. I know he was there but I cannot remember anything about him.

"He himself found his meteoric triumphs most unexpected. He was the first spectator to witness his own performances. When visiting he always sat with a broad smile on his face and seemed quite delighted. He was always unruffled and even-tempered, although when things did not run smoothly, if, for instance a costume did not fit or some other trifling matter upset him, he would suddenly become excited. But his attitude was never that of the spoilt darling of the public; he was always like the small child who complains but never demands.

"We hardly ever saw him without Diaghileff. Serge isolated him from the outside world, he even attached body-guards, who protected him night and day. It was usually Vasili Zouikoff, Diaghileff's devoted servant, sometimes Pavel Koribout-Kubitovitch, Diaghileff's equally devoted cousin.

"Years later, after the break with Diaghileff, Nijinsky turned up at my place in Paris unexpectedly and proved suddenly talkative. He wanted at all costs to make it up with Diaghileff and was full of plans and projects. He kept repeating that they were not doing what they ought to do in ballet, that everything ought to be quite different and that he would try to explain what he had in mind. I must confess that what he had to say was all very hazy and childish."

Four years spent in the constant companionship of Diaghileff had a disastrous effect on Nijinsky. Having cut him off from the outside world Serge, during that time, educated him despotically. He instilled, as it were, his own brains into Nijinsky. The thoughts forced up by this premature and hot-house system of education were hazy and faltering. This artificial spiritual growth, together with Nijinsky's readiness to be influenced by others, was fatal to him.

As a dancer he is unforgettable. Practically all his appearances, beginning with *Le Pavillon d'Armide* at the Maryinsky Theatre to the last Diaghileff production, were masterpieces. He was a born, God-sent dancer and a first-class dramatic artiste. His gracefulness, his lightness, and his *élévation* were quite unique. He *took time* to come down, it was a real illusion. I put this down to his will power.

As he sprang he must have believed that he was floating through the air and this belief communicated itself to the audience. It was a phenomenon which might be described as mass hypnotism.

My last meeting with Nijinsky was in painful and tragic circumstances. Diaghileff had a sudden idea that Nijinsky's mental sickness could be lightened if he could be transplanted to the surroundings of the ballet. In January 1929 Nijinsky was one of the audience at the Grand Opera, Paris, to witness his old ballet *Petrushka*. He sat in dead silence, a frozen smile on his face, staring fixedly and uncomprehendingly at the stage. Pointing at Leon Woizikovski, who was dancing Petrushka, Diaghileff asked him what he thought of him. "Il saute bien," answered Nijinsky, and again he was silent. They could get nothing more out of him.

After the performance Diaghileff took him on the stage. There his former partner Karsavina and many other friends and collaborators crowded round him. We were photographed. How happy and gay we all looked, yet I can never remember a more gloomy and melancholy occasion.

Nijinsky's daughter is already twenty years old. She is very much like her father but more beautiful. She has what the French call *beauté du diable*. A beauty, very piquant, she is noticed wherever she goes. A dancer of great talent, she is sure to make good in the ballet.

# 20

## KARSAVINA

IT gives me pleasure to sit down and write about Karsavina. It gives me pleasure because her name conjures up so many happy memories, and yet I find it difficult, because it is not easy to write of one on whom I can only shower praise. A charming, remarkably beautiful woman, and a gifted dancer, Karsavina soon, though not at once, stepped out of the ranks of the *Ballets-Russes*. No one imagined at first that this pleasing member of a family long connected with the ballet was to prove not only a great artiste but that the whole repertoire of the *Ballets-Russes* would depend on her.

She was taken into the Diaghileff company during the 1909 season as a *coryphée*, that is, in secondary parts. She was one of the two friends in *Le Pavillon d'Armide* and danced with Nijinsky and Fedorova. She danced with Nijinsky the "Dance of the Veil" in *Cléopâtre* and one of the dances in *Les Sylphides*. She had no leading parts in the first of Diaghileff's productions until, quite at the end of the season she stepped into Caralli's shoes as Armide. It was in this rôle, given to her quite by chance, that she first came under the notice of the Diaghilevians, when it occurred to them that here might be *the* ballerina, and steps were taken to make her famous.

Fokine, who for some reason had no faith in her, raised objections. He criticized her, accused her of laziness, foretold that she would never get anywhere, and, in short, did everything to stand in her way. It is not quite clear why Fokine shook his prophetic head over Karsavina in this way. Did he really fail to see anything in her, or was there some other, personal, motive? Whatever it was, the comparatively late appearance of Karsavina in the important rôles of the repertoire of the *Ballets-Russes* was undoubtedly due in some measure to Fokine's opposition.

During that first season, nevertheless, it became quite clear that the Diaghileff company could not depend on Anna Pavlova; she was not wholly "theirs" and seemed always to be looking somewhere ahead. It was apparent also that Caralli was quite unsuited to the Diaghileff repertoire. Yet it was absolutely essential that they should have a ballerina of their own. Diaghileff's friends talked to Karsavina and endeavoured to get to know her better. To their delight and surprise they found that she was not only an enchanting, gracious, and modest being, but far above her feminine milieu in culture. The painters could talk to her as an equal, which was a wondrously rare phenomenon in the ballet world. Her culture and her aesthetic sense were self-acquired. They discovered that she had read much, and to some purpose. She was preparing herself quite unnoticeably and in secret to be not only the great ballerina of the day but a truly educated artist. In time many of the Diaghilevians became her friends, she was invited to dinners and suppers, and actually became a member of their intimate circle, which was something more than even Fokine had achieved.

At the end of the season her husband, V. Moukhin, arrived. He was an amiable and unassuming man, an official in the Ministry of Finance. He seemed to be very astonished that he should be married to so rare a woman. Thus did the friends, one or two of whom had fallen in love with her, some tragically and all in vain, realize that she was married. She was, indeed, enchanting, not merely with the charm of beauty but with an appeal that was all her own, a great personal charm, and the simplicity of a pure heart. Karsavina, as a person, was very kind, very honest, and true. So far as I know there was not a single occasion when she refused to dance for charity. Not only in the circle of the ballet, but in the larger outside world, is it rare to meet one with so much decency and nobility of character. Her unique, high tinkling laugh had a childlike ring.

As early as 1910 Karsavina made her appearance as the firmly established prima ballerina of the *Ballets-Russes*. She took the principle rôles in the two big productions of the season: *L'Oiseau de Feu* and *Giselle*. Henceforth she was to be their own greatly beloved ballerina. Her success was enormous. Out of the modest Tamara Karsavina blossomed La Karsavina, a European name.

In 1911 she danced *Le Spectre de la Rose*, the ballerina in *Petrushka*, Echo in *Narcisse*, and, in short, all the big parts in the ballets. One cannot visualize Diaghileff's ballets at that time without Karsavina. She was indeed the "star." She deserved her great success. Gradually, not only by dancing but by hard work she developed into a ballerina of the first magnitude, technically perfect and a true dramatic artiste. Her own charming personality, fairy-like, poetic, and ideological, never failed to reach across the footlights. In her style of dancing she was the personification of what the Germans call "das ewig Weibliche."

329

It could not have been easy for her to appear every night on the stage as the partner of a genius like Nijinsky; she must have found it difficult to keep up to his level, to avoid criticism and comparisons. Karsavina emerged brilliantly from this trying position. No one could say: "What a pity Nijinsky's partner . . ." In her own enchanting way she proved a fitting partner for him. All those who saw them in *Le Spectre de la Rose*, in the *pas de deux* of that dreamlike idyll, remember not only Nijinsky but the entrancing figure of that young girl, Karsavina.

Her success was not limited to her work with the Diaghileff company. She became in time the favourite of St. Petersburg audiences and made many appearances at the Maryinsky Theatre. This became a complication in itself. It was not easy to free herself of her obligations to the Imperial Theatre and to remain true to her Paris friends. She had to make hectic train journeys between Paris and St. Petersburg, staying for only a few days and rushing direct from the railway station to the theatre for the evening performance. There were times when the *Ballets-Russes* had to change the order of the ballets in order to give her time to get from the station to the theatre and make up. She never let Diaghileff down; once her word was given she kept it, no matter what difficulties might arise.

Despite her beauty and the worship which her success brought her, Karsavina retained throughout her career that simple, open nature.

She married twice. Her first husband was Moukhin and her second Henry Bruce. When the latter came into her life it was obvious that she had fallen in love with him, and Moukhin put his own interests on one side and, refusing

PLATE XXIX

TAMARA KARSAVINA

PLATE XXX

ANNA PAVLOVA

to stand in the way of her happiness, gave her a divorce. Tamara Karsavina became Mrs. Bruce in Russia in 1917. When the revolutions came, first under Kerensky and later under the Bolsheviks, her husband, who was on the staff of the embassy, had to leave Russia. He returned for her in 1918 and took her to his own country.

Karsavina has given up the stage. She no longer dances— domestic happiness fills her life and has taken the place of art. It is very pleasant to think of her. Rarely does one find beauty, talent, happiness, and high moral qualities in one human being.

# 21

## PAVLOVA

ANNA PAVLOVA must rank with the few great phenomena in the history of art—the Divinities. To my mind
we have no right, even if we have the desire, to criticize
them.

Her art reached such heights, was so fine and so perfect,
the images she conjured up for us were so beautiful that
we ought to treasure them in our memories, where they will
delight us if only as recollections of the dim glories of the
past. If I were writing of the ballet in general, one of the
most significant portions of this book would have been
devoted to Pavlova. As I am writing of the *Ballets-Russes*,
as created by Diaghileff, this cannot be. Nor would it have
been possible if I had set out to write about the Imperial
Russian Ballet.

Anna Pavlova was unique. She pursued a lone artistic
trail, a trail quite unconnected with collective or creative
effects, so that in the choreographic sense there may
appear to be a tragic lapse in her life. She left no great
artistic memorial behind her and thus may be said not to
have made full use of the mighty gifts that had been given
her.

She was a born genius; with the exception of Nijinsky I
can think of no one who was endowed with such gifts.
Such rare phenomena as she and Nijinsky appear only
once in a century.

At a very early age, as one of the young *coryphées* in the Maryinsky Theatre, she stood out from the rest. The public recognized her from the moment she made her appearance, she could be detected by that inborn inimitable grace of movement, a grace which was both unusual and slightly melancholy, and by her own slender and ethereal person. No matter what dance the ballet was performing, she was all that one saw, nothing else mattered. The immediate and gripping hold that she had on the audience was extraordinarily powerful. I do not think she would have been a power on the films—in that "art" where personal contact between the artiste and the audience has been replaced by a soulless image on a screen. The direct influence, emanations, fluids, call it what you will, the name does not matter, but the phenomenon undoubtedly exists and as soon as you allow some mechanical contraption to become the intermediary between the artiste who possesses it and the person who perceives, you lose much, nearly everything that matters. Therein lies the secret danger of the gramophone and wireless and of the cinema, which is the most deadly where art is concerned.

Anna Pavlova possessed this quality of direct communication; her emanations reached the audience. In the beginning she did not possess great technique: as the years passed she attained proficiency in that direction, though she never became a technical virtuoso of the ballerina *di forza* type, like Geltzer and Kchessinskaya. But she had no need of this, such technical tricks as thirty-two *fouettés* and the *entrechats dix* would not have been of much use to her; there was more than sufficient technique in her free interpretation of her own flawless art.

Although she had dealings with *Mir Iskustva* as early as 1907, when she took the risk of incurring the displeasure of the management by taking Kchessinskaya's part in *Le Pavillon d'Armide*, it was obvious from the first season in Paris in 1909 that she did not wish to tie herself down to Diaghileff. She was late for the opening of the season and it was never quite clear whether this was an accident or whether she was waiting to see which way things would turn. It must have been during that season that she realized that in those surroundings she would never shine as she wished; the creators of the ballets were only concerned with the artistic excellence of the performance as a whole, the impression conveyed by the ensemble and the unity of the spectacle, and would certainly not suffer the ballet to become a frame, a background for any one ballerina, no matter how brilliant she might be. The overwhelming success of Nijinsky, moreover, seemed to put Pavlova in a secondary plane. In addition, Pavlova found herself besieged with offers from every important town in Europe and America.

By 1910 Pavlova was on her own. She had left the *Ballets-Russes* and was breaking away from the Russian Imperial Ballet. She became a nomad, a lone wanderer. She gave no consideration to the class of theatre in which she worked, she appeared in second-rate theatres, in music halls, in the company of jugglers and animal tamers. By doing this she made it impossible for herself to achieve any high artistic creations. She had extraordinary natural gifts, which were revealed even in the small sketches which she created. Her "Dying Swan," arranged for her by Fokine, was an unforgettable thing. With the realism of genius she conveyed the sad loveliness of the broken, dying bird.

But are we not justified in looking for more than this from a genius such as Pavlova? I think we are, and that is why I speak of her "tragic lapse" where choreography is concerned. In spite of this waste of her creative powers she performed great and invaluable work for this art: she may have done this unconsciously, without any particular end in view.

If you set off on a tour of the world, stopping at any place where fancy takes you, and ask any passing stranger if he has ever heard of the Russian Ballet you are certain to receive some such answer as: "The Russian Ballet? Why, yes. It is something fine and delightful, something beautiful . . . Anna Pavlova!" Travelling round the globe, from country to country and theatre to theatre, caring nothing for the quality of the theatre or the importance of the town, Anna Pavlova proved the great ambassadress of the ballet. In every corner, not only of Europe, but of every other continent she revealed her divine gift. Bandaged from head to foot to rest her aching muscles, so that only her nose and toes were to be seen, she would continue her pilgrimage—on to the next place, there to reveal herself again. In this sense her rôle was great and unique. She popularized the ballet.

It may be true that Anna Pavlova created no great stage rôle and had no part in the creative side of this new art, but it is not true that she did not *create* anything. She produced one of the most wonderful artistic creations of the age—herself, Anna Pavlova. Her own artistic characteristics are unforgettable. Airy, sad, and frail she was,

335

exquisitely winsome, poignantly touching. The two words "Anna Pavlova" conjure up in the minds of those who saw her a melancholy sentiment of unforgotten loveliness, bygone moments of delight.

In 1931 she was due to appear in Brussels. A few days before her opening night the world received news that she had died suddenly at The Hague. It was decided to go on with the performance. When the time came for her number the music of the "Dying Swan" was played and the single white ray of the spotlight moved over the darkened stage where she would have been dancing. The Queen of the Belgians, who was present in the auditorium, rose to her feet and the rest of the house did the same, their eyes following the white beam of light as it sought in vain for the vanished Pavlova. Could there have been any more simple or more fitting tribute to this supreme artiste?

# 22

———————

1 9 1 5 — 1 9 2 9

———————

IF the object of this book had been to tell the life-story of
Diaghileff, or the story of his artistic activities, or even to
give a historical summary of the Diaghileff ballet, then this
chapter would have come immediately after the chapter on
the year 1914. Also it would have been not a chapter but
a considerable section of the book. But when I commenced
to write I had not this in mind. I was interested in the
process which gave birth to a new art, I was stirred by
memories of the endeavours, difficulties, and failures, the
hopes, the joys, and the triumphs which attended this
birth, and it seems to me that it is precisely this period
which is of essential importance for the understanding of
contemporary ballet. It was in this period of Storm and
Stress during the romantic epoch of the *Ballets-Russes* that
this new branch of theatrical art was created. All that
followed were, in my opinion, merely more or less successful
variations on an already discovered theme. The temple
had already been built.

\* \* \*

After the War Diaghileff was a solitary figure. He began
to choose his own collaborators. He sought and found
them mainly in Western Europe amongst the "advanced"
painters and musicians of Paris, and also amongst Russians
who recommended themselves by their modernism. The

337

Revolution cut him quite off from Russia and destroyed his connections there.

The final attempt to attach Diaghileff to Russia occurred in 1917 during the so-called Kerensky Revolution. Under the chairmanship of Gorky a committee was organized to exercise supreme control over all artistic activities. This committee decided unanimously that Diaghileff must certainly be Director of Theatres. A lengthy telegram was dispatched to him, inviting him to accept this post and promising him complete independence and freedom in his management. The offer was obviously tempting. To receive an invitation to become a director with full honours of the theatres from which he had been so ignominiously dismissed, to undertake this immense artistic enterprise would, of course, have been a great triumph. But Diaghileff was not a fool. He had clearer and deeper foresight than anyone. He declined the invitation politely but firmly. A few months later the Bolsheviks came into power, and the Gorky committee was disbanded.

In pre-War days Diaghileff and his "parliament" were a single, united group. The members of the group had grown to manhood together, had fought side by side for their common artistic ideals, and had undertaken original creation together. When they ultimately arrived in Paris, bringing their ballets with them, they were hailed as innovators and revolutionaries. The *Ballets-Russes*, and consequently Diaghileff, became *le dernier cri* in art.

After the War the position altered. The united group, with whose members Diaghileff had reached maturity, whose leader he was, no longer existed. To remain the protagonist of all that was progressive in art he had to go

338

and seek for "advancedness," had to attract to his service collaborators who already had the hall-mark of *le dernier cri.* Before, he himself had created a revolution, now he had to search for one and follow in its wake. Picasso, Derain, Matisse, Marie Laurencin, Braque, Juan Gris, Pruna, Utrillo, and Chirico—all these painters had created a name for themselves independently of Diaghileff, and now brought to his enterprise their own patent brand of "advancedness." Among the musicians whose services Diaghileff sought we find fewer names who were already known for their modernism. De Falla, Eric Satie, Poulenc, Auric, Darius Milhaud, and Rieti composed ballet music for him, but Diaghileff often used old music, which, however, he adapted to suit his productions. In this direction Diaghileff retained his old love for making "finds," of reviving what had been forgotten. It was the remnants of that love for the past which had distinguished the *Mir Iskustva* friends.

In the post-War period Diaghileff's collaborators constantly change. The scenery is commissioned from one painter or the other, the music is composed by one or other of the "moderns," or unearthed in the archives of London and Naples and cut to a new pattern. There was no longer any permanent creative group, and consequently there is no creative continuity. There are nothing but "searches" and experiments. And what do "searches" mean? Is not the word in itself a confession that something is missing? Something important that must be found—creative achievement? And does not the word "experiment" imply uncertainty of the truth? Is there not here a doubt of one's creativeness?

339

But Diaghileff was so placed that he had no alternative. There was no powerful creative group to which he could firmly cement himself. Neither could he rest on his pre-War laurels. Before the War he had held the position of being the protagonist of all that was most progressive in theatrical art, and he could not withdraw from that position now; he must at all costs be *le dernier cri* which Paris, and following it Europe, considered him. He was compelled to go more and more forward, and before him lay no clearly marked path. He *had* to "search," *had* to "experiment."

These "searches" were far from being entirely fruitless. Much of what Diaghileff created in this period was both interesting and ingenious, sometimes even artistic—in short, successful. Many of the ballets of that time still remain in the repertoire and still interest and delight the spectator to-day. But there was not that compelling creative urge, that birth of a new art, which distinguished the early years.

In Diaghileff's post-War activities one cannot, in my opinion, discover any clear artistic principles. He introduced no reform and no revolution; one can only single out for praise—and great praise—separate productions.

The purely choreographical aspects of the ballets of this period come perhaps under another head.

The second revolution in choreography, which was only heralded in the Nijinsky-Diaghileff ballets of 1912 (*L'Après-midi d'un Faune* and *Le Sacre du Printemps*), dominates the post-War ballet. The rejection of the classical ballet of the five positions (points, etc.) is determined. Personally, I doubt whether this was for the good of ballet.

Every art must accept certain conventions, and ballet especially so. As we know it, this art is a hot-house growth based on the preservation of an age-long tradition. This tradition may be developed and freed of its unnecessary fetters—as Fokine did. But to abandon it entirely is to reject the basic conventions of the art, and the result is chaos.

The convention (artificial, of course) on which our music is based is tonality (the scale), and this convention is limitless in its possibilities of change and development. Even a score like that of *Petrushka* shows it; even the simultaneous use of two different keys is not a departure from the basic principle of tonality. But when a composer attempts to neglect this fundamental convention—the scale —and strives for complete atonality, in my opinion he only produces confusion.

Similarly, in my opinion, the basic convention of ballet is the classical dance with its five positions, points, *entrechats*, *pirouettes*, and so on. This is the choreographic scale. It is equally limitless in its possible developments. Allied with character-dances and mime, it offers a free field for the choreographer.

To create a new choreographic basis, a new school of ballet independent of the classic, is no easy matter. To do this takes decades, if not centuries. The chaotic jumble of "free" movements must be crystallized into a new "scale" of its own in order to create a new tradition, a new convention. Isolated cases may be successful, but on this style ballet cannot be constructed. Isadora Duncan was a miracle, but what is more of a nightmare than those ladies clad in Greek tunics who, following her example, danced on bare feet round the world?

In confirmation of my opinion, I may point out the

extraordinary tenaciousness of the classical dance. After nearly fifteen years of experiments in the new choreography the ballet has inevitably returned to the classic. In the *Ballets de Basil* the classical dance has again been revived, and Massine gives it more prominence and attention than he did before under Diaghileff.

In my opinion, this very tenaciousness proves that the classical dance is a sound foundation for ballet. The choreographer, of course, must know how to employ this basic principle, this "scale," must be a master of modulation, must learn to combine and interweave these "sounds," and must not be afraid of bold, original rhythms or of "dissonances" (grotesque). In a word, he must learn how to develop this basis to the full, but must nevertheless not forget that it is a basis and is not to be rejected completely. Fokine knew all this. The "Polovetz" dances and *Petrushka* are just such harmonic developments of the basic classical "scale" of dancing. Massine also, especially in his latest creative period, can do this.

The history of the gradual evolution of this exceedingly remarkable choreographer is interesting. From 1915 to 1929, almost without interruption, he produced the Diaghileff ballets. During these fourteen years he had seventeen ballets to his credit. From his first production (*Le Soleil de Nuit*) until *Le Pas d'Acier* in 1927 and *Ode* in 1928 he passed through the whole evolution of "search," "experiment," and modernism. During this period he was the only one of Diaghileff's creative collaborators to whom the word "continuous" can really be applied. The choreography of this period bears mainly the personal stamp of Massine, affected probably in some way by Diaghileff's influence, by his demands for novelty and modernism at any cost.

Towards the end of his life Diaghileff lost faith in this deliberate modernism, he thought more and more of a return to the past, he perceived the artistic blind alley into which his chase of *le dernier cri* had led him.

"One can't go on like this," he said to his friends. "No further advance is possible. One must return to the classic." Massine's evolution seems to have been parallel with that of Diaghileff, and he too lost faith in "revolution at any cost." His latest productions show a distinct tendency to return to the basis of classical ballet. In this he is undoubtedly Diaghileff's heir. He takes the path which Diaghileff perhaps would have taken if death had not intervened.

\* \* \*

Diaghileff made several attempts to return to the past in the post-War period. The chief of these was actually an attempt to go back beyond Fokine and the *Ballets-Russes* to Petipa and the Imperial Ballet.

This was the London production in 1921 of Tchaikovsky's *The Sleeping Princess* in its unabridged form and with the choreography of Marius Petipa.

Diaghileff wanted this production staged by Alexandre Benois. Even as a boy Benois had been very enthusiastic about this ballet and retained his love for it throughout the whole of his life. Through the medium of Prince Argoutinsky, then living in Paris, an active though secret correspondence with Benois was started. Benois was still in Petrograd, burning to escape from Soviet Russia and

343

to work for the ballet which he so much loved. Everything was prepared. Benois had procured a false passport, and the escape was organized. At the last moment, owing to someone letting out the secret, or in some other way, Benois's projected flight became known and nothing came of the affair. There was nothing to be done. Benois had to give up the work which was his constant dream. He has regretted it ever since.

After his disappointment about Benois, Diaghileff fell back on Bakst, who accepted the task with delight and in a very short time produced a complete set of splendid designs. In spite of the wonderful staging and the brilliance of the performers the ballet was not a commercial success. The presentation of a five-act ballet, a "grand spectacle," cost a great deal of money. Even to recover the expenses the ballet had to receive steady public support for scores of performances. Unfortunately, this was not the case. The box office did not cover the expenses, and at the end of the season all the properties, scenery, and costumes were sold by auction.

This put Diaghileff in a very difficult position. Paris had been promised *The Sleeping Princess*, it was billed to appear, and had even been specified in the contract. Something had to be done to get out of the difficulty. Diaghileff's solution was to give only the last act in Paris with the addition of the "Russian Dance" (Nijinskaya) and the "Chinese Dance" from *Casse Noisette*, also to Tchaikovsky's music. Benois's costumes and scenery for *Le Pavillon d'Armide* were used mainly, but costumes for some of the dances (for example, the "Chinese Dance") were by Goncharova. With this old scenery and in creased

344

costumes this act of *The Sleeping Princess* was presented in Paris under the title of *Le Mariage d'Aurore*.

Fifteen years later I was standing in the wings at Covent Garden during the rehearsal of a ballet. Beside me stood Arnold Haskell, and the following conversation took place between us.

P. L.: "Do you know, in one respect I resemble that 'old Russian gentleman' whom you depict in your book, *Balletomania*. The deep delight I take in *Le Mariage d'Aurore* proves it."

A. H.: "Yes, I too delight in it. It is my favourite ballet."

Haskell is probably the finest ballet critic of our day, with the greatest knowledge and understanding. But he is young. When Tchaikovsky and Petipa were creating *The Sleeping Princess* he was not yet born. Yet this ballet, compressed as it is in one act, appeals greatly to him. What greater praise could be given to the art of the classical dance?

Diaghileff's second attempt to return to the past was the Gounod Revival. This took place in Monte Carlo in 1923. The unearthing and revival of past masterpieces were the favourite occupations of the *Mir Iskustva* crusaders. In this respect, of course, the Gounod Revival is a return to the ideas and aspirations of the first creations of the Diaghilevians, when Benois reintroduced on the stage the *tutu Taglioni*, when the *Ballets-Russes* revived *Giselle*.

Benois was connected with this second return to the past. Having at length escaped from Russia, he arrived in Monte Carlo in 1923, and found Diaghileff in the mood of a man who has just been reprieved from hanging. Before the invitation to Monte Carlo he had been on the brink of an abyss. He had no money at all. In Paris one of the

345

performances had been stopped, and the bailiff was on the stage. Disaster seemed inevitable. The invitation to Monte Carlo saved the situation just in time. Diaghileff felt better and gayer. His friendship with the family of the Prince of Monaco was of the closest. They planned together the most ambitious projects and decided to revive Gounod.

They began with the production of the three-act comic opera, *Le Médecin malgré lui*. The scenery and costumes were given to Benois. In any French comic opera spoken dialogue is intermixed with the music. This was distasteful to Diaghileff, and he decided to replace these dialogues by recitative. This was no innovation. The dialogues in *Carmen* had long since been replaced in most productions and several recitative scores were composed for *Don Juan* after Mozart's death. Unfortunately, Diaghileff entrusted this work to the French modernist, Eric Satie. The music he composed for the dialogues was unsuitable and did not sound right.

A similar task for the opera *Philémon et Baucis* in the same Gounod Revival was performed much more successfully by another French composer. In this production, unfortunately, Benois, on his own admission, was not at his best. He had not wanted to undertake the work, and only gave way to Diaghileff's pressure. He was feeling unwell and over-fatigued. At that time Diaghileff was jealous of Benois's collaboration with Ida Rubinstein, and made scenes about it.

"Why do you do it?" he would ask. "Come now, do *Philémon et Baucis*, and show that you can do better for me than for Ida."

Benois allowed himself to be persuaded but, as was

346

generally the case with him, work undertaken against his will and under external pressure was not successful.

A third Gounod opera presented at Monte Carlo was the short two-act opera, *La Colombe*. The scenery and costumes for this were designed by Juan Gris. All these, together with the one-act opera-bouffe, *Éducation Manquée* by Chabrier, occupied two evenings.

It must be admitted that the Gounod Revival was not a success. What could be done in Russia at the beginning of the twentieth century could not be done in France. The Press was luke-warm about the Gounod festival, and it had only moderate success with the public and did not draw full houses. In some respects the French have little regard for the past, cannot look at it with unprejudiced eyes and see its living beauty. Revivals are not suited to the French public. It was impossible to revive Delibes, and even *Giselle* in 1910 was not a success.

The 1919 production of *La Boutique Fantasque* may also be considered a return to the past.

The choreography by Massine, it is true, was new; so were the scenery and costumes by the French painter Derain, and the music was even specially arranged for it. But the idea of the ballet was an old one. It is nothing but an up-to-date version of the old Viennese ballet, *Puppenfee*. The music in this ballet is also a return to the past. It is composed mainly of short unprinted pieces by Rossini.

Rossini left behind him not only *The Barber of Seville* and *William Tell*, but also the *tournedos* named for him. During the last thirty-eight years of his life he abandoned musical composition. The new music did not appeal to him

347

(he said about Wagner: "He has sublime moments but miserable quarters of an hour"), and he probably felt that his time was past. He devoted his attention to another favourite pastime of his—good food. Dining or supping with friends, between the *tournedos* and some other fancy dish, he sometimes composed snatches of music as a joke, short pianoforte pieces often only a few bars in length. Friends sacredly preserved these morsels of the respected composer. From these odd snatches and fragments the score of *La Boutique Fantasque* was composed.

Respighi, who arranged the score, did his task splendidly. The music sounds light and fresh and charming. The costumes and scenery were also quite successful, amusing, interesting, and simple. Massine's choreography, too, was effective. The alternation of amusing mime with the beautifully conceived dances of the dolls blended well and was pleasant to watch.

This ballet had a great and lasting success, retains its place in the repertoire to-day, and is as pleasing to look at as ever. It is not an important creative work, but as an accepted distraction it merits its continued popularity.

\* \* \*

I should also like to mention separately several productions of this period, not because they have any direct relationship with creations of the past, but because they represent, in my opinion, examples of real success in "searching," happy "experiments."

*Les Femmes de Bonne Humeur* was created in 1917. This is one of Massine's first efforts in choreography. If he can be accused of being to some extent mechanical, and consequently monotonous, it was, as a whole, well done. The music was by Scarlatti, and the arrangement by Tommasini was agreeable. It sounded fresh and gay, a little naïve but pleasant in the extreme. The staging was done by Bakst. At first in his designs everything was normal; perpendicular houses, etc. Then in a wave of modernism he decided that this would not do. After some thought he proceeded to place the same houses crookedly! Still, the result was quite good. The ballet as a whole was an excellent and interesting production.

The 1920 production, *Pulcinella*, was a first-rate ballet. Stravinsky and Diaghileff were struck with the idea of this ballet while attending open-air performances at Naples. They also hit upon the idea of using for it old music by Pergolese. Somewhere in London Diaghileff succeeded in unearthing a whole pile of unprinted music by this old composer. It is difficult to say whether this was authentic. Some musicians still maintain that it is not Pergolese. In any case it is of no importance. The music was charming and contained a wealth of lovely themes. This was just what Stravinsky required. He took the work in hand, and produced from the material an exceptionally witty score, a sort of instrumental satire. The result was a burlesque, a caricature of sentimentality, but the brilliant caricature of a virtuoso. This virtually original composition made under Pergolese's name would quite probably have been heartily approved by Pergolese if he had heard it. Picasso's staging was exceptionally attractive in its unusualness. In it everything puzzles, pleases, interests, and amuses.

As far as I know, this ballet has not been revived in the same form. This is to be regretted.

349

I also regret that the ballet *Les Dieux Mendiants* has never been revived. It is true that its production in 1928 was a slapdash affair. The scenery was from Bakst's *The Sleeping Princess*, the costumes from another ballet by Juan Gris, but then Handel's music was charming and the whole ballet, in spite of its heterogeneous character, hung together quite successfully owing to Balanchine's choreography. This was quite a common occurrence with Diaghileff. *Le Mariage d'Aurore*, also composed of bits and pieces, and compressed, still holds the boards; and among the early ballets *Cléopâtre* and *Le Festin* were patched together, even musically, from various odds and ends.

The ballet *Le Bal*, produced in 1929, was distinguished by a special, rather strange charm. This was perhaps due to Chirico, who staged it. Balanchine's choreography did not make any great impression, and the music by Rieti was quite undistinguished. One's whole attention was concentrated on the creation of Chirico, this master of delirium in painting. Owing to him the ballet had a strange, rather nightmarish effect, with classical elements linked to a kind of cubism.

The production of *Le Pas d'Acier* is interesting, in my opinion, not from the point of view of ballet, but because of the reasons which led to its production. Diaghileff at this time was considering the possibility of going to Soviet Russia. The Soviet poet Mayakovsky (who later shot himself) made his appearance about this time in Paris, and tried his best to arrange the matter. To facilitate the change-over, to bridge the gulf, as it were, *Le Pas d'Acier* was commissioned from the composer Prokofiev, who stood with one leg in Moscow and one in Paris. But the idea of

IRINA BARONOVA

PLATE XXXI

DÉCOR FOR "THE SLEEPING B
By

returning to the fatherland came to nothing. Diaghileff was fated not to work in Russia, either Imperial or Soviet.

I make no pretence in this chapter of giving a full description of Diaghileff's post-War activities. As I said before, that is not my aim. This period is outside my present sphere of interest, which lies in the history of the shaping of the *Ballets-Russes* from the scenic, musical, and choreographic points of view. In this last period I detect no such creativeness. I see occasionally highly successful productions, I see false steps, much wavering, much "searching," but I find no signs of the birth of a new art.

# 23

## BEHIND THE SCENES IN TWO THEATRES

*THE METROPOLITAN OPERA HOUSE, NEW YORK, 1916*

THERE is no place on earth that seems so strange, so fantastic and unreal as the ballet stage during an interval. In the wings and among the scenery at the far corners of the stage, mingling with the soberly clad workmen, are all kinds of strange figures—Egyptians from *Cléopâtre*, talking with graceful Sylphides in long white *tutus*, half-naked slave girls whispering to characters from *Carnaval*. As in a muddled dream these strange figures flit about, disappearing at one moment in the shadows, reappearing the next in the yellow artificial light. The workmen, arranging the scenery as if unconscious of the presence of this strange crowd, make it seem even more ephemeral and unreal. The scenery itself, seen at such close quarters, seems to be merely an incoherent jumbled mass of splashes of colour, huge daubs of paint whose only purpose is to frighten and bewilder you. The faces of the artistes are quite different from what is seen from the auditorium. The make-up is crude and artificial, the expression pre-occupied and serious. Here, for instance, is a sylphide, her face rudely daubed with wet white and streaming with large beads of perspiration. She is still panting and looks serious, pathetic. As she straightens the folds of her flimsy

352

*tutu Taglioni* her slender, ethereal figure seems in strange contrast with her tired white face.

In a corner in the shadows at the back of the stage is a little man of unusual build, dressed in a soft shirt and short pants. His behaviour is strange. With arms outstretched he jumps, up and down, without stopping, and always on the same place. Then suddenly he will commence some fresh mechanical movement. Standing on one leg he will raise the other, moving it forward, sideward, and backward. This operation he will repeat with the other leg, and so he goes on, first on one leg and then the other. This is Nijinsky at exercise. The perspiration falls like hailstones from his pale, slightly Mongolian face, and as you watch him going through these movements with such exactness and precision you are not quite certain whether you are looking at a clockwork doll or a human being.

Diaghileff walks slowly and languidly in the centre of the stage. He is in evening dress and his famous white quiff peeps out from the side of his sloping top hat. In his hand he carries a walking stick surmounted with a gold knob, in his eye is a monocle. The whole of his slightly corpulent figure gives an impression of weariness and boredom. He is accompanied by two ladies, who, judging from their rich furs and jewellery and their general air of superiority, must be of some importance and very rich. Without any attempt at exertion Diaghileff shows them his fairy domain. They pay no great attention to what they see, for them it is sufficient that they have been admitted on the stage, that a concession has been made to their "superiority." Diaghileff is as languid and pompous as a nabob—is he not the ruler of this strange kingdom! From time to time he draws the

353

attention of a workman, with his stick, to some forgotten trifle which has been left on the stage. Both he and his companions seem quite unaware of the presence of this strange crowd of multi-coloured ballet figures. They are only part of life, not of a dream.

It is at such moments that one gets a sense of the atmosphere of the ballet with its hothouse fragrance, for although dancing is one of the oldest of the arts, indulged in not only by the most uncivilized peoples but even by some animals, the display of this art through the medium of the ballet is unreal and conventional to an extreme degree. The ballet has been built wholly on cultural creativeness, distinguished from real life by the phantasies of its creator. A touch of realism would prove fatal to it. Combined with music it has found its domain in this intangible kingdom.

Ballets are dreams, sometimes light and poetical like *Les Sylphides*, sometimes tragic like *Petrushka*, sometimes nightmarish like *Le Sacre du Printemps*, but always dreams, never reality. No greater mistake in the conception of a ballet could have been perpetrated than in the staging of *Union Pacific*, in which a railway is being built and the dancers are placed in formation to represent railway lines. This is a perversion of the whole idea of ballet, an attempt to introduce realism into a dream.

So, like a strange, muddled dream, the stage of the Metropolitan Grand Opera appeared to me during an interval at the ballet.

From the wings during a performance everything on the stage is quite different. At the moment the opening strains of music are heard everything seems to become divided into two distinct and separate worlds. The stage is

354

illuminated with a bright yellow artificial light—in the wings everything is hidden in the bluish darkness where the same strange figures which during the interval were scattered about the stage are now crowded together. Everything is absolute silence, there is not even a whisper as in an atmosphere of concentrated expectation they await the moment of their appearance. They seem to exist only for the moment when they will emerge into this brilliantly lit atmosphere and take life in their own particular dream form. The workmen, in their everyday clothes, hide like mice here in the shadow where they cannot be seen. Their work is done and on the stage phantasy, a strange persuasive illusion, reigns. In the artificial light ethereal, feathery creatures flutter about like strange birds, meeting together, separating, forming circles and groups as in the performance of some unknown ritual.

From the wings you cannot see the audience, you can only sense the dark abyss of humanity for whom all this dream is created, you can hear the music, but somehow it seems a thing apart, something which has no relation to the actual performance. And, to you, what is happening on the stage is not clear. You know that it is all harmonious and co-ordinated, but it is directed towards this black abyss and only from there can it be understood. In this dark corner, where it was all prepared, you are outside the confines of this dream, you see something which is not within your realm.

Quite near me, almost at the edge of the blue shadow of the wings, stands a dancer. Her childlike figure is tense, in her white *tutu*, with funny little wings on her back, and, her shoulders and arms bare, she looks like some little child

355

or an insect. She awaits her cue. The moment arrives. Light as a feather she flies into the brilliant light of the stage. With a happy smile and softly swaying arms she commences a pyrotechnic display of *pirouettes, entrechats,* and *battements.* Her whole being is the embodiment of flight, extraordinary buoyancy, and joy of life. Her number comes to an end. With graceful leaps and the same happy smile she flies towards the wings and with one last bound reaches the blue shadows . . . and falls exhausted on the floor . . . a little heap of tulle. Her poor weak body is shaken by her quick, uneven breathing. With face drawn after the exertion she looks like an animal at bay. But the music continues . . . soon she must reappear on the stage. She rises slowly, as if with effort. She powders her tired and careworn face, rearranges her *tutu,* and once again, fairylike, with a happy smile, flies into the brilliance of the footlights.

When one sees the terrible physical strain imposed by the work of ballet artistes one cannot help but be astonished that their hearts stand the strain. The more fairylike the apparition the greater is the effort, the lighter the jump, the greater the tenseness, the contrast between the buoyancy of the apparition and the offstage weariness is enormous. The wings in reality seem to be the borderline between two worlds.

At the Metropolitan Opera House the hearts of the company off the stage were not very light. They had just torn themselves from Europe where war thundered. Many had relatives, brothers, and in some cases fathers— in the fighting line. In America they had entered into an

356

atmosphere of extraordinary prosperity. It was a time when orders for war material were pouring into the American market from a diseased Europe as from a horn of plenty. Money did not count. The Ziegfeld Follies and Bustanoby's Domino Room filled to capacity. Champagne flowed like water. The crowd in the Metropolitan Opera House was brilliant. I cannot remember ever having seen such a flashing of diamonds as I chanced to spy in the half-darkness of the *bel étage* boxes. The success was enormous but it was not reflected as in the ordinary way, behind the footlights.

Diaghileff himself was gloomy. It was the period of Nijinsky's action against him. Here, on his own stage, in his kingdom, he was compelled to tolerate a man who by legal proceedings was taking from him the last of his money, and this after he had moved heaven and earth to secure his liberation from an Austrian internment camp. Diaghileff was alone. He was in a difficult financial position, he had no new ballet creations, he was without hope. Behind the footlights his entourage pressed close upon him, they too were not gay, but preoccupied.

Should a lover of ballet go behind the stage? Does not the experience shatter the illusion? I think he can. A really artistic illusion will always remain persuasive and, no matter at what cost, belief in it can be revived. After all, every art is illusion. Take the lightest morsel of four lines of Heine, something which seems to have flowed so naturally from his pen, and in reality you have the fruits of pains-taking labour. If you search his manuscripts you will find probably thirty variations of these four lines. Every word

357

is weighed, pondered over, and worked out by hard labour. Only by years of painstaking practice could the pianist, with nimble fingers playing a Chopin mazurka, achieve such lightness of touch.

Art is illusion: its back-stage labour. The contrast between the dream of the ballet and the panting in the backstage shadows is the unavoidable law of every art, of every created work of beauty.

## COVENT GARDEN, LONDON, 1935

Twenty years have passed. It was not without some trepidation that I went along the dark corridors and through doors marked "Silence" to the half-lit stage. Once again I was behind the scenes at the ballet. What should I see? Not one of the "goddessess" of the art by whom at one time I had been held in thrall? Not one familiar face? Not one familiar figure? Everything new and strange? . . .

A rehearsal was in progress . . . some new choreographic symphony was being prepared: barefooted figures clad in dark tricots, like bathing suits, ran about the stage, leaping and forming groups.

Why did they all seem so tiny, just little girls? Could I be in the grip of the illusion which seizes a grown-up person who enters a room which in the days of his childhood had seemed so large? I became accustomed to it. It was quite true, they were young, extraordinarily young, their faces were almost childlike. It did not seem possible that any one of them was more than seventeen years old; I was quite certain that not one of them was born at the time of my visit to the Metropolitan Opera House.

358

In the far corner at the back of the stage stood Colonel de Basil, the man by whose efforts the Russian ballet lives and shines again. He is quite unlike Diaghileff in appearance. His long, lean figure gives him a sort of monastic appearance, he would probably look very well in the garb of a Jesuit. His whole manner in dealing with his difficult and complicated work is entirely different from that of his predecessor. De Basil is no pyrotechnist, no creator of fairy castles, he is a stubborn builder, consecutive and intelligent. Yet it seems to me that the Russian ballet of Colonel de Basil will endure and will be able to stand firmly on its own feet, that the beautiful art into which he has instilled new life will last. Diaghileff was a typical Russian, impetuous, sporadic, a gentleman, patron of arts. De Basil is also a typical Russian, but of quite a different stamp. His is the type of Russian, the careful, consecutive worker, which is not well known in the West, but a type which exists and is quite characteristic. In everyday life it can be recognized in the learned types of the old sectarian church, quiet, stubborn, and hard-working in the extreme. In art a striking example of the type is to be found in Rimsky-Korsakov, without whose enormous work practically the whole of Russian "national" music of the post-Glinka period would not have existed.

On the stage not far from de Basil stood a tall, well-built man. This was the producer, Serge Grigorieff, who, though still not old, is one of the outstanding personalities in the history of Russian ballet. From 1907 to 1914 he was the faithful assistant of Fokine. From 1914 to 1929 he was the closest collaborator of Diaghileff. From then to the present day he has worked unceasingly in the cause of

359

Russian ballet. He is a man who has not only seen and taken part in everything but who knows and remembers everything. Without him it would, perhaps, have been impossible to restage many of the old ballets. His choreographic memory is infallible, in addition to which he is familiar with and remembers most of the theatrical stages in the world. To me it seems that in the realm of ballet he is indispensable.

In addition to all this Serge Grigorieff is a delightful man. Calm, intelligent, and highly-cultured, he is not only a pleasant but a well-instructed conversationalist. To talk to him about the old days is extremely pleasant, and when he speaks of what he calls "the romantic period of the Russian ballet" you feel in his soft voice a special warmth and tenderness towards a treasured memory. Of Diaghileff he speaks with affection:

"I am glad that I lived during the lifetime of that exceptional man. It was not always easy to collaborate with him, one could not always foresee his reactions to this or the other fact. Everyone has some sort of inner foundation, as you might call it, from which all reactions take shape. Once you know the foundation you can foresee the reaction. But with Serge Pavlovitch the foundation was not stationary, you could never foresee definitely what the reaction would be. It would often happen that he would telephone saying that a certain matter was to be dealt with in such and such a way. I knew already, and did not hurry. Later the telephone would ring again. 'Did you do as I asked?' 'No, I haven't had time.' 'Very well, don't. I have changed my mind, you can do it so.' And in this way the instructions might be changed as often as six

PLATE XXXIII

TATIANA RIABOUSHINSKA

PLATE XXXIV

[Georges

TAMARA TOUMANOVA

times in the course of a day. But another time if they were
not carried out immediately he would be angry and would
begin to swear over the telephone. This perhaps seems
disorderly and confusing? Actually he had a very straight
and clear viewpoint and he, better than anyone else, knew
how to carry it through. Collaboration with Diaghileff
was always interesting and absorbing. In good days and
bad I always found in him a clear, vivid, and human
response, and always a warm and friendly attitude."

Serge Grigorieff values the past but he is also greatly
attached to the present and to the work he has in hand.
He is still young and full of vitality and loves his work.
In his early days, when assisting Fokine, he put aside his
personal career as an active dancer and, collaborating first
with him and then with Diaghileff, abandoned also a
career as a creator of choreography, but in the rôle which
he has chosen, the rôle of the ballet technician, he certainly
knows how to make himself especially valuable, even
irreplaceable.

In the ballet family of Colonel de Basil there are three
little "goddesses." To me, as an old man, they are infinitely
charming and dear, not only because they are young and
so brilliant, but also because, owing to them, all the purity,
all that is classic in the ballet art, everything that fills the
memories of my youth with poetry has been revived.
This new generation understands its predecessors, loves
them, and knows how to give a new freshness and power
to the almost forgotten art which they have inherited.

These three little goddesses—Irina Baronova, Tamara
Toumanova, and Tatiana Riaboushinska—are all three

marvellous. Technically they are streets ahead of anything I can remember. Not one of the bygone ballerinas (*di forʒa*) could do what these who are really only girls, perform with such ease. There was a time when the great patrons of art looked with approval on the thirty-two *fouettés* of La Kchessinskaya; Baronova and Toumanova can do thirty-two double *fouettés* with the same ease. Their virtuosity is amazing; in a classical dance you cannot detect the slightest effort, even the usual concentrated expression when performing a difficult *pas* is not to be seen: everything they do is fairylike, simple, and natural. You do not see that moment of preparation for a difficult movement which sometimes seemed to break the continuity of the dancing of the old ballerinas, the change of step is so facile and unnoticeable that you cannot see any jerkiness or jumping from one position to another.

In the old days those who studied the ballet divided ballerinas, like tenors, into two classes—ballerinas *di forʒa* and ballerinas *di graʒia*. Those of the first category were presumed not to have special grace, technique was their sphere of brilliance and lovers of ballet demanded of them not so much suppleness as virtuosity. Of such a type was the Moscow ballerina, Geltzer. This enthusiasm for pure technique sometimes caused a shade of acrobatism to creep on to the ballet stage. It is quite true to say that the possession of colossal technique may sometimes tempt the dancer to put that technique into the forefront to the detriment of the art itself.

I was not a little surprised to see how all three of the de Basil ballerinas had avoided this danger. Is Massine, the *maître de ballet*, responsible for this, or is it that among the present-day public there is a dearth of enthusiasts for *entrechats* and *battements* for whom these tricks were performed? I do not know, but the enormous technique, the virtuosity which these three possess never becomes the purpose but is always only the means; they are each three, in their own style, delightful dancers *di grazia*, each charming in their personal plasticity.

Baronova, Toumanova, and Riaboushinska started early. At an age when in the old days they would just have been leaving the ballet school they had already consolidated their positions and become world famous as ballerinas, they are the *wunderkinder* of Terpsichore, brilliant, delightful wonder children.

Irina Baronova is the youngest of the three. It is said that for the last three years she has been sixteen, not for the ladies' usual reason, but just the opposite. She was at first so young that they were afraid to admit her real age. In her case, however, it is difficult to speak of *wunderkind*. I know of no one more finished or perfect on the stage. In the classical *Le Mariage d'Aurore* she is brilliant, an absolutely perfect dancer. Not only is her technique superb but she possesses to the full the classical style. She is quite at home in the choreography of Petipa. At the same time Baronova is an accomplished mimic. She must be seen as the red-haired, ill-tempered *cocotte* in *Union Pacific* to understand her scenic ability. Every movement is lifelike, persuasive, and characteristic. If, after this, you see her in *Le Beau Danube*, flirting at the side of the stage in an innocent, girlish way with an artist, you will see clearly to what extent she has learned to transform herself from one type to another. I find it difficult to point to any defect in Baronova's art; to me she seems an absolutely perfect and finished artiste. If she is a *wunderkind* how can the *wunderkind* develop further?

Tatiana Riaboushinska also is charming. Her main virtue is inborn, one which cannot be acquired. She is as light as a feather blown in the wind. A jump by her is always a flight. On a crowded stage you cannot but notice this god-given lightness. Your attention is drawn involuntarily not only to this lightness but to the special womanly, yet childish charm of her movements. It is easier to speak of her as *wunderkind*. Her artistic personality perhaps still remains not quite developed or defined. She has still further to go in the purely scenic sense. As a ballerina she is perfect, the precision of her technique is wonderful. Her inborn gift is beautiful and it is ever present in her dancing. Perhaps as an actress, as a personality, there is still room for development. She is said to be seventeen—a whole lifetime with all its probabilities of excitement, happiness, and even sorrow, everything which forms personality, is before her.

I have left until last, as the English say, the "tit-bit"— the few words I have to say about Tamara Toumanova. She is my pet "goddess." Toumanova is a perfectly attuned, vibrating string. There is in her something intensive which is missing in the others. I will not speak of her technique, she has virtuosity to an extreme degree. What specially attracts me in her art is that inner fire, that sort of almost religious devotion to what she has in hand. Her dancing is inspired, in every movement you sense the tenseness of the spirit, it is a sort of terpsichorean prayer. For that reason her dancing is always full of a living, captivating temperament. Everything she does on the stage has warmth, there is not a touch of placidity or coldness in her. When one watches her, be it in a classical dance, be it in *Petrushka*, be it in some "Concurrence," one cannot watch unmoved. She always captivates me and for this rare delight of being enthralled, for being able to forget myself, I am always grateful to her from the depths of my heart.

This spiritual intensity is characteristic of the personality of Tamara Toumanova. Off stage she produces the same impression. Her large, dark eyes burn, her movements are full of life. You feel that everything in life has meaning to this girl. She speaks of her art with the passion of a devotee. She is still not satisfied, she still wants to go further, to reach a higher state of perfection.

"Technique?" says Toumanova. "We all have that. We are not afraid of any *fouettés* nor of any of the difficulties of the classical dance. But still we must work and seek to improve ourselves. It is not really so difficult to perform a perfect ballet *pas*, but one must know how to give continuity to each movement, to link it with the next until all are combined together as one whole so that in the end this same technique becomes unnoticeable to the spectator. One must work continuously with this in view, the ideal is still far off."

"In which ballets do you prefer to dance?"

"In the classics, of course. Not only are they more pleasing to dance but the public prefers them. In our repertoire—*Le Mariage d'Aurore, Petrushka, Les Sylphides* . . ."

I suddenly felt very old, a member of a long defunct generation. *Les Sylphides* . . . *Petrushka* . . . to me they still are revolutionary ballet, stamped in the conservative mind as "modernist" and "decadent." *Le Mariage d'Aurore*, the last act of *The Sleeping Princess*, with its choreography by Petipa, I can appreciate that as a real classic, but in my eyes there is a precipice between it and *Petrushka*. Perhaps, however, Toumanova is right and I am wrong. Looking back over the history of ballet during the past twenty years, it is more proper to allocate *Petrushka* to the past, to the Maryinsky Theatre than to the post-war era. But this *Petrushka* of 1911 to me is still young and contemporary: the controversy of the old days still remains with me, I have not yet learned to relegate it quietly to the category of the past.

But the past of these little ballerinas does not reach so far. The pre-war Russian ballet is as far back as they can go. They never saw the Maryinsky Theatre—they have not danced *Pharaoh's Daughter*, *The Bayadère*, or *Paquita*. The revolutionism of Diaghileff is beyond their understanding.

Time passes and with it all the excitement, all the delights, and all the tragedies of bygone days hide themselves, one by one, in the grey archives of the past. They all die down and become covered with the dust and cobwebs of history. All that remains of that pulsating life is a row of uninteresting books of reference, useful, but not exciting.

But if those same yellow documents fall into the hands of a man who has lived in the past, the shadows take shape before him, his heart will flutter, the old excitements and pleasures will grip him with renewed strength, and he will lose himself in reverie.

Will he know how to pass on to his youthful neighbour even a small part of the excitement which holds him?

Will there be found in this book even a few words which will bring to life before the young reader some of the romanticism of those long dead years?

# INDEX

## BALLETS, OPERAS, ETC

369

# PERSONAE

373

# INDEX

William II, Emperor, 179
Woizikovski, Leon, 318, 326
Wolkonsky, Prince Serge, 39–42,
47, 272

Yurgensson, 60

Zarine, Leonide, 11

Zheltouhin, 62
Zilotti, Alexander, 295
Zimin, 203
Zografo, Mme, 61
Zouikoff, Vassili, 238, 245, 249,
250, 263, 325
Zucchi, Virginia, 57, 58, 60, 283,
287, 313